EYE OF THE TIGER
A Hundred Years of LSU Football

By Marty Mulé

LONGSTREET PRESS
Atlanta, Georgia

ACKNOWLEDGEMENTS

Special thanks to Dr. Jesse Coates, who shared memories of his father's efforts a century ago.

Also the insights of Bud Johnson, Paul Manasseh, Paul Dietzel, Billy Cannon, Carl Maddox, George Bevan, Gaynell Tinsley, Bill LeBlanc, and Gaynell Kinchen were invaluable.

And for the notepads and memories of Bill Bumgarner, Pete Barrouquere, Peter Finney, John Jones and Bob Roesler.

And Bob Christ, who somehow made sense of it all.

Photographs courtesy of the LSU Sports Information Office.

Published by LONGSTREET PRESS, INC.
A subsidiary of Cox Newspapers,
A Division of Cox Enterprises, Inc.
2140 Newmarket Parkway
Suite 118
Marietta, GA   30067

Printed in the United States of America

1st printing, 1993

Library of Congress Catalog Number 92-79660

ISBN: 1-56352-090-7

This book was printed by Semline, Inc., in Braintree, Massachusetts.

Cover design and book design by Graham & Company Graphics, Inc.

PREFACE

March 6, 1993

For a few years after I finished playing football and left LSU, I struggled to get up the steam to attend a game at Tiger Stadium.

As I recall I did go once with my old roommate John Adams, but we left early, a minute or two after the second-half kickoff. I was a lot like the fellow who loses his one true love and finds himself unable to consider another. I was sick for something I could never have again — sick and lonesome and jealous, too. I wanted to be 18 again, new to the purple-and-gold adventure, and not some has-been who'd been put out to pasture. "I'm not a fan," I remember saying time and again, generally on fall Saturday nights.

"I'm a player, for heaven's sake! A player!"

On occasion now, I'll dream about LSU and football, but almost always the dream will have little to do with what I experienced back in the late 1970s. For instance, I'll dream I'm dressed out for practice, riding a bus to the Ponderosa practice fields over by the river. I look around me at all the fresh-scrubbed faces. They are boys, and here I am, 35-years-old, with love handles and skinny arms, and a few sad wrinkles around my eyes.

I'm in awful shape and I figure I'm heading out to die. Maybe it'll happen during calisthenics, or maybe later, during team offense or three-on-three drill. Somebody will hit me or look at me too hard and I'll break into a million pieces. The windows of the bus are wet with condensation, and I write this on the glass with a finger: Help me!

In this dream — this nightmare — I do not reach the practice fields. I'm smart enough to wake myself up as soon as the bus doors swing open, and when I come to I always feel lost and empty. Enough real demons populate the mind than to have to deal with invented ones, but there I lay in a puddle of sweat, trembling and cold, wondering why four short years of my life still mean so damned much to me.

Ernest Hemingway once said that Paris is a moveable feast. I used to really like that line, but then I went to Paris and discovered that the city was actually more immovable than moveable, and that if you wanted to feast you'd better have plenty of money. LSU football was my moveable feast. To this day I carry it with me wherever I go, and I find myself talking about it to strangers in cities thousands of miles from home — in Portland and Seattle and Chicago and L.A. and Miami. I recollect in restaurants with names I can't pronounce. A shot of alchohol usually gets me going, and I become nostalgic, painfully so. I babble on to whoever will listen, exaggerating my accomplishments, adding digits to the win columns of the teams I played on.

Once in New York I was having lunch with a couple of magazine editors, and one of them asked me this question: "Is Tiger Stadium as haunted as they say?"

My reply was hackneyed but honed. "Durn right it's haunted," I said, hammering a fist to the table. "Once you've been there it chases right after you the rest of your life."

At a party in Paris I demonstrated how to "scoop block" to a room full of literary types clasping glasses of champagne. A chair was the noseguard, a book cabinet the backside linebacker. I gave the chair a proud forearm shiver as I raced past it en route to the cabinet, whose wealth of precious collectibles trembled as I approached. I was pretending to be clearing the way for some old friend — for Charlie or Hokie or LeRoid or Jude. I was a lineman again, willing to lay down my life for the team. A gaping hole to my rear was the result of my efforts, and I instructed one of my fellow partygoers to hurry and run through it. "The goalline's over there," I said, pointing to a crease in the linoleum. "Come on, man! Don't you want to score?"

Another time, in Washington, D.C., I found myself in a park just up the street from the newspaper office where I worked. Somebody had rounded up an imaginary football, and I was demonstrating how to deep snap for punts. I showed how to properly address the ball, and how to fire it back with a perfect spiral. On this particular occasion I hadn't even been drinking, but there I was under a canopy of sun-dappled plane trees, making a fool of myself and scaring the pigeons silly.

I sent one invisible orb after another just above the punter's knee, hitting the spot exactly. It's a good thing no one told me to sprint downfield 40 yards and tackle some idler picnicking on the grass, because I probably would've done it.

Let me speak now of some of the things that often come back to me, that live on in memory, and that will probably follow me to the grave.

I remember Broussard Hall and its crazy purple carpet and sweating yellow walls. I remember running gassers in the August heat, running until it seemed no pain in this life could be greater, and nothing would ever hurt more. I remember prime rib dinners and giant butter cakes with icing designed to resemble football fields. I remember all those happy hands to shake, and souvenir programs to sign, and little kids with golden heads of hair to muss.

I remember letter jackets with big roll collars and giant fuzzy "L's." I remember Coach Mac in his golf cart, wheeling across the Ponderosa with his cap slightly askew. I remember going as a team to a movie every fall Friday night, the lead bus holding the offense, the rear one Big D. And long Saturday afternoons locked in our rooms, waiting for the 6 p.m. ride to the stadium. And I remember that ride — through screaming crowds of fans dressed in feverish color, and sort of parting on a biblical scale as the buses made their way to the Tiger Den.

I remember jock straps and ankle wraps and new white jerseys with your name printed on back. I remember running through the goalposts as the band rose up with noise, and feeling that my legs had never been lighter, nor my heart stronger. And all the fans on their feet, and a caged Mike the Tiger roaring his loud, deadly promise. And quarterbacks barking signals that used to mean something, "Red 19, red 19 . . . hut Hut HUT! And almost hyperventilating before the game had even begun.

I remember sitting in the chute before the opening kickoff, and both the bright and dark smells there, and assistant coaches nervously striding among their troops, saying whatever came to mind: remember this, remember that, look out for this, look out for that. And the pep talks, God almighty I remember those pep talks. My senior year I was captain of the offense, and there I was giving my first of many, the words all running together. "The cream will rise to the crop," I remember saying, really mixing things up. What I got then wasn't cheers but laughter, a big, deep, humiliating rumble. We went out and won anyway; we kicked them but good.

It never rains in Tiger Stadium, not even when it storms. Oh, yeah. I remember that, too.

But I couldn't tell you any of the scores. Well, there was the time we routed Rice 77-0 back when I was a sophomore. We scored 11 touchdowns that night, and after each one I had to snap for the extra point. Perhaps as a way of getting back, or of venting their frustrations, those sorry Rice Owl bastards lined up three men across center and unloaded as soon as the ball left my hands, and before I could even get my head up. Eleven times that night I found myself flat on my back, gazing off at the stars above Baton Rouge. Try having to watch that on film Sunday afternoon in front of your teammates and coaches. Snap, crack . . . splat! "Bradley! They're killing you, son! Killing you! Have you no pride? Have you forgotten who on earth you are?"

You remember. But better than the games and the seasons you remember the fellows you met and befriended, your teammates. It's always amazed me to think that you joined the program a total stranger, with nary a friend on the squad, and four or five years later you left as a brother to about a hundred. You knew their habits, good and bad. You knew the kind of music and cologne and women they liked, and you knew to trust them. These were relationships forged in the hope of glory, and they were the kind that held up, that never died.

Each of us who played is a pearl on a chain, it comes to me now, and the chain runs back a hundred years. I'm proud to have been one of the many, and grateful, too. I wish there was someone in particular to thank. Those were great days.

John Ed Bradley
Novelist, freelance writer
Captain of the 1979 Tigers

INTRODUCTION

The voice from the television barely penetrated consciousness: "LSU football coach Bo Rein, returning to Baton Rouge from a recruiting trip to Shreveport, was killed when his plane crashed in the Atlantic Ocean."

There was no sense in standing there in the den anymore. This was obviously a dream.

Unfortunately, as day overhauled dawn that unforgettable morning, it was stark reality. Rein was the new head football coach of the Tigers, the successor to Charlie McClendon, and on the job a total of 42 days.

That morning of 1980 always served as a benchmark for me, not only because of the tragedy but because it was a lesson of which I'd always had thoughts but never verbalized before: When covering LSU, be prepared for anything.

The steam-heat history of LSU athletics has always been pulsating, a long gold line of excellent athletes and thrilling competition. But the politics and the colorful characters behind the scenes have been just as interesting as what happens on the field. Let's face it, Huey Long left a larger legacy on Tiger football than some of LSU's coaches.

There has always been a cult of personality at LSU, where individuals have often loomed almost as large as some of the great Tiger teams. Say "Billy Cannon" and the first thought to a Louisianian is his incredible 1959 run against Ole Miss; Say "Dalton Hilliard" and the 1982 "Night it Rained Oranges" Florida State game is frequently remembered.

That's what we wanted to do — provide background and personality to the histories that have already been done on LSU. What was a sentence or passing mention before is a chapter here, adding what we hope is depth to earlier works.

LSU, though, is in the midst of tough times on the football field. It enters its second century of football with an unprecedented record of four straight losing seasons. That performance, because they played right away and for all four seasons while teammates were redshirted, made defensive back Derriel McCorvey and kicker Pedro Suarez the losingest Tigers in history.

And yet, you wonder if they are. They both played with distinction, and McCorvey in particular is the personification of the type of student-athlete Charles E. Coates envisioned when he coached the first LSU football team in 1893. "He thought athletics and scholarship went hand-in-hand," Dr. Jesse Coates, son of the coach, said.

In a way, Charles Coates must have had athletes like McCorvey in mind.

After the Tigers' 2-9 season of 1992, in which he made All-SEC second team, McCorvey received LSU's highest award for scholarship in classical languages, in his case, Latin.

"I think this would have appeal to the classical schoolmasters, who always elevated the ideal of mens sana in corpore sana — a sound mind in a sound body," said Robert Edgeworth of the department of Foreign Languages and Literatures.

"It really moves me, because it kind of lends credence to all my investment in my academics," McCorvey said, "not just to be a typical jock, more concerned about football than anything else in life."

McCorvey, twice a member of the SEC Academic Honor Roll, is the youngest of ten children. Every one of his siblings has earned a degree. So has his mother, who finished high school, college, and graduate school while raising her children. What a story, what a legacy.

It's one of the behind-the-scenes tales you just know would normally be recounted somewhere near that all-seeing, all-knowing beautiful tiger eye Bob Brodhead painted on the field of Tiger Stadium in the '80s. There are eight million stories in Tigertown.

It's always been sort of startling to realize where, how and how often Tigers pop up in our everyday lives. Those moving pictures of the young American flier George Bush being picked up in the choppy waters of the Pacific during World War II were taken by a young submarine officer, Bill Edwards, who a year before was holding down the line at LSU. For better or for worse, a non-athletic Tiger named James Carville was the master-mind behind Bill Clinton's 1992 presidential campaign which ousted Bush from the White House. Of coarse, Hubert Humphrey got his advanced degree from LSU, and Rex Reed, who advises us all on what movies to see, saw plenty during his time at the Ole War Skule. And Dr. James Andrews, the world's foremost practitioner of sports medicine recieved far more renown operating on Bo Jackson than he ever did as a Tiger pole-vaulter.

And former press-box announcer Sid Crocker lived through a troika of circumstance very few could equal. Crocker was stationed at Pearl Harbor on December 7, 1941; three years later, he took part in the Normandy landing; and 14 years after that, he was in Tiger Stadium the night Billy Cannon made his fateful Halloween night run.

Still, when football is the discussion, names like Cannon, Huey Long, Ganell Tinsley, Tommy Casanova, and Jim Taylor will always be the stepping stone for the Tigers.

And Bo Rein. I'll never forget that night when his ghostship, and the two unconscious passengers, flew 1,500 miles off course, and over Raleigh, N.C. where his little girls were sleeping, maybe dreaming of all the glory their daddy would reap at LSU.

Charlie McClendon was preparing his last team for his last game, a Tangerine Bowl game with Wake Forest. Rein said he would not make public comment or meet with the press until after that game was over.

The week before the tragedy, Rein agreed on the telephone that it was time for Louisiana to get to know him better, so he set up an interview.

Then fate intervened. Jerry Stovall, a former Tiger great and a former Tiger assistant, was recommended to step in by athletic director Paul Dietzel. The LSU Board of Supervisors hastily called a meeting for 10 a.m. that Saturday.

The proverbial hair on the back of my neck rose while driving to that meeting. That was exactly the time of my appointment with Rein.

TABLE OF CONTENTS

THE 1893 KICKOFF

1

"It struck me," said Dr. Charles E. Coates, "we ought to have that sort of thing."

He was speaking of football.

Coates, a young chemistry professor just recently hired from St. John's University in Maryland, had just arrived to teach at Louisiana State University. He found what he considered an essential component to the "whole" man, as idealized by the ancient Greeks, surprisingly lacking.

"He felt scholarship and athletics went together,"

THE FOUNDER — *Charles Coates brought football to LSU in 1893.*

Dr. Jesse Coates, the son of Charles Coates, said in 1993, a hundred years after his father coached LSU's first team. "That those ingredients together made the complete man." That ideal would be especially important at a school like LSU. Founded as the Louisiana Seminary of Learning and Military Academy only 33 years before Coates' arrival, the school's first superintendent was William Tecumseh Sherman, a man who would gain infamy as the Union general who torched Atlanta.

LSU retained a strong military personality for three-quarters of a century,

OLD TIMERS — *The oldest known photograph of an LSU squad: the 1894 Tigers.*

relishing its heroes and strong officer corps it sent to war so that even now it is referred to as the "Ole War Skule."

In 1893 LSU was essentially a military seminary of 300 cadets and 19 faculty members. A former athlete at Johns Hopkins University in Baltimore, Coates was surprised to find no football, no tennis and only a little baseball at LSU.

He and Dr. H.A. Morgan, later the president of the University of Tennessee, decided to rectify the situation. They enlisted some players, and for equipment they nailed cleats on leather shoes. There were no uniforms, but they began trying to teach the rudiments of the game.

Coates, in a 1937 issue of the *LSU Alumni News*, wrote, "Morgan and I did the coaching quite poorly. I taught the boys the Leland flying wedge and the turtle back."

An old friend of Coates', T.L. Bayne (known as 'Nervy' Bayne, according to Coates), was at the same time trying to develop interest in football in New Orleans and at Tulane.

They agreed on a match, the first college game in Louisiana, and it was a reflection of the innocent times. Before the first blow was given, their friendship and the good relations between the schools allowed Bayne, a former Yale player, to travel up to Baton Rouge several times to help Coates and Morgan get the LSU team prepared.

Bayne, like generations of coaches after him, got one look at LSU and started poor mouthing.

"They're much bigger than we first thought," said Bayne to the New Orleans press. "Why, Billy blazes, they must average at least 160 pounds."

The hard work put in by the athletes of the state university impressed others, too. "When boys study as hard as they play football," said one newspaper, "there are going to be some intellectual lights in

Louisiana."

While LSU was practicing, Tulane was playing. Bayne's charges took on the Southern Athletic Club, and lost, 12-0, in Tulane's first organized game a week before the scheduled meeting with LSU on November 25.

Sportsman's Park in New Orleans was the site of the first Tulane-LSU football meeting, played on Nov. 25, 1893. There was only one man on the field who weighed more than 200 pounds-Tulane center Walter Castenado — but by all accounts the 1,500 fans witnessed a powerful display of primitive football by the home team. Uniforms consisted generally of pullover sweaters, lightly padded khaki pants, shoes with improvised cleats and long stockings of various colors and shades — and often leather noseguards, and almost always long, bushy hairstyles that they believed would cushion head contact.

Football then was basically a game played and determined by battering ram tactics and roughhouse, physical play. Legal piling on was the cause of many injuries.

"We had flying wedges, revolving wedges and all sorts of power plays," Edwin F. Gayle, a 155-pound freshman back on the LSU team, recalled in 1971. "You'd line up about 15 yards down field, get a flying wedge into motion, and it was just a question of how many you knocked out."

In this instance it was LSU who was knocked out — quickly.

In just two plays, tackle Hugh Bayne, brother of the coach, scored the first touchdown in Tulane history, racing 30 yards behind a flying wedge. He slipped at the goal and pitched, face forward, onto the lined stripe marking the end zone and suffered slight burns about the eyes from the lye. His face white with the stinging substance, Bayne missed the conversion.

LSU had one brief moment of satisfaction in their football inaugural. A goal-line stand forced the Tulanians to struggle for one of their seven touchdowns.

With a first-and-goal at the four, following an LSU fumble, Tulane employed the wedge and ran straight at the defense. For two minutes the lines pushed back and forth at each other before the referee, none other than Coates, yelled "down," in the manner plays ended in the Gay Nineties.

Tulane was held at the two after the allotted three downs, but an infraction against LSU gave the home team another opportunity and Tulane finally shoved the ball into the end zone three plays later.

The 34-0 battering of LSU becomes far worse when it's realized touchdowns in those early days counted for only four points. Six more points were added to Tulane's seven touchdowns by way of three PATs, which then counted for two points.

Gayle claimed to be the only athlete to play the entire game, which was an upset in itself considering one memorable collision. "We played without helmets," Gayle said. "I remember I bumped heads with the Tulane quarterback once during the game. Fellow named (Walter) Lewis, he was a redhead. I dove into the line at the same time he did, and we met head-on.

It knocked both of us out, and because he was vital to the Tulane team, and because we didn't have adequate subs, they just had to stop the game until we were ready to play again."

LSU captain Ruffin Pleasant, later the governor of Louisiana, also had to be helped from the field.

After it was over, the LSU contingent, players and fans, boarded a special train for the return trip to Baton Rouge. It was the first time a train was ever used to transport a student body to a football game, so Tulane and LSU made football history right off the bat.

The thrill of beating LSU was to last only a little while, however, for Tulane wasn't to enjoy beating its up-river opponents again until 1900. And the friendly competition which marked the early games was an early casualty as the series quickly became a contention of intense proportions.

"After that first game," Gayle said, "we went out and hired us a professional coach (A.P. Simmons). He brought in a couple of tough boys from Wisconsin

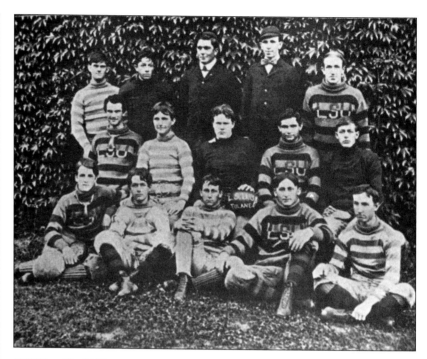

PRIDE — The 1899 Tigers pose with a football from their 38-0 conquest of Tulane that year.

with him, and the next time we played Tulane (in 1895) we turned the tables (8-4)."

That turned out to be the only season — the only game — Coates ever coached. He would become renowned in scientific circles for his work in sugar production and chemistry.

Coates never lost his interest in LSU football though, attending games through the 1930s. His son said Dr. Coates reacted like any other fan with cheers in victory, and with jeers in an occasional defeat.

Jeers? Boos? From a former coach?

"You know what they say," reminded Jesse Coates, "when you pay for your ticket . . ."

WHEN THE TIGERS WERE PELICANS

2

Tigers by any other name are, of course, tigers.

Still, it is, at first blush, an odd appellation for an area in which tigers have never been a indigenous creature. And yet it carries such an emotional charge.

There is, of course, an intricate story involved.

LSU, then a military seminary, played without a nickname its first three football seasons, though the team was called the Baton Rouge "boys" by the New Orleans papers which covered them in the 1893 LSU-Tulane inaugural, the first college game played in Louisiana.

By 1896 the team had its first mascot — a greyhound named "Drum," the pet of the LSU commandant of cadets, a Lieutenant Gallop, U.S.A. — and a growing natural identification with a native Louisiana animal: the pelican.

Justin Daspit, a member of the 1896 team, explained in a 1929 interview with Maud O'Bryan of the New Orleans Item-Tribune that as LSU entered the 1896 season its team was known as the Pelicans, and even had pelican insignia sewn on their jackets.

But that 1896 team was a fighting bunch, the first exceptional LSU squad and one which played with uncommon ferocity. LSU was 6-0 and outscored its opponents 136-4.

That season LSU defeated Centenary, 46-0; Mississippi State, 52-0; Texas, 14-0; Ole Miss, 12-4; the Southern Athletic Club, 6-0; and Tulane through a forfeit. (Tulane was leading 2-0 in the second half on a safety when Tulane attempted to substitute a player not enrolled in school. LSU objected, and Tulane said it would not play unless this sub could play. As a result, the officials awarded the game to LSU.

Fans were taken with the team, and it wasn't long before someone known only to history made a double-barrelled connection with Louisiana history and likened the LSU team with the "Louisiana Tigers." Which is why the Tigers are the Tigers.

The original "Tigers" were fighting men of the Civil War, the Louisiana brigades in the Army of Northern Virginia. They are proudly referred to in the 1899 LSU Reveille as the "veritable Tigers of Jackson and Lee."

The use of the word "Tiger" among Louisiana troops goes at least as far back as the Mexican War, and there were several in the War Between the States, including the Rapides Tigers, Calcasieu Tigers, Beauregard Tigers, and the Tiger Rifles of Captain Alexander White of the First Special Battalion. But the description almost surely came from the Seventh Louisiana Infantry which came from Acadia, according to Dr. Mark Carleton of the Louisiana State University history department. This particularly ferocious bunch often charged with Bowie knifes and returned with necklaces of Yankee genitals, ears and other body parts.

The State Seminary of Learning, then located in Pineville, closed because of the war. A professor of ancient languages, David French Boyd, enlisted to find one of his former cadets, John Workman, the sergeant of his company. The board which oversaw the school asked Boyd to avoid a commission so that he might return as soon as the academy could be re-opened. When it was clear the school would not reopen until after the war, Boyd, the commissariat of the First Louisiana Brigade, attained the rank of major.

The "Louisiana Tigers" of the Army of Northern Virginia, including the Donaldsonville Cannoniers and Zouave troops from New Orleans, were instrumental in turning the tide in the South's victory of the first battle of the Civil War, Bull Run, by routing a Northern brigade under General Burnside.

The Tigers continued to distinguish themselves throughout the war, fighting fiercely and dying in terrible numbers — gaining further fame at the Battle of the Shenandoah Valley and all the way to Gettysburg.

It was written that the words "Louisiana Tigers" chilled the Union troops, and that Northern soldiers fleeing into Washington after the first battle of Bull Run explained their actions by panting out: "Damn those Louisiana Tigers! Born devils every one of them."

A Union account of Gettysburg read: "The 'Louisiana Tigers' were met by heavy artillery fire . . . they were massacred, but kept charging clear into the Union lines. The 'Tigers' were merciless, bayoneting the artillerymen at their cannon . . . The Rebel charge was broken, the 'Tigers' cut to pieces."

General Ewell said afterward, "The Louisiana brigade and their gallant commander gave new honor to the name already acquired on old fields."

Boyd came out of the

A Tiger on the run.

gested the sobriquet "Tigers" in conference with his players. But that was 43 years after the fact, and his memory may have been playing tricks. No reference can be found of the nickname "Tigers" before 1896.

There's another little historical inconsistency here.

Coates said the morning of November 25, 1893 — the day of the first Tulane game — he and several of his players went to Reymond's store to buy colorful ribbons with which to adorn their uniforms, and found that two Mardi Gras colors (purple and old gold) were in the most supply. The other primary Carnival color, green, had not yet come in.

That is how, legend says, LSU got its royal colors of purple and old gold.

But there are a couple of problems with this scenario. First of all, why would there be such a plentiful supply of Mardi Gras colors in November when the event doesn't take place for weeks afterward. In 1894 Mardi Gras fell on February 6, a month and a half after the Tulane game. Indeed, two days before the alleged trip to

war to become the second superintendent of the Louisiana Seminary of Learning, and must have been pleased when the 1896 LSU team began being referred to as the Tigers, the honored namesakes of his distinguished fighting unit.

Ironically, the description of "Fightin' Tigers," which sounds like it came from a battling military unit, did not. That nickname came rather late to LSU. Paul Dietzel gave his first team, the 1955 Tigers, that name because of its scrappy nature. It stuck.

Dr. Charles E. Coates, the first coach of LSU, said in his 1937 LSU Alumni News article that he sug-

Reymond's store, and the chance procurement of those particular colors, the New Orleans Times Democrat reported, "all the young ladies are preparing purple and old gold streamers for the occasion."

Actually, seven months before, when the LSU baseball team defeated Tulane, 10-8, in the first intercollegiate athletic competition for both schools, although David French Boyd chose blue and white as the school colors years before, the LSU team wore ribbons of purple and old gold.

Actually, LSU's purple-and-gold colors, like its nickname, may be rooted in the Civil War.

Nearby the original campus, on Third Street, was a watering hole renamed at the start of the Civil War called "Sumter's Saloon" to commemorate Louisiana's succession. The place was decorated in bunting of purple and old gold, perhaps to match the piping of a fighting unit. A Confederate cannon was half buried in front, and is said to still be there, though now fully covered.

At the very beginning of the Civil War, the Seventh Louisiana regiment was presented a beautiful flag with a pelican on a dark field by the Pickwick Club of New Orleans. More than 20 years later, in 1883 — a full decade before LSU ever kicked off a football — the corps of cadets was presented a flag by a ladies' organization in Baton Rouge, perhaps the same one, or a replica, carried by the Seventh. It bore the image of a pelican and the state coat of arms.

The reported description read: "The flag is of handsome purple silk, fringed with gold."

THE HUNDRED YEAR WAR: *LSU VS. TULANE*

3

Marvin "Moose" Stewart made his way through the Tigers and Greenies milling about the field, shaking hands, and found Tulane coach Ted Cox.

"Hey, coach," said Stewart when he found Cox on the sideline. "Do you need me yet?"

LSU had just defeated the Green Wave, 41-0, to cap the 9-1-0 regular season of 1935, a season in which Stewart made All-America at center.

No one was much interested in Stewart when he came out of Picayune,

Mississippi, as a high school senior. He took it upon himself to travel to New Orleans and try out for the Tulane team. After the workouts, Cox told Stewart, "Go back to Picayune, and, if we need you, we'll call." Of course, Tulane never did call. Not only did LSU call, but obviously profited by Cox' mistake.

That kind of one-upmanship has pocked this series ever since the two schools began their gridiron war a century ago. It began as extremely friendly competition, and quickly

turned into internecine warfare–bloodless but blood-broiling.

These two rivals not only despise each other, they can't even agree on their won-loss records.

THE BEGINNING, 1893-1923

Tulane and LSU didn't play in 1894, but it's noteworthy that after the Olive and Blue, which was Tulane's awkward nickname at the time, lost all four of its games the Tulane student newspaper recommended construction of a special dormitory to house its athletes, who lived all over New Orleans, so they could follow a special — and presumably Spartan — regimen. A few weeks later that suggestion was followed up with another for contributions for the athletic dorm and also to use in order to hire a professional coach: "A man fresh from this year's game, and thoroughly familiar with the new plays and schemes that have come into effect."

A month later, when the contributions were counted, a grand total of $25 had been collected.

Still, there was a wistful innocence about the "gentleman amateurs" who played the sport then, one which allowed the Tulane Banjo, Mandolin and Glee Club to travel to Baton Rouge for the 1895 LSU match for the purposes of cheering for its team during the game, and to give a concert later. After the LSU victory, one of Tulane's stalwart performers, Cartwright Eustis, sang in the concert. His selection was a popular song of the day: "I Been Hoodooed."

In 1894 the Tulane Athletic Association advocated a Southern body to enforce codes of conduct to make football safer from "the dangers of professionalism." This led to the formation of the Southern Intercollegiate Athletic Association (SIAA), sort of a regional forerunner to the NCAA. To Tulane's embarrassment, one of the first major decisions handed down by the SIAA was the banning of the school from competition for the 1897 season after a dispute with LSU the preceding year. Coach H. W. Baum played an ineligible athlete — George Brooke, who had an outstanding reputation in Pennsylvania where he apparently played before seeking admission to Tulane law school.

Tulane was leading 2-0 late in the game when LSU began a long drive downfield.

When LSU reached the four, Tulane attempted to insert Brooke, who was not registered in school, into the lineup. LSU protested immediately and vigorously, and the officials agreed with its contention. Tulane refused to finish the game and the referees fixed the score at 6-0, LSU.

Strained relations ensued, and, indeed, the series almost died a premature death.

But before it reached the crisis stage, LSU put together two remarkable outings against its "city" foe. LSU ran a stunning 111 plays from scrimmage against Tulane in 1898, resulting in a total 726 yards — 6.5 yards per carry. The Tigers weren't held for downs or forced to punt in gaining a 37-0 victory. The following season, LSU rolled up 639 yards against Tulane. That 1899 Tulane team didn't score a point and went 0-6-1.

Revenge was quick in coming, though, and in 1900 Tulane got its first victory over the Tigers since the inaugural, and did it with a team that became a measuring stick of sorts. Tulane president Edwin A. Alderman, who took office the previous year, seemed acutely embarrassed by the 1899 team's poor showing and urged potential athletes to offer their services.

In a stunning turnaround, not only was Tulane unbeaten in 1900 with a 5-0-0 record, but it didn't give up a point, beating its opponents cumulatively 105-0. LSU went under 29-0, and Tulane gained 380 yards in scoring its five touchdowns while surrendering a meager 36 yards to the Tigers. But for Tulane kindness the score probably would have been higher. Tulane consented to calling off the remainder of the match because of nightfall with 10 minutes to go.

"The Tulane team covered itself with glory," Coach H.T. Summersgill said with proud emphasis, by beating "the gridiron gods of Louisiana State University."

The Tulane-LSU game had clearly become an emotional blood-letting.

The rivalry was taking on immense proportions in the interests of people who only a few years before had no interest whatsoever in football. Mrs. Charles E. A. Gayarré , widow of the famed historian and jurist, wrote to a companion on the day of the Tulane-LSU game of 1900 that a meeting of her social club brought "a rather sparse collection of members for it seems that (football) has for our ladies now more attraction than intellectual entertainments. It was a contest between Tulane

and State University. Of course Tulane triumphed."

That Tulane triumph of 1900 also marked the first time in the series cheerleading was orchestrated.

A "Rooters Club" was organized for the LSU game by Louis Bush, captain of the 1896 team. Bush "was armed with a huge megaphone," according to the *Daily Picayune*, "through which he issued orders to the faithful."

One of the cheers went:

Rah! Rah! Siz! Boom! Ah! Rah! Rah! Tulane!
Hippety Huss Hippety Huss!
What in —— is the matter with us!

A shocked reporter wrote that the cheer was "faithfully given as sung before a thousand ladies yesterday."

It was after the 1901 game that the infant series almost died. On the field, Tulane won 22-0, but its key player was a back named Howard Crandell, who scored on a sensational 65-yard run on the first play of the second half, then kicked the PAT. But LSU protested Crandell's participation and charged

he had accepted pay for his services with the Bernhards, an independent football team, and thus was a professional.

Crandell's eligibility was challenged, and again the SIAA ruled in LSU's favor.

Tulane refused to accept the ruling, and today both universities list the game as a victory.

Even the pre-game build-ups began to take on tones of all-out war rather than college competition. Before the 1905 Tulane-LSU game the *Tulane Weekly* carried a story with a wild-eyed message: "Every day brings us nearer to our battle with Louisiana State University and every day we witness numerous exclamations very much like Cato's 'Carthago delenda est' . . . 'LSU must be destroyed.' "

Apparently the excitement of that 1905 game, in which the Tigers won 5-0 on the last play, caused the *New Orleans State's* reporter to omit the score completely. The *State's* headline read: "LSU beats Tulane in Close Finish." But no score was given in the lengthy story. The only mention of the ultimate outcome came in the second-to-last para-

HOSS–Tom Dutton is one of LSU's greatest lineman ever.

MATCH MADE IN HELL — the Tulane "Goat" checks out a paper tiger, 1913.

graph: "The timers announced there was only eleven seconds . . . . LSU gathered themselves for a mighty rush, made it and carried Smith over for a touchdown, the first score made . . . quite a deal of money changed hands on the result of the game."

Jim Fourmy, who was the 1905 LSU quarterback, said 80 years later that it was the big game of his career, and Tulane was always the big game of all turn-of-the-century Tigers. "It was Tulane," Fourmy said, "and no matter what, you just had to beat Tulane. We always played them in New Orleans. It meant more money to the schools. We had 5,000 (actually it was closer to 6,000 in 1905, and after that ticket prices went up a hundred percent, to one dollar) for one game with Tulane."

Heated charges were made again after that 1905 game, this time by Tulane, which contended LSU played several ringers, including two brothers named Smith from Michigan, one of whom scored the Tigers' lone and late touchdown, and who came South for nothing more than to play a little football and see the Mardi Gras.

When Tulane made its case to the SIAA, it was referred to the vice president for the district of Louisiana, Mississippi and Texas: Colonel Thomas S. Boyd of LSU.

Boyd ruled in favor of the Tigers.

Because of the growing antagonism between the schools, only two Tulane-LSU games were played between 1902 and 1911, causing two of the best teams in Southern football to miss each other completely.

In 1908 Tulane won seven of eight games, losing only to Baylor 6-0. In that era of the four-point touchdown, Tulane outscored its opposition 113-24. Of course, that was also the season of LSU's first truly great team which swept through its schedule 10-0, and tallied 442 points to 11 for its composite foes. LSU defeated Baylor, 89-0.

By the midteens the fans started getting in on the football act, and thrills not supplied by the players were often provided in the stands. In 1914 the cheerleaders agreed to a show of friendship by coming to the middle of the field for a joint yell. But a fight was narrowly averted when an LSU banner was torn down during the milling about.

Three players were tossed out of the 1915 game, an exceptionally rough contest, and afterward the ejected athletes attempted to settle their differences, resulting in a riot - a sad situation that again threatened the series.

The late Bill Keefe, sports editor of *The Times-Picayune* for more than half a century, said that period was when the series was at its worst. "We had riots in 1915 and 1917," Keefe said in 1966, "and I suppose that would have to be when the rivalry was its hottest.

"Tulane freshmen and some drunks were responsible for the riot here (in New Orleans) in 1915. I didn't mince any words in hitting the Tulane officials for lack of police protection. After the 1916 game in Baton Rouge, the Tulane team was pulled off its trucks and beaten by the fans. There was only one policeman at the game, and I really criticized the LSU officials for having just one policeman on hand.

"The next week, a delegation of LSU people, headed by Gov. Stubbs, came in to see my publisher, D.B. Moore. They claimed I had been unfair in my criticism. Mr. Moore asked me about it. I told him to wait a minute and ran and got the column I had done the year before, blasting the Tulane people. Mr. Moore read the column and turned to Gov. Stubbs and the delegation and said, 'Gentlemen, you don't have a complaint.' I never heard any more about the column."

Tulane's 28-6 triumph in 1917 was one of its more significant outings against the Tigers. It was the first victory against the Ole War Skule since 1904 and, perhaps even more important-

DIED

—

On the State Field

THANKSGIVING DAY

TULANE'S GOAT

Interment will be on

L. S. U. Parade Grounds

at 4:30 Wednesday

All Tigers be on Hand

A sign welcoming all comers to the funeral of the Tulane "goat."

ly, it marked Tulane's first successful try at beating LSU on the Tigers' home field, no doubt spurring the impetus for several more wins before the start of the rivalry's second stage. It was big enough for Tulane to celebrate by cancelling classes.

LSU coach Irving Pray glanced at Tulane's 6-0-1 record going into their 1919 meeting, and told his men, who were 5-2, they were 21 points better than the "Goats," as the Tigers referred to their football adversaries. He then proceeded to point out the weaknesses of the

Greenbacks after their 7-7 tie with Georgia.

Meanwhile, Tulane had fun with a fake tiger, complete with a scaffold and coffin, for a mock hanging after the anticipated victory. LSU won, 27-6, as Pray predicted, and the Tiger cadet corps stormed across the field at game's end, destroyed the scaffold and confiscated the coffin.

The next day there was a funeral procession in Baton Rouge for the "Tulane Goat." Mourners followed the hearse to the LSU parade grounds as the Tiger band played a dirge. As the coffin was lowered into a grave on the field, the goat was given a military salute — three shots from a cap pistol.

A year later Tulane returned fire. Playing under the presumed inspiration provided by Rosa Hart, college football's first woman cheerleader, Tulane brushed aside Pray's Tigers, 21-0.

Afterward, *The Daily Reveille*, LSU's student newspaper, ran a story headlined: "IMPOSSIBLE TO BEAT TIGER." The writer said, "It was hard luck to lose, but we're not beaten. If the Goats didn't get the heavy end of it once in a while, he'd be peeved and want to quit."

F. Edward Hebert, sports editor of the 1920 *Tulane Hullabaloo*, countered by saying the contest was "the greatest football game ever witnessed by people in this section (of the country). Deny it if they will, that old 21-0 score will rub in good and hard."

Though no one realized it at the time, the series' first stage was nearing its

THE GOAT — LSU students line up to show their Tulane "Goats."

close with Hebert's self-proclaimed "greatest game." Both institutions were on the verge of bigger and better football achievements.

COMING OF AGE, 1924-1949

Clark Shaughnessy, one of football's most renowned coaches, laid the foundation for Tulane's finest period of gridiron excellence and the Greenies' greatest era of domination over LSU — the Roarin' 1920s and the Great Depression of the 1930s.

The Green Wave won 12 of the 20 LSU games between 1920 and 1940 — 52 percent of all Tulane victories in the first century Greenie-Tiger football games. Tulane, in fact, was 10-3-2 against LSU over the 15-season period bracketed by 1920 and 1934.

In fact, when LSU took a 7-0 lead in the 1931 game, a game Tulane eventually won 34-7, it marked the first time the Greenies trailed the Tigers since 1926. It was that kind of decade in the series.

For example, in 1924, the year generally accorded as the start of big-time

FIRST GAME — The Tigers played their first game ever in Tiger Stadium on Thanksgiving Day, 1924, versus Tulane.

GREAT GRAB- Pete Burge leaps from a crowd of Greenies and snags a pass from Abe Mickal which gave LSU a 7-7 tie with Tulane in 1933.

football in Louisiana, the Green Wave won eight of nine games — and soured the dedication of LSU's Tiger Stadium with a 13-0 thumping. (Tulane, in fact, won five of its first six appearances in Tiger Stadium.) A year later, in 1925, Tulane went unbeaten (9-0-1) and posted a significant 18-7 victory over Northwestern, one of the better teams in the Midwest.

LSU, under coaches Biff Jones and Bernie Moore, also was making strides.It was inevitable, with both programs in high gear, that

SALUTE — The Tiger Band salutes Louisiana Governor Leche prior to LSU's 33-0 defeat of Tulane in 1936.

some memorable games were on tap.

One of the most noteworthy plays in LSU history came in the 1933 game in which the Tigers ran 41 rushing plays and gained yardage only 19 times. But quarterback Abe Mickal was seven of 11 passing that day, and one of his completions was a 13-yard touchdown pass to Pete Burge. The pass was high, as if Mickal was throwing it away. Burge, in the end zone, was trying to free himself from a cluster of Greenies. He leaped near the back line of the end zone, got one hand on the ball, and somehow, came down with the ball in his possession.

"He came down flat on his back," Mickal said. "It was remarkable."

The 1934 Tigers were 6-0-2, and riding an 18-game streak without a defeat, heading into the Tulane fray. The Green Wave was 8-1. An invitation for the host berth in the inaugural Sugar Bowl was in the offing for the winner.

LSU had a 12-7 lead with three minutes remaining when the Tigers punted out of their end zone to Bucky Bryan. Bryan took the kick at midfield and, on a crossing pattern, flipped the ball to Monk Simons who went the distance, despite being hit by several Tigers. The PAT gave the Green Wave a stunning 13-12 victory, and the Sugar Bowl berth.

Just as in the 1915-1917

THE RAG — *Spoils of victory in the LSU - Tulane rivalry.*

LAY DOWN — *Despite a tenacious defensive effort, Y.A. Tittle and LSU settled for a 6-6 tie with Tulane in 1947.*

period, in this era, particularly in 1935 and 1938, when as many as 15,000 fans duked it out for three hours after the game, fights in the stands were commonplace. As is often the case, the students acted the most maturely. The two studentbodies agreed on a proclamation that made three points: (1) the football field was neutral and off-limits to students; (2) a rectangular flag with colors of blue (for Tulane) and purple (for LSU) bearing the seal of Louisiana would be awarded annually to the winning school; (3) the presentation would take place at a banquet of the two student councils after the game. It was originally called a "truce flag," but became known as "The Rag," and an integral part of the series.

The most important "rag" to Dan Kirschenheuter was the patch from the canvas pants worn by Tiger Steve Van Buren in the 1943 game. Then a 17-year-old Tulane freshman out of Warren Easton High — also Van Buren's alma mater — Kirschenheuter kept the torn cloth as a life-long souvenir of that 27-0 Green Wave victory. "That win didn't just happen," he recalled. "If we were preparing for someone like Mississippi State, Coach (Monk) Simons had us work three days on them and one on LSU."

But World War II took the steam out of a lot of college programs, and Tulane was no exception.

If, somehow, a football fan in 1948 could have looked into the future, he would have been thought daft reporting results of the Tulane-LSU series.

THE LONG RUN, 1949-72

Tulane, in the late 1940s, was a football force to be reckoned with. The Green Wave had the look of a team destined to reach the heights of the sport, while the Tigers were floundering.

Among Tulane's nine victories in 1948 was a 46-0 pasting of LSU, the Bayou Bengals' worst Tiger Stadium defeat in history and the biggest Tulane margin of the series.

Tulane, in essence, went from one of its proudest moment into near oblivion. There would be close games — and tie games — during the ensuing 24 years, but no Tiger trophies.

With All-American fullback Eddie Price and a host of talented lettermen returning for 1949, Tulanians had every right to expect another powerhouse. They got a good team, one which won the Southeastern Conference championship but lost to an 8-2 Cinderella Tiger team that defeated three conference kingpins, including Tulane, en route to a Sugar Bowl berth that was the Wave's until the 21-0 loss to LSU.

Prognostications always abound before a big game, but in 1949 college kids proved the most able forecasters of all. Before the Wave-Tiger clash, students broke into Tulane Stadium and painted "LSU 21, TU 0" predictions on the ramps. They also planted rye grass seed on the playing field, which sprouted in large block letters "LSU" on the day of game and whose dark imprint remained visible on the turf even after it was cut.

And 21-0 was exactly the score of the upset that day.

"There wasn't a good ballplayer out there for us that day," admitted Charles Cusimano, then an LSU guard and later a member of the school's governing board. "Tulane's third team was better than our first team. But the difference was the scouting report and that we were more hungry."

It has sort of been that way ever since — with LSU on top — and not because of less emphasis by Tulane.

In fact, the Greenies went into half the LSU games between 1950 and 1956 as the favorite. In 1951, when six-point underdog LSU prevailed, 14-13, a New Orleans sportswriter was reminded of how Tulane students kidnapped LSU's mascot the season before and was prompted to quip, "Tulane's students should have kidnapped the (LSU) coach instead of Mike the Tiger."

Tulane raced to a 13-0 lead against a highly-favored Tiger team in 1954, only to fall 14-13. A year later the same thing happened and LSU needed a fourth-quarter touchdown

PLAY IT AGAIN — LSU has defeated Tulane by the score of 62-0 three times (1958-61-65).

to get out with a 13-13 tie.

Andy Pilney's 1956 Tulane squad, which defeated Ole Miss and Navy, giants at the time, was victimized by a super-human effort by Jimmy Taylor when he scored seven points to Tulane's six, and prevented two touch-downs with sterling defensive plays.

But two years later, with the first of the 62-0 deba-cles, it became obvious a serious discrepancy existed between the programs. Amazingly, LSU won by that exact 62-0 score three times in seven years.

In the 1965 game, with the Tigers toying with the Greenies, the LSU place-kicking team switched roles when the usual kicker Doug Moreau held for the usual holder, Billy Ezell. The PAT was missed. "We decided to do it right there on the field," said Moreau, who said Charlie McClendon wouldn't have allowed it if they had talked about it on the side-lines.

Because the PAT was missed, a few minutes later, with the score 60-0, LSU went for two, and Moreau made the catch for the two-point conversion. "Once

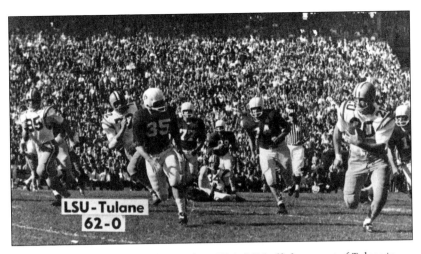

ROLL IT UP — Billy Cannon darts in for a TD in LSU's 62-0 conquest of Tulane in 1958.

we realized it was there," said Moreau, "we wanted it." They got it the hard way. After Don Schwab scored LSU's 60th point, Pat Screen's pass to Moreau for the two-point conversion was batted away. But Tulane was holding, and LSU lined up for another shot at 62-0 — and got it.

The reason LSU wanted to rub it in apparently was that the Greenies, according to the Tigers, showed little grace in 20-0 and 13-3 defeats to LSU the past two seasons. Moreau said Tulane made comments that bordered on insult.

"We've been waiting for this game for a year," said Screen with satisfaction. "They cut us pretty deep with some of their remarks after last year's game.

Coach McClendon always taught us to be gracious after a game. We had trouble with Tulane the last two years — but we won. And we said complimentary things about them. But they ran off at the mouth pretty good after last year's game."

And paid dearly for it.

THE LAST QUARTER-CENTURY

The rivalry started heat-ing up again with the arrival of Jim Pittman at Tulane in 1966.

Under Pittman, Tulane reinstituted a physical edu-cation department and made a commitment to its football program.

A spunkiness thought long gone from Tulane re-emerged under Pittman, and the 1967 Tiger game was the first show of real strength by the Green Wave in years against LSU.

The Bayou Bengals, on their way to the Sugar Bowl, had little problem in assuming a 27-7 halftime lead, but to the amazement of the Tiger Stadium crowd, the Greenies refused to fold and closed the gap to 34-27 before a late fumble allowed LSU another touchdown.

That Tulane showing becomes more impressive when it is realized that the year previous, in a 21-7 game, the Green Wave scored its first touchdown on LSU in six years.

In 1972, the schools learned how much football really can be a game of inches — which turned out to be the microscopic difference between victory and defeat in perhaps the best game ever played between the rival schools.

Playing LSU off its feet, the Bennie Ellender's Green Wave held Bert Jones (who was sacked seven times for a minus 74 yards) and the Tigers without a touchdown for the first time since 1948, but three field goals gave the Tigers a 9-3

lead with 57 seconds to play. In that time, quarterback Steve Foley took Tulane on a 67-yard drive. The last play of the game came with the Wave at the five with no timeouts left. Foley hit back Bill Huber two yards away from Tulane's biggest victory in 24 years. The ball was thrown slightly behind Huber and he had to reach back for it, giving Tiger defensive back Frank Racine enough time to come up and make the tackle inches from the goal.

The next year, in the last LSU-Tulane game to be played in the old Sugar Bowl Stadium, and the second straight year the game was held there, Tulane held LSU without a touchdown, again, for the second consecutive year, and beat the Orange Bowl-bound Tigers, 14-0.

After a quarter-century, Tulane finally managed to beat the Tigers.

And it's happened since. LSU later fell to Tulane in three of four games (1979, 1981, 1982).

Still, during the same two-decade interim, the Tigers have won 16 of 20 games against the Green Wave.

It's a percentage LSU should be content with.

Still, almost 30 years after that last horrendous score, there are Tiger fans who won't be happy until the Tigers again duplicate the infamous 62-0 difference between the programs.

"Remember," one said sternly. "62-0 isn't a score. It's a way of life."

ALL IN THE FAMILY

4

Like father, like son, the saying goes. Football at LSU, its faithful like to think, is a family affair. There is a certain pedigree that gives substance to the notion.

Some of the most notable latter-day Tigers grew up sitting on their daddies' knees, listening to their football exploits. Most of them true, too. The sons followed in their paw-pads.

Bert Jones was a second-generation Tiger, of sorts. His father, William "Dub" Jones, was a half-back with uncommonly good potential when he played for LSU as a fresh-man in 1942. Unfortunately for LSU, because of wartime circumstances, Dub was at Tulane in its Navy V-12 program in 1943. World War II was probably the biggest single event of the 20th Century and it added an extra little dash of history to the LSU-Tulane series in the form of Dub Jones.

The Tigers defeated the Greenies, 18-6, in '42 with Jones tottin' the ball. In 1943, after Jones switched sides, Tulane beat LSU, 27-0, making Jones the only man ever to play for LSU when it beat Tulane, and for Tulane when it beat LSU.

There also has been All-American tight end Billy Truax (1961-63), whose son Chris toiled in the Tigers' offensive line (1988-91). Guard Ruffin Rodrigue (1986-89) was preceded in the trenches by center Ruffin Rodrigue, Sr. (1962-64). Robert Stovall (1906-09), a center, and his brother, halfback Rowson Stovall (1907-09) played together, and quarterback Hefley Stovall (1927-28) followed his father and

STRANGE — Clarence "Pop" Strange was the first of three Stranges to play at LSU. His sons Charles and David would star in the purple and gold years later.

uncle to LSU. End Norm Stevens (1922-25) finished his college career 25 years before his boy, quarterback Norm Stevens Jr., started as a Tiger. Eddie Ray (1967-69) was a bone-crunching fullback while his son, flanker Scott Ray (1990-93), took up pass receiving as a Tiger.

There's more than a brotherhood among Tigers. A Tiger, it's often noted,

can't change his stripes. It's in his genes.

Clarence "Pop" Strange was a starting tackle on LSU's 1935 and 1936 Southeastern Conference championship teams.

"I was scared to death when I first got here," Strange said in 1977, just before his retirement. "I was one of 112 recruits. I weighed 192 and there was only one tackle smaller

than me. When a coach said, 'All tackles over here,' there were 17 in the group."

There was incentive to be among the regulars, in those days roughly the first 30. "The guys who played ate like kings," Strange said. "Steak, potatoes, dessert, the trimmings. All you wanted. The scrubs ate cold cuts."

Strange was able to hold

REACH OUT — Charles "Bo" Strange (72) lunges for Rice halfback Roland Jackson in 1959.

There are a lot of LSU fans just like me," Curly Brisset said. It is a sobering thought.

There are fans, and there are fans. There are few clusters of fans though, with as intense devotion — and apparent compulsion to show their colors — as LSU fans.

They don't just paint little emblems on their face for a cutesy close-up during a television game. There are those who wear simulated tiger-skin outfits to games. "We like to show our colors — or stripes," one sniffed.

There's another who has a standing offer to pay anyone $1,000 if they catch him not wearing purple socks.

When Brisset made his statement to an almost disbelieving Douglas S. Looney of Sports Illustrated in 1979, he carried a photograph of his $200,000 New Orleans home. The four antebellum columns, fence, gate and mailbox were all painted purple and gold. A painting of a tiger graced the double front doors.

"When I was having the doors put up," Brisset said, "my neighbor was sneaking around in the bushes and I heard him call to his wife in this anguished voice, 'Gloria, he's at it again.'"

That's not the best. Many years ago, with Brisset and his pregnant wife, Rosemary, at a game, he told her what he wanted to name their child. Rosemary, just as disbelieving then as Looney was later, said, "You wouldn't dare."

Twenty years later their son, Billy Cannon Brisset, was a student-manager for the football Tigers.

down a spot at the training table, and when he was finished playing he spent most of the ensuing 44 years on the LSU staff. He was, in fact, present for 17 of LSU's first 19 bowl games.

Strange was the Tiger director of recruiting, and he recruited his two sons to follow him on the Bengal line. Both were starters, Charles "Bo" Strange from 1958 through 1960, David Strange from 1963 through 1965.

Bo Strange, now a noted physician, was a sophomore tackle on the White Team in 1958, and was the

target for Coach Frank Howard when Clemson played LSU in the Sugar Bowl.

Clemson mapped its game plan with Strange in mind and aimed its power running game straight at the 202-pounder, who responded with a heroic performance in LSU's 11th victory of that season, 7-0. Clemson never penetrated the LSU 20, and Howard

admitted afterward his strategy didn't pan out the way he figured. Howard said in his opinion Bo Strange, not Billy Cannon, deserved the MVP award.

"After looking at all of the LSU pictures," Howard said, "we figured Strange to be the weak link in their line. We figured we could drive him back 10 yards at a crack and planned our offense to run right over

HANDS — Ken Kavanaugh, Sr., starred in the 1939 contest with Holy Cross, scoring four touchdowns.

LIKE FATHER . . . — Ken Kavanaugh, Jr. donned the purple and gold from 1969-71.

him. But as it turned out, he was the toughest man on the field."

No single family contributed as much to Tiger football as the Kinchens of Baton Rouge. Gaynell Kinchen played on the Chinese Bandits from 1958 through 1960 and was in on a couple of LSU's biggest plays of the era.

Kinchen recovered the Ole Miss fumble that led to the Tigers' first touchdown in the 14-0 1958 victory. Then, two years later in Oxford when LSU was a three-touchdown underdog,

Kinchen helped foil the Rebels' perfect record and national championship aspirations in a 6-6 tie with a timely sack of quarterback Jake Gibbs.

Gaynell's brother, Gary, played center for the Tigers from 1960 through 1962.

Twenty-four years after his last game in a Tiger uniform, Gaynell's son, Brian, started his LSU career. Brian Kinchen became an All-SEC tight end, whose late touchdown catch of a Tommy Hodson pass gave LSU a thrilling 26-23 nod over Georgia in 1987.

A second son, Todd, was an All-SEC split end in 1990 and 1991. Todd, who was an extremely talented, exciting performer, took a swing pass against Texas A&M in 1990 and turned it into a breath-taking 79-yard touchdown that not only spurred LSU to a 17-8 upset but had wide-eyed fans comparing it to Billy Cannon's run against Ole Miss 31 years before.

Ken Kavanaugh, who succeeded Gaynell Tinsley at end, was one of LSU's all-time finest players, very possibly the finest pass receiver in Tiger annals, an All-American who finished high in the Heisman Trophy balloting in 1939 when Iowa's Nile Kinnick was the recipient. Kavanaugh, who led the nation in receptions that season with 30 for 531 yards, was the first lineman to be awarded the Knute Rockne Memorial Award, and later was a National Football Foundation and Hall of Fame inductee.

Thirty years after his last LSU game, his son, Ken Kavanaugh, Jr., who grew up in Pennsylvania as his dad worked as a coach and scout in professional football, was cavorting around Southern football fields as an outstanding split end for the Bayou Bengals. Ken Jr. had a fine career at LSU, though he didn't have as much flair for the dramatic as his daddy, who once scored seven consecutive touchdowns, an LSU record, and set another record for scoring 54 points, most ever by a lineman.

Kavanaugh Sr. was also involved in one of LSU's most memorable football moments. The Tigers were leading Rice, 6-0, in the third quarter in Houston when the Owls drove inside the LSU one. The Tigers hadn't given up a point in its two previous games, but this looked to be a sure thing.

Of course, as we all have learned, there is no such thing as a sure thing. As Red Vickers hit the line, he was smacked hard and the ball went flying out of his arms. Kavanaugh pulled the fumble out of mid-air, and he took off for the other end of the stadium on his long, lanky legs. A hundred yards later he was in the end zone to ensure LSU its third victory in three games.

That was the team which would lose only one regular season game — the infamous "hidden-ball" 7-6 chicanery at Vanderbilt. "If Vandy doesn't beat us," Kavanaugh said with a sad shake of the head, "we might have gone to the Rose Bowl instead of Alabama."

Second-ranked Holy Cross was LSU's second opponent of 1939, and the Tigers were treated rudely in Worcester, Massachusettes Crusader coach Joe Sheeketski taunted the Tigers in the press, hinting he might start his

AHEAD OF HIS TIME — Ken Kavanaugh, Sr. was arguably the finest offensive receiving threat of his era.

second team against LSU. "They laughed at us," Kavanaugh remembered. "They were asking us what we made the trip for."

Kavanaugh virtually sewed up a spot on the All-America team with an eye-catching day. He scored four touchdowns in a 26-7 upset. Tailback Leo Bird hit Kavanaugh with three touchdown passes, and Kavanaugh, with his flair for the unexpected, intercepted a lateral and sped 80 yards for his fourth touchdown. Those are the kind of LSU stories, you'd have to believe, that are handed down from father to son, from Tiger to Tiger.

CHRISTMAS IN HAVANA

5

What U.S. football team first played on foreign soil and when?

Answer: Harvard vs. McGill University of Montreal, Canada, on October 23, 1874. Actually, what they played was rugby.

But there was a time, in 1907 to be exact, when the Louisiana State Tigers represented a small band of pioneers, missionaries really, for true American-style football. Their trip was a milestone. It was the first appearance by a United States football team, playing uniquely American football, in a foreign country.

The LSU season was supposed to end after a 48-0 thumping of Baylor. But the high-for-time score must have caught someone's fancy in, of all places, Havana.

Cubans not only were crazy about American football, but took the University of Havana team to heart as it beat opponent after opponent. Football picked up fans by the thousands on the island-nation, and they gloried in nationalistic fervor by beating every American service team in the area.

This was less than 10 years after the Spanish-American War, and the Cubans deeply resented the U.S. military presence on their island. The American soldiers and sailors didn't have to be reminded to "Remember the Maine!" The hull of the sunken battleship could still be seen above the waves in Havana harbor, a grim remembrance of what the men on the U.S. Navy ships then at anchor in Havana, and the soldiers at a nearby garrison, Camp Campbell, viewed as treachery.

Cuba was a prickly tinderbox. Feelings were running high on both sides, and almost anything could have lit the fuse to a political incident. But by the end of 1907, the Cubans wanted badly for Havana to take on a U.S. college team with some standing, which was thought necessary to validate Havana's football prominence.

When LSU coach Edgar Wingard got the invitation to play on Christmas Day, he leaped at the opportunity for an exotic trip and more football, even though it meant keeping his 13-man team in training an extra month.

A group of excited Baton Rouge fans raised $2,000 — no small amount at the turn-of-the-century — for Wingard to bet in Cuba, though it may have briefly looked like a sucker bet. Wingard found the Cubans were combing the island for ringers, to bolster the Havana University team. Apparently, the Cubans meant to get that football validation one way or another.

But it was the servicemen and other Americans that most worried Wingard. His team was met with inordinate hospitality from countrymen, the military

whose own football teams had lost to the Cubans and who saw the Tigers as the redemption of their national honor. Every time the Tigers ran into other Americans they were treated to drinks and a food spread. Somehow, the Tigers survived a diet of daiquiris, and a dish of arroz con pollo, a combination of stewed chicken and saffron rice. It was a dietary combination that had Wingard concerned, along with the nonchalant attitude exhibited by his players.

If that weren't enough, a huge crisis arose at the last minute. At the eleventh hour, University of Havana authorities pulled out of the promotion, apparently developing cold feet that the attraction wouldn't draw.

Another group of speculators stepped up, however, and were successful in selling the game as a sort of turn-of-the-century Super Bowl. The sideline seats were filled with Cuban aristocrats and high government officials who paid $10 apiece, a rather hefty sum in those days. Elsewhere there was a large contingent of U.S. soldiers

EL RUBIO VASELINO: Doc Fenton starred for the undefeated 1908 Tigers.

and sailors.

The servicemen made politicians nervous at the Christmas Day gathering. They made a large cheering section, and began a series inflammatory chants of a decidedly ethnic nature that put officials on edge.

The pregame yells included one which went:

"Lick the Spicks, kill the Spicks
Rah! Rah! Rah! Louisiana!"

Wingard's Tigers couldn't help but notice an unusual display on the Cuban bench: a long row of drinking glasses, each filled with wine. Every so often, during warm-ups, the Cuban players would run over and gulp one

HAVANA — LSU torched the University of Havana, 56-0, in Cuba in 1907.

down.

A.C. Infante-Garcia — a 300-pound lineman who had been recruited since the season just to handle LSU's W.M. Lyles, a superb guard who in that era was considered a near-giant, weighing 200 pounds — ran to the sidelines and chug-a-lugged several glasses of wine. George "Doc" Fenton, LSU's sensational 22-year-old sophomore, eyed him, then cryptically advised Lyles to "Hit that guy in the stomach with your head and he's done for."

The promoters made a killing. The game drew 10,000 spectators, and the game was barely underway when Lyles drew a bead on Infante-Garcia's bulging belly, which couldn't be contained by his tight jersey, and fired right in. Recalled Fenton: "The big guy sprouted like an artesian well. I give you my word. We nearly had to swim out of there."

The rout was on. The Tigers were off to a 56-0 runaway, scoring 10 touchdowns (they counted five points each until 1912) and six conversions. The Cubans never came close to scratching the scoreboard.

The afternoon was filled with derogatory yells of the American servicemen, and the sky often filled with blue caps. Every time LSU scored, sailors from the U.S.S. Paducah and U.S.S Dubuque threw up their caps and let go with their insulting chants.

The red-haired Fenton had several spectacular runs, and finished the game with his jersey ripped and torn. It was Wingard's custom to soak Fenton's woolen shirt in a mild acid solution to weaken the fabric — creating perhaps the first tearaway jersey. Cuban fans gave Fenton a new moniker — "El Rubio Vaselino": the Vaselined Redhead.

Doc

6

"Doc" was his name, and football was very definitely his game.

It's a name that will live as long as his game is played at LSU.

George Ellwood "Doc" Fenton was an extraordinary athlete with matinee idol looks. Known as the "Artful Dodger" on the fanciful sports pages of the day, and at other times called "the Kandy Kid," Fenton was universally known as "Doc" because his father traveled as a singer with an old time Indian medicine show.

Doc Fenton put LSU on the football map.

The legend of LSU's first football great has grown with time, but hear what his contemporaries said of him: "When the ball was snapped," said Coach Mike Donahue, whose great Auburn team of 1908 lost to Fenton and the unparalleled Bayou Bengals of '08, "he was capable of rushing off in any direction. He was the consummate football player, born to run. He lived and loved the attacking side of football."

"I saw Jim Thorpe,"

said Troy Middleton, LSU president in the 1950s, "but Doc Fenton was a better player." Mississippi A&M (now State) coach Fred Furman, who not only lost the recruiting war for Fenton but two games in large part because of him, said Fenton was the "greatest quarterback I ever saw on a field."

At the time, LSU had been fielding a team for less than two decades. And apparently the way Fenton got into a Tiger uniform would set off alarms in the offices of the NCAA these days. But it was the way

THE GREATEST — The 1908 Tigers were arguably the finest team of the early years of LSU football.

things were done then, during this period when Southern schools went North for coaches as well as players, and as far as LSU was concerned, one player in particular: Fenton.

Fenton's career began with St. Michael's College in Canada and continued at Mansfield Normal in Pennsylvania, where he played four years at end. You have to wonder about the eligibility rules of the day when you have Fenton recalling that after four seasons at Mansfield, he had offers from LSU and Mississippi A&M.

"I guess you could say I was one of the first of the boys from the Pennsylvania coal country to come down here to play football," Fenton said in 1958. "I got all the fundamentals playing rugby in Toronto. I learned how to kick on the run, and I learned how to operate in an open field."

He chose LSU for two reasons: a slick-talking coach named Edgar Wingard and the nickel beers in Baton Rouge. When Wingard, a Pennsylvanian, recognized Fenton's fondness for a brew on a visit to Louisiana, he reminded Doc of the blue laws back home, as well as in Mississippi.

Wingard went about building his team around Fenton, whose background in rugby and soccer made him a dazzling broken-field runner. Since linemen carried the ball as much as backs in those days, Wingard kept Fenton at end, using him on a variety of reverses, along with double and triple laterals.

Other than a trip in which LSU played — and lost — two games in two days to Texas and then to Texas A&M, Wingard's carefully recruited team improved as the season wore on, all the way to the season-ending game with Baylor. The Bears were prohibitive 5-1 favorites.

Fenton got the ball on the opening kickoff, and instead of returning it, he sent a 60-yard punt downfield. A surprised Baylor player fumbled the boot, and LSU's Les Stovall picked it up and trotted across for a touchdown in the game's first 17 seconds. The Tigers went on to win 48-0 as the bookies committed hara-kiri.

That was the game which sent LSU to Cuba on Christmas Day, and a 56-0 massacre of the University of Havana.

That show-no-quarter football conquest was a harbinger of things to come in 1908 — a season like no other in LSU annals.

Wingard moved Fenton to quarterback, which meant the 165-pounder would be handling the ball on every play. With Fenton at quarterback, which he at first resisted, LSU produced one of the finest teams of football's early era. For decades afterward, it was the standard by which every other Tiger team was judged. It probably still should be.

LSU, which averaged an unheard of 180-pounds andwith equally unmatched speed, must have been viewed as a team of supermen in 1908, a season of almost incomparable glory — and suspicion.

Consider this: The Tigers, in the era of the five-point touchdown, were actually close to achieving "point-a-minute" status. LSU scored 442 points in 450 minutes, and surrendered only one touchdown in their 10-0-0 season. Even a safety LSU gave up was hardly earned. It came at Auburn, and Fenton said, "I was kicking from behind my own goal, and an Auburn tackle broke through to block it. The ball was bouncing around, so I picked it up and was getting ready to run it out when a fan reached over the rope and cracked me over the head with a cane. It knocked me cold."

LSU that season was a team the likes of which had never been seen in Dixie. Jim Halligan, a pioneer football official who worked all of the Tiger games that memorable season flatly maintained in an interview with Peter Finney of the *New Orleans States-Item* almost a half century later that the 1908 Tigers was the finest team ever to come out of the South. "They had the lateral pass down to perfection," Halligan said. "All of the backs were big, fast, triple-threat men who handled a football like a basketball. Fenton's knack of kicking on the run was fantastic. All of them were masters of the change of pace, stiff-arm, blocking on the run."

The sensational Tigers, however, were also the object of finger-pointing. Vanderbilt, then a real Southern power, Tulane, and Auburn, which gave up the only points of the season in its defeat by LSU, began a whisper campaign of LSU "professionalism." And the more the Tigers won, the louder came the accusations.

They were picked up by Grantland Rice, a Vanderbilt graduate who was a sports editor in Nashville, who charged LSU was playing with "ringers." Rice said he could prove that six players, including Fenton, were paid salaries to play football.

LSU President Thomas Boyd asked for an investigation. Ultimately, the eligibility of only one player, halfback Mike Lally, came into question. During the summer, Lally sang in a movie house in Tonawanda, N.Y., and played baseball. When he was on the road with the baseball team, Lally paid a baritone to take his place by endorsing over one of his baseball checks to the singer. That check, brought before the Southern Intercollegiate Athletic Association, was the only evidence brought against LSU.

In fact, Lally, who was dismissed from the team in 1909, was allowed to return in 1910.

None of Rice's allegations were proved, nor was LSU found guilty of any serious charges. The essential clearing of LSU of "professionalism" though, never seemed to quite catch up to the accusations.

As it turned out, Auburn, not LSU, was generally recognized as the Southern champion, a ruling ignored by Tiger fans, particularly when many, like the *Memphis Commercial Appeal*, did give the Tigers their due, calling Fenton, Lally and guard William Hillman the South's best at their positions, and ranking LSU as the best in Southern football — LSU's first true championship.

When the team returned from its final game, there was a civic banquet and parade down Third Street led by Gov. J.Y. Sanders. Wingard was presented with a gold-handled umbrella.

Still, it was a season that refuses to fade in Tiger memory. If converted to today's scoring system, the 1908 Tigers would have tallied 508 points. An illustration of LSU's potency is its 34 touchdowns of more than 20 yards, and eight of 60 or more yards. Fenton, who scored 36 touchdowns in three seasons, totalled 125 points in '08. Even though it was accomplished in the day of the five-point touchdown, it's a figure that 85 years later no other Tiger has yet equalled.

"In 1969 we erased almost every offensive record in the LSU book," said former LSU coach Charlie McClendon. "Except the 1908 records," he quickly amended. "I think those records will stand forever."

The Fenton era came to a close with a 6-2 record in 1909, with Doc saying of John Mayhew, the new LSU coach, who was a 1906 All-American halfback at Brown: "He spent his time trying to prove he was a better broken-field runner than me.

STRANGE DAYS- An LSU punt hits the goalpost and bounces into the arms of a Mississippi A&M player for a TD in 1922.

The Voice of the Tigers

7

There he goes. Dances through the middle of the line, BREAKS FREE, at the 30 . . . 40 . . . 45 . . . ROOOLLLLLLLED out of bounds near midfield. First and 10, Tigers.

John Ferguson, many times.

John Ferguson, broadcasting a horrible 1950 football game, turned to his colorman.

The analyst — Gordon McClendon, founder of the Liberty network — was fast asleep, head tossed back, mouth wide open and emitting a sound close to the rhythmic blasts of a train whistle. "I prefer to believe it was the game and not the broadcast," Ferguson sniffed. The score was 33-7.

Forty years later, Ferguson turned off the mike. The rich baritone voice with the very proper personality that served LSU as a distinct signature — as much a part of the Tiger imprint as Billy Cannon, Bert Jones or Pete Maravich — signed off.

Ferguson stepped away from the radio broadcasts he had done continuously since 1961 — and intermit-tently since 1946 — in 1984. But he had retained his status and identification as Voice of the Tigers on TigerVision, the school's cable outlet, though those telecasts were a stopgap, generally a step below the more attractive Tiger games which were often carried on network television.

But that too eventually was relinquished, and by the 1987 season, for the first time in 40 years he had no broadcasting duties. "It's not hard giving up this (TigerVision)," Ferguson said in 1987. "It was much harder giving up radio.

John Ferguson, the longtime Voice of the Tigers.

That was my career."

Ferguson chose to concentrate his energies on the Tiger Athletic Foundation, the fund-raising arm of the athletic department of which he was director. As much as Ferguson relished his role as Voice of the Tigers, he realized his less-publicized duties may well have been more important to LSU.

"Making footprints" is the way Ferguson described his fund-raising efforts, which in large measure fuels the program.

"I knew I'd be good at this," Ferguson said with a chuckle. "Years ago (former ticket manager) Jack Gilmore asked me to help him get rid of six tickets in Section eight, East Side.

Sold them in 10 minutes."

In 1942, Ferguson, then a recent graduate of Louisiana Tech with a degree in chemistry, sold an El Dorado, Arkansas, radio station owner named Fletcher Bowes on his budding talents.

"What makes you think you can do this?" Bowes roared at the suddenly shaking applicant. "Because," Ferguson said, working up enough courage to retort thinly, "I'm better than anyone you have."

He got the job, doing everything from sweeping floors to announcing Cotton States League baseball, 70 hours a week at $17.50.

It took awhile, but Ferguson worked his way to the Texas League, and then to what he described as "the Big Leagues then and would be the Big Leagues now."

One hundred forty-four missions as an Army Air Corps transport pilot over "the Hump," the Himalayan mountains between India and China, in hellish weather conditions at the earth's ceiling, Ferguson said made him whatever he became.

"I was always the youngest man in my crews, just a kid of 22," he recalled. "But I was always known as the 'Old Man.' I wasn't a fuddy-duddy, exactly, and I wasn't really a military man. But I was a military pilot, and I carried a lot of responsibility. I took it seriously. "

The material Ferguson piloted over the Hump supplied the B-29s that were bombing Japan, and occasionally the Chinese Communists who were fighting the Nationalists and the Japanese.

"We didn't know who we were going to end up backing," he said, "so I guess we were playing footsie with everybody. They weren't any different from any of the other soldiers we came in contact with."

There are moments that live in a man's soul forever. Ferguson's came when he took aboard 50 Chinese troops destined for training in India. It was 1945 and China was suffering.

The troops ranged in age from 11 years to over 70.

The cargo area, where the troops were, wasn't pressurized. Ferguson began to worry when the swirling weather over the Himalayas began buffeting the transport more than usual. To escape the storm, and for better visibility, Ferguson took the plane higher. And higher.

"It was sickening," he said. "No one said anything. When we landed I didn't move for a moment, then told the crew not to bother going to the cargo area. I didn't want to see it, and I knew they didn't. No one could have survived.

"We went to sign our flight papers, then walked slowly back out to the runway. The cargo door opened and one soldier struggled out. We couldn't believe it."

While the crew helped the one Chinese soldier, another staggered out. Within an hour every one of the 50-man contingent stood at attention in a raggedy line along side the transport.

"There wasn't," said Ferguson, "a dry eye on the base."

A year later, Ferguson was at LSU working on a master's degree in broadcasting. WJBO radio, which had just successfully bid on the Tiger football games, inquired about

Ferguson's availability. He almost knocked down the door trying to get into the radio booth.

Ferguson insisted that LSU team, the 1946 Tigers, was the very best he ever saw.

"There was a quarterback named Y.A. Tittle, a punter named Rip Collins who was the best in LSU history, Ray Coates, an excellent back. That team, filled with returning war veterans, was six deep everywhere."

A halfback, Joe Glamp, from Mount Pleasant, Pennsylvania, who lettered in 1942 before going to war, is Ferguson's favorite example of just how good that team was.

"Glamp was unhappy about his playing," Ferguson said, "and went to see Coach Bernie Moore. Moore told him there just wasn't that much opportunity for him at LSU."

Glamp later started three seasons for the Pittsburgh Steelers.

Still, the 1946 Tigers lost one game — 26-7 to Georgia Tech — and were tied 0-0 by Arkansas in the infamous "Ice Bowl."

Ferguson said the Tech loss was "just one of those

games. But Tech scored on the last play of the game, and seconds later the stadium lights went out. (Coach) Bobby Dodd took his team off the field and never kicked the extra point. He added insult to injury."

In the Cotton Bowl, played in a blustery snowstorm, LSU ran up 15 first downs to Arkansas' one, and gained 271 yards to the Razorbacks' 54, but couldn't score.

In the almost four decades in which Ferguson was the voice of the Tigers, he said some of LSU's finest efforts ironically came in defeat. The scintillating 17-12 loss to a superior Southern Cal team in 1979, which hinged on two late controversial calls, was the best game Ferguson said he ever saw the Tigers play. A 3-0 defeat to Notre Dame in South Bend during the 1970 season got second billing.

LSU's 28-8 thumping of the Irish in 1971, and Bert Jones' 17-16 last second miracle against Ole Miss in 1972 are next on his all-time list.

The worst game Ferguson could recall was a 3-3 "clinker" with

*P*art of the reason Tiger Stadium turns so loud at games, particularly big games, is that LSU fans are world-class party people before kickoff and after it's over. But it's not the only picture.

Pre-game festivities in Baton Rouge hotels and lounges normally begin heating up about sundown Friday night and continue through Sunday morning. But the stadium tailgate crowd is far more family oriented.

Tailgate cookouts, an art form in the stadium parking lots, are an LSU ritual that is decades old. Amid cold beer and boudin, highballs and hogshead cheese, the Tiger faithful get a game face on.

"It's just a big party, that's the thing," said George Kalil, one of the Tigers' most devoted fans. "We'll take a TV along and watch the afternoon college game," Kalil, a former LSU football player, said. Kalil parked in the same spot from 1952 through 1991, when LSU assigned a special spot closer to the stadium for him, but he remembered his old camping grounds near the south end of Tiger Stadium with fondness. "We knew everybody around us, and everybody brought something different to eat. We were right where the visiting team would pass, and we would wait to yell at them. It was good-natured."

And it's not always easy being a football fan from New Orleans, Kalil said. You have to be dedicated.

"If you're a Saints fan too, it's rough. We get back home from LSU about 12:30 Sunday morning. You have to get up and go to Mass, and then get to the Saints' game by 11 o'clock," he said. "By Sunday night, you're dead tired."

As far back as the 1940s, Kalil took it upon himself to escort promising students, those with high academic potential, around LSU and show them around the buildings and professors they would most need to know about. Many schools have such academic recruiting tactics now, but Kalil was doing it almost a half century ago, and without official sanction.

"I was a poor boy from Rayville when I came to LSU," Kalil said. "LSU fed me, clothed me, gave me an education, gave me my life, really. I've always felt I owed LSU, and that was one way I tried to pay LSU back."

---

clearly dominated, Jones completed passes for four first downs and eventually the winning touchdown," Ferguson marveled. "Magnificent."

Billy Cannon's 89-yard punt return that beat Ole Miss 7-3 in 1959 is Ferguson's runner-up performance, although, ironically, he didn't broadcast that game. In 1958 and 1959 Ferguson was doing the Southwest Conference Game of the Week, causing him to miss LSU's national championship season and Cannon's run, the most storied play in Tiger history.

Through good games and bad, Ferguson's trademark was terse reporting which gave every opponent its due and offered no excuses for the Tigers.

"I've always felt the listener should know what's going on," Ferguson said, "and I've never been a cheerleader.

"We always prepared, and we approached each broadcast as our business — professionally. We wanted to be second to none in that regard; we were sensitive to that.

"But we also wanted it clearly identified as a Tiger

Tennessee in 1964.

Bert Jones' heroics against Ole Miss, Ferguson said, was the finest individual performance he ever witnessed.

"With 3:02 remaining, against a team that had

THE VOICE — John Ferguson's voice boomed LSU football games across the country every Saturday on WWL radio for decades.

broadcast — and from Tiger Stadium. I think we pulled it off."

LSU's Saturday night spectaculars were easy to broadcast, Ferguson said. From the late 1950s to the late 1980s LSU generally produced very representative teams. The Saturday night power of two clear channel stations, one in New Orleans, one in Shreveport — at a time when few schools played at night — gave the Tigers a "wonderful public relations window."

"I was in the right place at the right time," Ferguson said. "I started doing LSU football in the heyday of football broad-

casting, the '50s and '60s. Before then, the game wasn't as popular. And in the last 10 years or so, with cable, with more and more teams playing at night, the market has become fragmented. There was never a better time for broadcasting (than during Ferguson's professional prime)."

And he did it in good times and bad, doing a game in 1968 two days after his father died, and another in 1979, a day after his grandson was born.

The networks, of course, were not unaware of Ferguson. He did U.S. Open golf, the Liberty Bowl for seven years, the

Sugar Bowl for NBC radio, American Football League for ABC, New Orleans Saints games, and Southeastern Conference basketball.

"I decided this is where I wanted to live," he said, "but I accepted just enough network work to satisfy myself that I was at least in the same league with some of my colleagues."

The very first AFL game telecast out of Denver (versus the Oakland Raiders) was broadcast by Ferguson, who was aided by the Broncos' public relations man, Paul Manasseh, who later became LSU's sports information director.

But Ferguson remembered that 1960 game mainly because of a horse show at midfield during halftime.

"A horse embarrassed himself in front of the cameras," Ferguson said with a hearty laugh. "And when the cleaning man went out with his scooper, the camera stayed on him all the way out . . . and all the way back. It seemed like forever."

Nothing, of course, is forever. Ferguson always promised himself he would get out of the broadcast booth by the time he reached 50. That was in 1972. "Fifty just got here a lot faster than I expected it to," he said.

It could have been coincidence, but when controversial athletic director Bob Brodhead surrendered WWL-radio, which reached 43 states on those Saturday night football games, as the Tigers' flagship station, the impetus to nudge Ferguson out of the broadcast booth may have been provided.

Brodhead put the broadcast rights up for bid, and they went to WJBO, the Baton Rouge station where Ferguson began his career, for $1 million.

"I begged him not to do it," Ferguson said. "I told him if the deal (with WJBO) wasn't too far gone, to buy his way out if he had to. WWL was that important."

When WJBO became the anchor of the LSU network, Ferguson was asked to do one half of play-by-play and new announcer Jim Hawthorne would do one half. Ferguson felt the suggestion was demeaning, and declined. "I told them I would do one more sea-

son, the last on the WWL contract, then step aside."

Joe Dean, Brodhead's successor, eventually got the Tigers back on WWL-radio, and Hawthorne has been a solid replacement for Ferguson.

In personal demanding times as those surely were, Ferguson harkened back to his days flying "the Hump."

A steep drop into a northwest Indian valley after an exhausting flight, onto a cobblestone runway just as the stormy skies sapped the last rays of visibility, ran through Ferguson's memory bank.

"That's what I mean about that experience making me what I am. After flying "the Hump," things that seem overpowering to some people seem a bit trivial to me. I think I have a sense of what's important."

Ferguson hasn't been "the Voice of the Tigers" since the fall of 1986, but he continued spending his Saturday nights where he spent them for most of the previous four decades - in Tiger Stadium, usually from the press deck. He admitted football isn't nearly as enjoyable, though, as

when he was on the mike. "The game," Ferguson said, "just isn't as focused to me."

What was focused was a sense of mission — leaving footprints — that Ferguson exuded with an energy and enthusiasm that belied his almost seven decades.

"Sixty-six is startling?" Ferguson asked rhetorically in 1987, and with a hearty laugh.

"Figure out how many minutes there are in 66 years. There isn't a minute in my life that I haven't loved."

THE ALL-AMERICAN BOY

8

Who would have thought the All-American boy would be Syrian?

Abe Mickal was everything Americans love to see embodied in their college heroes: seemingly a near-super human athlete, a triple-threat on the football field, with an intellect to match, and old fashioned values and virtues.

Mickal was a real-life model of Jack Armstrong, All-American Boy, covered in LSU glory and the red, white and blue.

But Mickal knew what performing under pressure meant long before he ever flung a football. He was born Ibrahim Khalil Mickal in what was then Syria, in an area which was partitioned after World War I and is now part of Lebanon.

Turkish soldiers fiercely fought Moroccan troops, who took up arms for France during Mickal's youth, and bands of outlaws roamed the land for whatever they could get from the people. "They ransacked the country," Mickal said of all the armies. "We had to defend ourselves."

Two women brandishing rifles with bandoleers crossed over the shoulders are featured in a family photograph, with little four-year-old Abe also in the picture and also wearing a bandoleer.

"There was one bandit who was called 'The Bloodshedder,' " Mickal recalled, "who killed people, then piled the bodies on a caisson to frighten the townsfolk. The men of our town, Talia, pulled the wagon out because of the sight and smell, and many youngsters tried to help. I fell and struck my head on the wheel." Seven decades later, the scar is still on Mickal's forehead.

ABE — LSU halfback Abe Mickal was named a Louisiana state senator by Louisiana Governor Huey Long.

Yet, if he hadn't been placed in such an angry, wretched land, there might never have been such an LSU legend as Abe Mickal.

Abe's father, Khalil Mickal, had migrated to the United States early in the century with a brother, Toufick. They settled in Jeanerette, Louisiana, with relatives who helped them get started in the business of peddling merchandise to the farmhouses of the area. The brothers became natu-ralized citizens in 1903.

But when the brothers' father became seriously ill, they decided one would have to return to care for him as long as he lived.

Khalil went, and, in the midst of that crushing mis-ery, met his wife and began raising a family. It was diffi-cult at first as the entire household had to sleep on a dirt floor.

Najla, the oldest daugh-ter, was born in 1911, and Abe came in 1912. Abe's mother was pregnant with another child, Chafik, when his father returned to the United States in 1914. He was to send for the fam-ily as soon as he could, but World War I intervened.

Abe was seven when Khalil was finally able to bring the family over. Khalil settled in McComb, Mississippi, where he opened a general store. It served a need in McComb, and the Mickals had a rela-tively comfortable exis-tence — though Khalil worked long and hard. Two other children came along as the Mickals were estab-lishing themselves as the epitome of the American Dream.

Meanwhile, Abe was making a name for himself at McComb High where he became one of the hottest and most memorable names in the history of the school. Mickal was a sensa-tional athlete and won 12 letters in his four years, and excelled equally in the classroom.

Only the classroom — and his after-school work in the store — was impor-tant to Khalil. "Because my dad wanted all his children to work," Mickal recount-ed, "he was against my playing football. I'll never forget my first game in high school. I was holding the ball for the opening kickoff when he ran into the stadium and pulled me off the field."

It was after that Khalil found how much his customers enjoyed sports. Even the mayor came by to see if he could get Khalil to relent. Eventually he did, though Khalil didn't close the store to see Abe play a game, until his boy's senior season in 1931.

That game was against Brookhaven on Thanksgiving Day, and Khalil and four other elder countrymen went to see their first football game. Abe had a good day, scoring three touchdowns as McComb won easily.

"When I got home, Dad and the others were waiting," he said. "All they could say was, 'Damn it, when you got the ball you ran into a pile. On the other side of the field there was no one. Why didn't you run there?' The air went out of my balloon."

Few others were questioning where Abe ran. By that time everyone in the South — no, everyone in college football — knew of Abe Mickal, an extraordinary passer, runner and kicker.

One of the religious brothers at St. Stanislaus in Bay St. Louis, Mississippi, talked to Mickal of the glories of Notre Dame under Knute Rockne, which is how long-distance recruiting was done at the time. Notre Dame seemed to be Mickal's first choice — until the news that Rockne had been killed in a plane crash.

"I kind of lost interest after Rockne died," Mickal said. "Things were different then, and you couldn't just get up and go to South Bend, Indiana, unless you were sure you wanted stay there for a while. I wasn't completely certain."

Mickal gravitated toward LSU, where he had developed a close relationship with Tiger assistant Ben Enis. "He used to drive over for Sunday dinner, when driving from Baton Rouge to McComb took hours and hours, and the family loved to see him," Mickal said. "Going to LSU seemed a natural thing."

Mickal quarterbacked three of LSU's finest teams and counted All-Americans Gaynell Tinsley and Marvin "Moose" Stewart among his teammates. The Tiger teams of 1933-35 never won fewer than seven games and went a cumulative 23-4-5, while Mickal played a role in at least four of the biggest football memories in LSU history:

■ The first came in 1933 against Tulane, which had won nine and tied two of the previous 14 LSU-Greenie games. Trailing 7-0 just before the half, Mickal had the Tigers as close as the Tulane nine before losing three yards. Mickal seemed to throw a pass away, sailing it high over a clump of green-shirted defenders in the end zone.

Suddenly, end Pete Burge seemed to fly straight out of the green cluster, caught the ball with one hand at the height of his leap, and came down on his back — with the ball. That tied the game, 7-7, which is how it ended.

■ The second came in 1934 against Southern Methodist in Tiger Stadium — the game in which Huey Long threatened to have the Barnum and Bailey animals scrubbed in cattle dip to prevent disease if the

OUCH–Rough-and-tumble action from early era of LSU football.

circus' starting time wasn't changed to prevent a conflict with LSU.

LSU was behind 14-7 with four minutes to go when SMU punted and the Tigers took over at their 28. Mickal immediately arched a rainbow down the middle that grazed the fingertips of a blazing — and open — Walter Sullivan, a sub.

On second down, according to legend, Mickal faded back, back, back to the LSU 15 before digging his cleats in and heaving a diagonal shot to Sullivan who had just cleared the last Mustang defender. Sullivan pulled the ball in as he flew by the LSU 30 on the east sidelines and cruised into the end zone.

Tiger Stadium rained confetti and programs after the play, which, until Billy Cannon's 1959 run against Ole Miss, was considered LSU's most exciting.

"Some people say it went 65 yards in the air, some say more," Mickal said. "It might have been 55 yards for all I know." John McKeithen, later governor and a rival to Long as LSU's biggest fan, was sitting in the stands and gushed, "I'm telling you, gentlemen, the ball was in the air 70 yards!"

■ In the 1934 Vanderbilt game, the one in which Long pressured the Illinois Central railroad to let LSU students travel to Nashville for a $6 round trip ticket,

Mickal quarterbacked the Tigers to a 29-0 victory, the Commodores most lopsided defeat in 14 years.

Long, who was so smitten with Mickal's talents he used to visit practice and help the quarterback take off his jersey, was so overcome he proposed making Mickal a "state senator."

Coach Biff Jones was furious when he heard of the idea, and told athletic director Red Heard, "Look, I can't run a ball club like this. It's bad for morale making a spectacle of one player." When Heard gently expressed Jones' sentiments to Long, the Kingfish said: "Hell, Red, I'll make them all senators."

On his national radio

show, humorist Will Rogers recounted the story saying they were trying to make senators of their football players in Louisiana. Rogers added an aside: "Maybe they ought to try making something of their senators."

To Mickal's credit, when told to report for the installation, he refused to go. Heard finally prevailed on Huey when he pointed out a state senatorship could jeopardize Mickal's amateur standing because of the $10 per diem.

■Mickal, in the 1936 Sugar Bowl, his final game as a collegian, shone along with TCU's Sammy Baugh and teammate Bill Crass in perhaps the finest kicking game ever played.

On a muddy field, in a 3-2 Horned Frog victory, these are the startling punting charts.

Baugh:
   Regular punts: 60, 50, 69, 35, 43, 39, 51, 56.
   Out of bounds: 51, 49, 34, 47, 26.
   End zone: 49.
Mickal:
   Regular punts: 54, 41, 65, 44, 43.
   Out of bounds: 31, 43.
   End zone: 48.
Crass:
   Regular punts: 45, 46, 25.
   Out of bounds: 35.
   End zone: 64.

Baugh shaded the LSU tandem with a 47-yard average compared to their 45-yard average. But, Lord, what an exhibition!

The only thing unusual about it for Mickal was coming in second. He was not only a superior quarterback, he was a dean's list student, president of the student body, undergraduate commandant of the LSU cadet corps and recipient of the Golden Sabre as the outstanding cadet in ROTC, and a varsity debater.

Mickal went on to become an M.D. and was head of the Department of Obstetrics of the LSU Medical School in New Orleans when he was inducted into the National Football Foundation and Hall of Fame in 1967.

What accomplishment, what a life.

The model of the mythical All-American Boy, it's hard to disagree, could well have been imbued with the traits of the lad from the village of Talia, Syria.

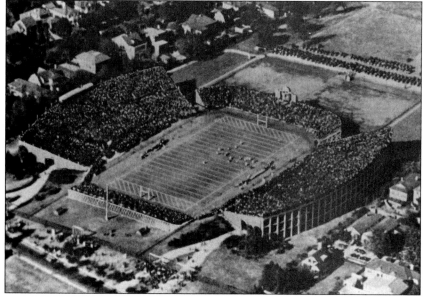

SUGAR BOWL — An ariel view of Sugar Bowl Stadium the day of LSU's first-ever bowl game versus TCU in 1936.

"EVERY MAN A TIGER"

9

Huey Long looked the man straight in the face and asked, "Did you ever dip a tiger? Or how about an elephant?"

It was a curious question under unusual circumstances, but the publicity man for John Ringling North's Barnum and Bailey Circus expected the unexpected when summoned to the Baton Rouge office of Louisiana's U.S. Senator, the Kingfish.

"You know we have laws in this state, mister," Long said while pacing behind his desk, "and the way I interpret them, every one of your animals will have to be dipped when they cross the state line. We can't take a chance of your circus bringing in disease."

It was a naked display of childish petulance, but the advance man understood its meaning: that unless the Ringling Brothers' extravaganza, traveling across Texas at the time, cancelled a performance that conflicted with LSU's 1934 home opener against Southern Methodist University, the senator intended to meet the caravan at the state line with king-sized vats.

The circus was cutting into advance sales for the Tiger-SMU game, and Long dusted off Louisiana's ancient sanitary code and uncovered a little-known animal-dipping law. He was now waiting as the excited publicist put through a long-distance call to North. With all the cards in his possession, which is the way Long liked to play power politics, nobody was going to call the Kingfish's bluff. The circus was rescheduled.

Long's shenanigans with the LSU football team and band were as well-known as his "Share-the-Wealth" philosophy. As governor a few

KINGFISH — Huey Long had a dynamic influence on LSU football in the 1930s.

and hightail it down the field in Music Man fashion.

Long was a politician by profession, but a coach at heart — especially after a Tiger victory when there was plenty of glory to go around. During the games, Huey took his customary seat — on the bench, where he could hear the coach give advice and offer some of his own. The Kingfish always said he and Vanderbilt coach Dan McGugin, whom he admired, were just alike, except that, "He tells his team what to do before the game and I tell the LSU team what to do during the game."

And also the coaches.

In 1930 Long leaped out of his "neutral" governor's box at the Tulane game when the Tigers were on the Green Wave seven yard line and fell on his knees and beat his fists on the earth for an LSU touchdown, to no avail. Tulane won, 12-7, and Long later rehired Coach Russ Cohen after having fired him on the spot.

Always optimistic on pregame football matters, Long couldn't fathom the concerns of coaches who were well aware that just the capricious bounce of the ball is sometimes the most

years earlier, he had invited several players—Ed Khoury, Bill Butler and Sid Bowman — to live with him at the mansion, and it was not an unusual sight for him, after returning home after ramming laws through a rubber-stamp legislature, to order 22 chairs into the ballroom so his boarders could demonstrate LSU's latest play. He fed them so

much sour milk in the interest of nutrition that Khoury ballooned from 240 pounds to 300.

A perennial sophomore when it came to LSU football, Huey sometimes would show up in the dressing room before a game, passing out hamburgers. At halftime, he would take over the marching band he eventually built into a 240-piece unit

important factor in the outcome of a game. Long especially got irked by the pessimistic views of the dour Cohen. Once in Shreveport, the day of a game against Arkansas, Huey found Cohen nervously walking the floor of his hotel room.

"What's wrong," asked Huey.

"It's that Arkansas bunch, governor. They've got me scared to death."

Long wiggled a finger to bodyguard Joe Messina. "Go scout Arkansas," ordered Huey. And Messina took the elevator to the hotel lobby where the Razorbacks were milling about. A few minutes later, Messina returned to Cohen's suite with his report: "They don't look so tough to me."

"You see, coach," soothed Long, throwing a consoling arm around the coach's shoulder. "You're worrying over nothing."

Cohen, it turned out, had reason for concern. Arkansas won, 32-0.

And there was never a logical reason for an LSU defeat to Long. "Arkansas has no reason ever beating us," reasoned Huey, "because we've got more paved roads in this state than they have."

Another reason was material. Huey always figured LSU had the best. And, if not, he'd help get it. One day in the summer of 1931, Red Heard, LSU's athletic business manager, rushed to the mansion after an excited call from Long, who shoved

Heard's face into a newspaper clipping detailing the heroics of one Art Foley of New Mexico Military Institute.

"This boy may be the finest football player in the country and I want him to play for LSU," Long said. "I'm not leaving anything to chance. I want you to find out where that boy lives and go out and get him. And I want you to leave right away."

Heard, at the time, was supervising the installation of lights in Tiger Stadium, obviously a major project. But when Long said go . . . "That evening," Heard said, "I was headed west on a train to Eufaula, Oklahoma."

A day and a half later,

EUFALA FLASH — Art Foley played just one game as a Tiger in the first night game ever played in Tiger Stadium, 1931.

the weary Heard arrived in Eufaula only to find that Foley was vacationing with his family in Mineral Wells, Texas. Heard took a bus to Mineral Wells, located the Foleys, and soon was out on the golf course with Art.

"He was a high-class boy," Heard said, "and I explained I had come all the way from Baton Rouge to recruit him. He was an avid golfer and welcomed a partner, so we played every day for a week and then I followed the family to Eufaula and we played some more.

"All the time, I was reporting back to Huey. Although I knew nothing about the boy's football ability other than what I had read, on the golf course he looked like a great athlete. Huey was happy to hear this and, by the time Art returned to Eufaula from Mineral Wells, he had a new set of golf clubs, a present from Huey."

Foley said he'd report to LSU, but the Kingfish was still taking no chances. Heard was sent back to Oklahoma in the fall to escort him to Baton Rouge.

The Saturday after Labor Day, with LSU scheduled to hold its first scrimmage, a limousine drove onto the field inside Tiger Stadium. Out stepped the Kingfish who opened the rear door — and then Foley stepped out. The senator walked the halfback over to where the team was huddled and turned him over to Coach Cohen. With a wave of the hand to all present, Huey jumped back into his limousine and drove off with a contented look.

As a junior-college transfer, Foley, a 6-foot-3, 175-pound triple-threat athlete, was eligible immediately but was not ready for LSU's opener against TCU in Fort Worth because of a tooth infection, and the Tigers lost, 3-0. The following week, however, Foley made Huey Long look like a shrewd judge of talent. Repeatedly breaking loose, Foley scored three times, zig-zagging 56 yards for one touchdown and returning a punt 62 yards for another as LSU demolished little Spring Hill College of Mobile, 35-0, in the first night football game played in Baton Rouge.

Although Spring Hill was no football barometer, Long was ecstatic. Even Cohen, who had been dubious of Huey's recruit from the start, was excited. It

turned out Spring Hill would be Foley's first, and only game for LSU.

"The bad news came in a hurry," Heard said. "A few days after the game, Art began to hemorrhage in the shower. A specialist was called in and he advised Art to give up football and return home where the drier climate might hasten his recovery."

Long was crushed. "He not only felt sorry for the boy, but indebted to him," Heard said. "Before Art left, Huey gave him a new Ford sports car, a red one, to drive back to Oklahoma." Art Foley had little time to enjoy his gift. Within a few months, he was dead of tuberculosis. Huey wept when Heard broke the news.

A tear or two was probably shed by Cohen, too, because the Tigers finished its mediocre 5-4-0 season with a 34-7 defeat to Tulane, which also finished his coaching career.

That's what brought Biff Jones to the kingdom of the Kingfish. Jones, the head coach at Army from 1927 through 1929 was hired only after receiving the blessing of Chief of Staff Douglas MacArthur. Jones

was a close friend of the general and, at the time, was serving as an assistant athletic director at West Point. MacArthur had Jones detailed to LSU as an instructor in military science so he would not have to resign from the Army.

Strong on organization, Jones quickly assembled a big time staff for LSU's considerable talent and soon had the Tigers at the top of Southern football. After a 6-3-1 record in 1932, the Fightin' Tigers were unbeaten (7-0-3) in 1933.

Louisiana was running a high football fever by the fall of '34. This was the reason the Kingfish, with the highest temperature of all, would tolerate no opposition — or competition — from a circus or, a few weeks later, from a railroad.

That 1934 season is best remembered in Louisiana as "the year of the Nashville Special," the time Long announced he would lead a mammoth invasion of Tennessee "to repay Andrew Jackson for saving New Orleans."

No LSU student, Long decreed, was going to miss the Vanderbilt game because of a lack of funds, despite an official of the

BIFF — *Biff Jones speaks to his first LSU squad, 1932.*

Illinois Central Railroad trying to explain that cut rates for students were out of the question. The Kingfish simply telephoned the railroad president, pausing to mention that it would be a pity, "If our legislature was to raise the assessment (of railroad bridges) from $100,000 to $4 million."

The railroad president saw the light, and agreed to a $6 fare for a round-trip that normally cost $19. Once the fare was established, Huey appeared on the LSU campus passing out an estimated $3,000 in loans of $7 per student — $6 for the fare, $1 for meals. Some students wrote IOUs on laundry slips.

Six special trains carried them to Tennessee, and the Kingfish led 5,000 students, 1,500 ROTC cadets, and a 125-piece band through downtown Nashville. Said *The Nashville Banner* in a front-page headline: "Nashville Surrenders to Huey Long."

Serving as cheerleader, bandleader and waterboy, the Kingfish overshadowed LSU's 29-0 victory over an unbeaten Vanderbilt team.

But nothing changes things like disappointment.

Long never set foot in a classroom at LSU, having studied law at Tulane, but he despised Tulane, and was furious when the Green Wave upset LSU 13-12 in Baton Rouge to win a trip to the first Sugar Bowl. A week later, Tennessee whipped the Tigers. This double jolt had Long on edge. With LSU trailing Oregon, 13-0, at halftime in the final game of the 1934 season, he could no longer control himself.

The Kingfish stormed into the LSU dressing room demanding to talk to the team. Jones refused. "I'm sick of you losing games," Long snapped. "You'd better win this one."

Jones shot back: "Well, senator, get this: win, lose or draw, I quit."

"That's a bargain," Long said.

In the second half, LSU came back to win, 14-13 — but Jones kept his word. He quit.

"I was right there when they started talking after the half," said Dr. Abe Mickal, then the Tiger quarterback.

Mickal and Jones stayed fast friends for years, each visiting the other through the years. "So I know how he felt," Mickal said. "Biff didn't want to quit, and Huey didn't want him to quit. They both said things they didn't mean. The problem was the *Associated Press* got hold of the story. Both Biff and Huey tried to get them to kill it, but AP wouldn't. Once the story got out, there was nothing anyone could do. Biff had to resign to save face, otherwise it would look like he was caving in. But he didn't want to leave."

Finding a top replacement was a concern for Long. First he felt out former Tulane coach Clark Shaughnessy, who wasn't interested, and then he arranged a rendezvous with Alabama's Frank Thomas at the Roosevelt Hotel in New Orleans, when Bama stopped off on its way to the Rose Bowl. Thomas verbally agreed to terms: $15,000 for himself

and $7,500 each for two assistants of his choosing.

The Kingfish ordered Red Heard to accompany Thomas to California to make certain the Tide coach wouldn't change his mind. But it was Long who had a change of heart. Heard picked up a paper on the West Coast with the headline: "Kingfish Appoints Bernie Moore Coach."

"After I left with Alabama," Heard later said, "Huey called Dan McGugin, former coach at Vandy and a man he respected, for a recommendation. Dan recommended Bernie, who had come to LSU as an assistant in 1928, the year Huey was elected governor. In 1933, Bernie took a five-man track team to Chicago and brought back the NCAA championship. Huey flipped over this. In hiring Bernie, he was hiring what he promised LSU fans — a coach with a reputation."

Still, Long wanted to cover all his bases. He called McGugin back and asked for a play that "would score every time." Dan diagrammed something he called "No. 88," and the Kingfish went over

it with Bernie Moore.

Bernie Moore, later the commissioner of the Southeastern Conference, recalled the circumstances.

"Huey was a senator and had come to Baton Rouge from Washington for a special session of the legislature. He told me the session was called to pass another law against Standard Oil.

"I said to him, 'Senator, why don't you go to Hot Springs and rest up for the football season. We're gonna have a pretty good team.' As usual, he was excited. He had hired the bandleader from the Blue Room in New Orleans to take over the LSU band. Together they had written 'Touchdown for LSU,' and 'Miss Vandy,' a ditty Huey planned to introduce on a return trip to Nashville in October. But Huey was determined to pass those laws, and I guess this determination helped alter Louisiana history."

Just days afterward, Huey Long was shot in the State Capitol, and two days later was dead.

And LSU never did run "No. 88," the play guaranteed to go for a touchdown every time.

THE GREAT TIGER

10

He sat in the bright sunlight, like a fluffing, contented cat.

The pride of the Tigers prowled LSU's parade grounds on Saturday, April 17, 1993, the day the school commemorated its football centennial, and everywhere were tigers of all sizes, shapes and ages.

The 1958 national champions, with Billy Cannon at tailback, lined up and ran a play.

Abe Mickal, a quarterback from the '30s, and Bert Jones, a quarterback of the '70s, threw spirals.

Fat men in "Root Hog" T-shirts still were surrounding running back Charles Alexander, who played in the 1970s.

But there was no mistaking Gaynell Tinsley, the greatest of the Great Tigers, nuzzling in the warmth of remembrance and recognition. He, by virtual unanimous consensus, is the Tiger by which all Tigers are measured. Not Cannon, not Tommy Casanova, not the storied Y.A. Tittle, but Gaynell "Gus" Tinsley.

He was LSU's first consensus All-American, and not so coincidently when LSU named its Early Years (1893-1937) Team of the Century, Tinsley was the only unanimous selection.

Bernie Moore, who coached LSU while Tinsley was playing end, and whose 1936 team finished second in the first Associated Press in 1936 with the sinewy, raw-boned end holding down his line, once said unequivocally, "Tinsley could have made All-American at any position. He was so tough, he made blockers quit. He's the greatest lineman I ever saw."

"That," Tinsley recalled, "was the finest complement I ever received. But," he hastened to add, "to be

Gaynell Tinsley, the Greatest Tiger.

MEET AT THE QB — Jeff Barrett and Gaynell Tinsley (24) close in on TCU's Slingin' Sammy Baugh in LSU's first bowl game, the 1936 Sugar Bowl.

a good football player requires a little talent," Gaynell Tinsley said slowly and with thought, "and a lot of luck."

Tinsley's point was that being in the right place at the right time often counts for more than sheer talent. In his case, it was no doubt a combination of factors.

Consider: Moore's Bengals not only won two Southeastern Conference championships with Tinsley terrorizing opponents, with the 1936 team named the nation's best in the Deke Houlgate poll and second in the first Associated Press poll, with an unbeaten streak of 19 regular-season games, a

record marred only by a 6-6 tie with Texas, and allowed only 13 points in their last seven games of the 1936 season.

There's no question that Bernie Moore was in the right place at the right time when Tinsley fell into his lap.

Tinsley, from Homer, Louisiana, played high school football under a pair of coaches who were Tulane graduates, and was all set to play in college as a Greenie. But he was persuaded by a neighboring high school principal, an LSU man, to go along with a couple of boys heading to LSU on his way to New Orleans, and to stop off and at least give

LSU a look-see. He did, and as it turned out, never again saw Tulane as anything but an adversary.

"When Gus was a freshman," Moore once recounted, "Biff (Jones, then the head coach) asked me to bring over the frosh so the varsity could work on punt protection. He was at left end. The ball was snapped. Gus rushed, knocking the blocker into the punter. They lined up a second time and he did the same thing. Biff was pretty hot, so he ordered it a third time. Darn if Gus didn't do it again. Biff turned to me and said: 'Take that damn team back where it came from' "

Clarence "Pop" Strange, who played at LSU in the 1930s, where he was a teammate of Tinsley, and coached at LSU for almost four decades, who was there during the times of Taylor, Cannon and Casanova, said, "I'd have to say Gaynell was the best I ever saw, yes. Of course, when this question comes up, you always think of Jimmy Taylor and Billy Cannon. Don Hutson, who played for Alabama, made a lot of those all-time teams, but Gus was a better football player."

At 6-foot-3, 215-pounds, Tinsley was considered to be the prototype end of the era because of his mobility. An astonishing force on defense, Tinsley also became a dangerous offensive threat. LSU scored a national high 281 points in 1936, and Tinsley alone scored 48 points.

LSU led Arkansas, 13-7, in 1935 when Tinsley went out with a broken nose. "It was smashed, all over his face it looked like," Strange recalled. "When they started marching, he came in, made three tackles for losses, then went out." And the Tigers won, 13-7.

Interestingly, when Texas Christian shaded LSU, 3-2, in the 1936 Sugar Bowl, the Horned Frogs' quarterback "Slingin' Sammy" Baugh was hounded all afternoon by the Tigers' line-crashing end.

Baugh and Tinsley teamed after the following season in the Chicago All-Star game against the Green Bay Packers. The All-Stars won, 6-0, on a 47-yard pass play from Baugh to Tinsley.

Tinsley went on to become an All-Pro with the Chicago Cardinals and was widely considered to be the

GAYNELL — Gaynell Tinsley, who starred in the purple and gold from 1934-36, coached the Tigers from 1948-54.

premier defensive end in football, although his offensive skills remained considerable. In a 21-14 aerial showcase in which the Cardinals defeated the Washington Redskins, Tinsley scored all three of the Chicago touchdowns — and gained a lasting legacy. A headline the next day read: "Gallopin' Gus Leads Cardinals Over Redskins."

Tinsley set a NFL record of 675 yards in pass receptions in 1938, a season in which he caught 36 passes. To put that in perspective, the Cardinals' No. 2 receiver, Doug Russell, had 12

receptions. The next season, Tinsley tied Don Hutson's NFL record 41 receptions. When he quit pro ball after only three seasons to go into coaching, Tinsley was the NFL's fourth-ranked career pass catcher.

Both Pop Warner and Bronco Nagurski recognized Tinsley as one of the game's premier figures. Both selected Tinsley to their all-time college football All-American teams. Nagurski said of Tinsley: "Never have I seen an end who could do everything so well."

THE WALL GAMES

11

Bill Arnsparger, when he was coach at LSU from 1984 through 1986, instituted a practice of recording the scores of extraordinary performances on the walls of the Tiger Den, where the LSU team enters Tiger Stadium. Called "Wall Games," they represent extraordinary performances worth remembering long after they are played — the kind of games on which tradition is founded. Carrying Arnsparger's idea further, these, in no particular order, are among the "Wall Games" of a century of LSU football.

LSU 7, OLE MISS 3
Tiger Stadium
Oct. 31, 1959

He gallops eternally, like the Headless Horseman riding through Sleepy Hollow. Each Halloween Billy Cannon makes that same eerie and bewitching run, in grainy black-and-white film, across Death Valley.

All the cosmic tumblers had to be aligned, it was written, when LSU and Ole Miss played football Trick-or-Treat on Halloween in 1959's Game of the Century — a game that more than a third of a century later still has that kind of sheen.

Both teams were undefeated with 6-0 records, LSU was ranked No. 1, Ole Miss ranked No. 3. A combined total of 13 points — two field goals against the Tigers, one touchdown against the Rebels — had been scored against those sturdy defenses. "Ole Miss," recalled Cannon, "was as good a football team as could have been fielded in those days."

Interestingly, new and stronger floodlights had been installed in Tiger Stadium since the 1958 season. With the 100 percent humidity, according to *Baton Rouge State-Times* Dan Hardest, "the foggy field assumed an unearthly quality under those lights." And obviously added to the dramatic setting.

Cannon very nearly became the game's goat in the first quarter. Bobby Franklin bottled LSU up at its five. On a 10-yard gain, Cannon dropped the second of three first-half fumbles. Billy Brewer recovered on the 20, and in four-plays Ole Miss was planted on the Tiger four. Somehow, some way, the defense held, and Bob Khayat kicked a field goal.

As it was, a 3-0 lead would have been enough against most opponents. After gaining the advantage, and with the Tigers constantly playing in the shadows of their own goal, Rebel coach Johnny Vaught wanted LSU to handle the slippery ball. One lapse, one mistake, and he felt the Rebels could finish the kill.

A third-quarter Cannon interception was carried to the Ole Miss side of midfield, but Wendell Harris, five-for-five in field goal attempts going into the fray, missed. Vaught's cat-and-mouse strategy had LSU on the ropes. By the fourth quarter the Tigers seemed worn and beaten for the first time in 18 games.

With 10 minutes remaining, though, Vaught's tactics blew up. Cannon drifted back to his five to field Jake Gibbs' third-down punt, Ole Miss' most consistently effective play of the night.

"We had a rule of not handling kicks inside the 15," Cannon related, "but I had broken four tackles on a previous punt, although I didn't get much out of it, and it was getting late. I thought, 'If I see a chance I'm going to try to bring it back.'"

The ball bounced high, and right into Cannon's arms at the 11. He was hit several yards upfield, shook off the tackle, and maintained his balance. Richard Price made a futile attempt at the 19, and Jerry Daniels slipped off the suddenly steaming Tiger runner. At the 25, a Rebel mob enclosed around Cannon, but in a millisecond he came busting out. By the time he passed Vaught at midfield, eight Rebels had gotten at least a hand on Cannon, and only Gibbs, 10 yards straight ahead, still had an opportunity to stop him. "I figured Jake was waiting for me to cut back on him," Cannon said, "so I gave him a little juke and went inside. . . . I know people say you can't think like that during the heat of a game, but that's how I got past Gibbs."

Hardesty wrote of the hair-raising play that Cannon was like "a white-shirted ghost wearing jersey No. 20."

Tiger Stadium erupted with ear-splitting emotion, and Cannon was mobbed in the end zone by teammates — and others. "I was so tired I could barely stand," Cannon said. "After I gave the ball to the official a guy in red corduroy jacket came racing out of the stands. I had my hands on my knees trying to catch my breath, and the fellow started pounding me, really clobbering me on the back, and I was too tired to stop him. Donnie Daye finally pulled him off me, and I don't know whether he'd just won a million dollars or lost a million dollars."

The suspense wasn't over, though. A silence crept over the stadium as more and more fans caught sight of a penalty flag near midfield. Finally, the touchdown was officially signalled. Ole Miss had been in motion on the punt. Harris' conversion made the score 7-3, LSU.

In a surprise move, Vaught inserted sophomore Doug Elmore at quarterback to pull the game out in the remaining 10 minutes. Starting at the Rebel 32, Elmore ignited a long, arduous march, flinging his backs against the Chinese Bandits and slowly worming into position for victory. "I was getting oxygen on the sidelines, watching Doug pick up first down after first down," Cannon said. "I thought to myself, 'Here's the best run I ever made in my life, and we're going to lose!'"

When Ole Miss penetrated the LSU 23, Coach Paul Dietzel sent the White Team back in. But the advance continued. The drive reached the seven with 90 seconds remaining. In the three ensuing plays, Ole Miss

worked itself to the LSU two yard line, forcing a win-or-lose, fourth and goal situation. Elmore slammed off-tackle where Warren Rabb stopped his progress, and Cannon finished the tackle one yard short of the goal. LSU regained possession with 18 seconds left.

"That," sighed a relieved Dietzel afterward, "was the greatest run I ever saw in football."

Years later Vaught was asked jokingly why he didn't trip Cannon when he passed within a couple of feet of the Rebel coach on the run.

Vaught answered that since no one else on his team seemed able to stop Cannon, he didn't think he could either.

LSU 28, NOTRE DAME 8
Tiger Stadium
Nov. 20, 1971

"Irish Stew at LSU" was the *Sports Illustrated* headline, and those few pithy words completely summed up one of most memorable nights in Tiger Stadium history.

The Fightin' Tigers had been spoiling for another

crack at the Fightin' Irish since their titanic struggle at South Bend the season before when Notre Dame squeaked past LSU, 3-0, on a field goal with less than three minutes to go. Added to the fuel was the Cotton Bowl two years before when the Irish decided to break their long-time bowl ban after LSU thought it had an agreement with the Dallas classic.

Coach Ara Parseghian was bringing a team he said was physically the best he'd seen during his tenure at Notre Dame. The seventh-ranked Irish were 7-1, and LSU was 6-3 with back-to-back defeats to Ole Miss and Alabama.

An emotionally-fried crowd at long sold-out Tiger Stadium was waiting in the night, despite national television coverage.

What they all witnessed was an awesome — and unforgettable — display of Tiger football.

Coach Charlie McClendon threw the Irish defense a curve before the first play was run. His No. 2 quarterback, Bert Jones, went out with the first offensive unit instead of the previous starter, Paul Lyons.

McClendon, who made his decision after the coin flip, was playing a hunch, not only that the strong-armed Jones could do serious damage to the Irish secondary, but that Jones, at 6-foot-3, would be able to see over the huge Notre Dame line better than Lyons, who was 5-foot-10.

In less than three minutes, Jones drove the Bayou Bengals 77 yards to a 7-0 lead as he hit his cousin, Andy Hamilton, on a 36-yard touchdown strike.

Notre Dame came right back — only to get a taste of what was in store the rest of the night. The Irish drove inside the Tiger one. The crowd was howling, almost as one.

On fourth down, Notre Dame was four inches from a first down, one foot away from the tying touchdown. Behind an offensive line which averaged 250-pounds and dwarfed the Tiger defenders, Andy Huff went churning off the

IRISH STEW — The LSU defense halts Notre Dame's Andy Huff during a stirring goal-line stand in LSU's 28-8 victory in 1971.

right side. Skip Cormier, LSU's 205-pound defensive end, penetrated and made initial contact. Then Louis Cascio, a 205-pound linebacker, fought through a double-team block to stand Huff up, with Lloyd Frye, another 205-pound linebacker finishing off the job.

Shortly thereafter, Notre Dame was threatening again with a third-and-two feet at the LSU 10. Frye stopped the runner for no gain. Parseghian, obviously, couldn't believe what he was seeing and again passed up a field goal attempt to go for it on fourth down. LSU

should have made a believer out of him, because sophomore defensive back Norm Hodgins eluded a blocker as he fired into the backfield and nailed quarterback Cliff Brown for a three-yard loss.

Notre Dame's frustration put the crowd in a near-feeding frenzy. People sitting side by side could barely hear each other through the din.

For a third time in the first half, Notre Dame came charging back to the LSU three, where, on fourth down, the Irish decided to go for the touchdown. This time, though, Brown went to

STUFF — LSU All-American Warren Capone spearheaded LSU's staunch defensive units of the early 1970s.

the air. He rolled to his right, and lofted a pass intended for Larry Parker into the end zone. Frye seemingly came out of nowhere, reached cleanly over Parker's shoulder and batted the ball away.

After sophomore line-backer Warren Capone intercepted Brown, finally giving LSU breathing room, it took Jones exact-ly eight seconds to increase the lead. With 1:14 remaining in the first half, he again hit Hamilton for 32 yards and a 14-0 lead.

Notre Dame hadn't sur-rendered a touchdown in the second half in its pre-vious nine games, or in the fourth quarter in 20 games. LSU was deter-mined to break those strings and did, building a

28-0 lead — and in the process stopping the Irish again in close Tiger territory, this time at the 19 — before the Irish got a face-saving touchdown with two minutes to play.

Jones, the surprise starter but from then on a fixture on LSU's starting unit, finished the night seven-of-nine for 143 yards and figured in three of the Tiger touchdowns. He blossomed into an outstanding quarterback indeed, LSU's only All-American at that position, Hamilton caught seven passes against the Irish, including one from Lyons, and scored three touchdowns.

But the pumped-up Tiger defense — spearheaded by linebacker Ronnie Estay, who was in on 17 tackles — really highlighted the night, and was largely responsible for what was, at the time, the worst defeat of Parseghian's Notre Dame career.

There was only one question about LSU's performance, but it was answered by *Baton Rouge State-Times* columnist Sam King. "It's amazing how the Goodyear blimp managed to circle Tiger Stadium without hitting any of the LSU football players," King mused in print. "They, too, were that high."

The impressive victory put LSU in the Sun Bowl, where it defeated Iowa State to finish 9-3.

The defeat stung the Irish almost as much as their victory did LSU the year before. Greg Marx, the Irish's 6-foot-5, 235-pound defensive tackle reflected Notre Dame's frustration. As LSU was attempting its fourth PAT in the final quarter, Marx gave Tiger guard Lloyd Daniels a shot to the leg. As the two got up, in a voice dripping with sarcasm and frustration, Marx said to Daniels, "Well, how do you like that, you (censored)?"

Daniels got up, pointed to the scoreboard, and answered, "Okay. And how do you like that?"

LSU 14, ARKANSAS 7
Dallas, Texas
Jan. 1, 1966

A common Chinese prayer is the entreaty: "Please keep this house safe from tigers."

It's safe to say the Arkansas Razorbacks, circa the mid-1960s, adopted the adage late on the afternoon of January 1, 1966 — probably about the same time a heady band of LSU Tigers were tearing apart a red jersey bearing the numerals "23" in their Cotton Bowl dressing room.

In Louisiana, especially for those living near the Arkansas border, a new war cry was adopted: "Soo, pig, phooey."

LSU had just pulled off the near-unthinkable: Previously undefeated Arkansas — in clear position to claim a second consecutive national championship, victor over 22 straight opponents, and the highest scoring team in the country — was beaten by a Tiger team which lost thrice during the regular season, and a team which never seemed to hit on all cylinders until the Cotton Bowl.

It took a miracle for LSU, big losers in two of its defeats, to Ole Miss (23-0) and Alabama (31-7), to even be in Dallas, much less pull off the biggest bowl upset in school history.

Though the team was highly regarded before the season, with talent that produced four future pros, including All-Americans tackle George Rice and flanker Doug Moreau, Charlie McClendon's history of quarterback injuries continued at mid-season. He had lost his starter four straight years at that point.

Nelson Stokley went out early with a blown knee against Ole Miss and the steam seemed to immediately leave the Tigers, one possible reason why they were flattened by the Rebels and offered only token resistance the following week against Bama. This was McClendon's fourth season as head coach at LSU, and that two-week period was, by far, his low point.

On the other hand, it also cleared the way for the high point of his early Tiger reign: the startling upset of the Razorbacks.

LSU was only in the Cotton Bowl because of circumstance and political intrigue. After it became apparent third-ranked Nebraska, the Cotton Bowl's first choice, would play Alabama in the Orange Bowl, SEC commissioner Bernie Moore became the middle man in helping provide SEC teams to both the Sugar and Cotton bowls.

Kentucky was ticketed for New Orleans, and Florida would go to the Cotton, although the Gators voted for the Sugar. Once Florida coach Ray Graves told his team they would have a possible shot at Arkansas, though, they jumped at the idea.

The Missouri Tigers complicated things, however, and Moore worked a switch. Kentucky, which had beaten Missouri, 7-0, in the season opener, agreed to accept a Cotton Bowl invitation if it defeated Houston, and Florida agreed to take the Sugar Bowl provided it defeated Tulane. The Gators beat the Green Wave, but Houston upset Kentucky.

No sooner had that score rolled in when LSU AD Jim Corbett, a master of persuasion, was on the phone selling his team.

Suddenly LSU, with a 7-3 record, was in a major bowl, against a major, major opponent.

Razorback coach Frank Broyles knew his second-ranked team was at a psychological disadvantage, although Arkansas led the nation in scoring with 32.4 points a game and had a running tandem of Harry Jones and Bobby Burnett which averaged 7.7 yards per carry.

Also in Broyles' favor was the decision of the Associated Press poll to take a final poll for the first time after the bowls. The reason was three undefeated teams, Michigan State, Arkansas and Nebraska, all with legitimate arguments for the No. 1 ranking.

And yet McClendon wasn't as frightened as outsiders suspected. He was well aware that anything less than a perfect game plan — and execution — could result in humiliation.

But McClendon also knew his team was not a sacrificial lamb, and that it had a chance. In fact, McClendon privately felt that he just might throw at Arkansas the best rushing offense the Razorbacks had seen. Lost in its gaudy record, but not to the LSU coaching staff, was an interesting tidbit: The Razorbacks surrendered more than 400 yards in somehow beating run-oriented Texas, 27-24, during the regular season. A healthy LSU, Mac knew, was a very good offensive football aggregation.

LSU, a nine-point underdog, practiced for a month with the scout squad all wearing red jerseys with the numerals "23" on them, the implications being obvious: The Tigers did not want to end the year as just the latest Razorback victim.

And, to McClendon's delight, the Arkansas fans played right into his hands. When LSU got to Dallas, the Hog faithful made a point of mocking the Tigers with the smirking question, "LS-Who?" As the Tigers left the hotel on their way to the buses that would take them to the Cotton Bowl, a little old woman wearing one of those red Porker hats in the lobby shrieked at the sight and yelled loudly, "Look, they're actually going to show up!"

There was some doubt early as the Tigers, unranked and, in some quarters, unwanted, were surgically sliced up. The Razorbacks cut through the LSU defense early for 87 first quarter yards and the lead as Bobby Crockett made a Houdini-type grab, then tippy-toed 16 yards down the sidelines.

Surprisingly to some, the Tigers didn't fold. Instead, it was as if cold water had been thrown on their collective face. Another Hog drive ended with a missed field goal. Then LSU took over.

Pat Screen, who took over when Stokley went down, did so again. Stokley came in to start the series, giving his team a lift before reinjuring himself seven plays later. Screen again picked up the torch.

Screen guided the Tiger offense, which had a slightly different look from the one Arkansas studied on film. Joe Labruzzo, a dangerous, 5-foot-9, 170-pound tailback was lined up deeper than usual so he could pick his options on the fly, depending on how the Razorbacks lined up.

The Tiger offensive line took control, blowing the defense off their heels. Labruzzo cut back behind the blocks of 6-foot-5 strongback Billy Masters, 6-foot-6 tackle Dave McCormick and wide back Danny LeBlanc.

And, perhaps as a indication that fate was finally going to smile on the 1965 Tigers, LSU got a monumental break when Screen, playing a second and 16 from midfield, called a pass to Masters. Razorback Tommy Sain reached out and tipped the pass. He spun around and had control for a second, but the ball flew out and into the grasp of Masters who turned it into a 14-yard gain.

Nine plays later the score was 7-7 as Screen guided LSU 80 yards in a convincing — and crunching — 16 plays with Labruzzo scoring the tying touchdown from the three.

Arkansas quarterback Jon Brittenum slightly injured a shoulder and momentarily had to leave the game. Two plays later defender Tommy Fussell hit backup Ronnie South, causing a fumble which Tiger Bill Bass recovered at the Razorback 34.

It was the fading moments of the half, and Screen went for the knockout, but with body blows. Once LSU reached the 19, Screen ran Labruzzo five straight times at left tackle.

He finally went in from the one, and with 18 seconds remaining until intermission, LSU held a stunning 14-7 lead.

Emotional highs are part of football, but LSU assistant Doug Hamley said he never experienced anything like that halftime.

"We couldn't hold the team in the dressing room," he said. "They got up four times and tried to leave, but Coach McClendon had to hold them back because the bands were still on the field." Another assistant, Bill Beall later pointed to marks on the floor where the caged Tigers pawed on the concrete waiting for the halftime show to end. "I knew they were ready," McClendon said. "That is, I felt if this team wasn't ready to play, I could never be sure of any team in the future."

Defensive heroics filled the second half, as the Tigers were determined to let the shaken Razorbacks make the mistakes. Crockett made another amazing leaping catch to the LSU 15. On the next play, a steaming Jim Lindsey swung left on a reverse and had two blockers ahead of him when he was cut down by Ernie Maggiore's feet.

"I had been coming up fast to turn the wide stuff in," the lineman explained with a grin. "But they had been running in the alley between me and Fussell. This time I threw my body to the inside to cut him off, but when I saw him turn to go around me, I threw out my legs and caught him in the shins."

Lindsey, who had a chance of reaching the end zone, wound up with a six-yard loss, and the Arkansas drive eventually ended with a missed field goal.

Later cornerback Jerry Joseph, who was victimized on Crockett's touchdown, intercepted a late throw to him at the Tiger 20 when LSU disguised a zone. "It could be they weren't expecting that type coverage," Joseph said.

The record crowd of 76,000 was either depressed or hysterically happy a few minutes later when the game clock finally wound down. Arkansas very definitely not only lost a game but the national championship. Michigan State was upended by UCLA in the Rose Bowl, and, later, Nebraska was beaten by Alabama in the Orange Bowl. The No.1 tag ended up going to Bama, with a loss and a tie on its record, after keeping the national title the year before despite losing to Texas in the Orange Bowl — which was part of the reasoning in the AP's waiting until after the bowls to vote.

To LSU, though, the Cotton Bowl victory was its greatest postseason moment. Afterward McClendon and Corbett clutched joyously on the field with Mac shouting, "We shoved it up their ass!"

The whooping Tigers tore the red jersey bearing number 23 to shreds in the locker room before Charlie Mac stood on a trunk to be heard over his shouting team, quieted them and said what even then they must have suspected. "The rest of your lives," Mac told them, "you won't ever forget what you did today."

LSU 9, GEORGIA TECH 7
Atlanta, Georgia
Nov. 17, 1945

The place of Red Knight in Tiger history was assured by his place-kicking, even though he was LSU's leading passer in 1943 and the leading rusher in 1945.

Georgia Tech was playing its first season under Coach Bobby Dodd. LSU was 5-2 going into the Ramblin' Wreck contest, but Knight, obviously a key component for Bernie Moore's Bayou Bengals, had reinjured a knee the week before against Mississippi State and wasn't expected to play in a game where every man would be needed — and at his best.

"I wasn't even supposed to make the trip to Atlanta," Knight said. "But (assistant coach) Joel Hunt talked Coach Moore into taking me. (Trainer) Marty Broussard worked on me during the night before the game, and had me all taped up that day."

In a bruising defensive game, each team managed one touchdown. Y.A. Tittle, who replaced

OLD POSSUM — Bernie Moore served as LSU head coach from 1935-47 and compiled a record of 83-39-6.

Knight as LSU's place-kicker, however, missed the PAT after the Tigers' first quarter touchdown. When Tech scored with less than five minutes to play it appeared the Tigers would go home 7-6 losers.

Tittle began surgically slicing up the Yellow Jacket defense after a long kickoff return, however, and reached the Tech 21 with less than a minute to play.

"(Teammate Ray) Coates asked me in the huddle if I could kick a field goal," Knight said, "and I told him I could. Clyde Lindsey, our captain, asked for one more play, and Tittle passed to (Doug) Sandifer for a five-yard loss — and out of bounds."

This placed the ball on the hashmark, 18 yards from the sidelines. As the Tigers scrambled for their last play, they were penalized five yards for delay of game.

From the spot where Coates, the holder, placed the ball to the goal posts was a distance of 42 yards. That was quite a kick for a cripple in 1945, and from a severe angle. The kick was unerring, though. The

heavily-taped Knight fell down after the follow through and had to be helped to his feet.

The dramatic 9-7 victory was LSU's first over Tech, and easily the biggest in the Tigers' 7-2 season.

LSU 21, AUBURN 20
Tiger Stadium
Oct. 25, 1969

A note from an LSU professor a few days before the Auburn game on how spoiled Tiger fans had

become was brought home to Charlie McClendon.

It read:

"Dear Mac, You're passing too much and scoring too many points. The games aren't interesting anymore. Please make them closer, but be damn sure you win."

LSU was squarely in the path of Auburn's Touchdown Twins, the sensational sophomore pitch-and-catch combo of Pat Sullivan and Terry Beasley. The schools hadn't met in 27 years, but the Bayou Bengals were 5-0-0

SAND MAN — Dan Sandifer scores in LSU's 9-7 upset victory over Georgia Tech in 1945.

at midseason and Auburn was 4-1-0. Both knew they would have to turn in a peak performance in order to keep their sensational season going.

LSU put in a surprise on the game's first play from scrimmage. With the ball at the Tiger 32, Andy Hamilton lined up at tight end rather than split end. Quarterback Mike Hillman took the snap and pitched out to tailback Jimmy Gilbert. Gilbert moved as if on a sweep to the left side, then pulled up and unleashed a rainbow to Hamilton who had broken free.

LSU led 7-0 seconds after the kickoff.

Sullivan and the Plainsmen recovered, and took a 14-7 lead just before the half, but LSU was driving again. Mark Lumpkin attempted a field goal, which was wide, but Auburn was guilty of an infraction on the play with 30 seconds remaining until the half. With the second chance, Hillman speared Jim West for a touchdown — and a 14-14 halftime deadlock.

The Tiger defense had its paws more than full with Auburn. Linebacker George Bevan, an All-

SURPRISE — Andy Hamilton scores off a halfback pass to open the 1969 Auburn clash. The Tigers went on to notch a 21-20 victory.

America that season, said his position coach, Doug Hamley, may have saved the day with improvisation.

"We were in a 4-3 (defense)," Bevan recalled, "and couldn't handle them. Doug huddled with us on the sideline, and drew up a new defense with his finger in the ground. 'See how this works,' Hamley said of the new 5-2."

It was enough to slow Auburn down a bit, and LSU went ahead 21-14. Auburn came back, though, with an impressive fourth-quarter 95-yard drive that made the score, 21-20. As kicker John Riley came in everyone was wondering if LSU could put together one last thrust to get back into field goal range.

Bevan, though, felt he had a chance to block the

PAT and save the offense all that energy. "We had a strong outside rush when Bill Thomason blocked their field-goal attempt in the second quarter," Bevan said. "This time the man who was supposed to block me moved to the outside again, so I came inside him and caught the ball on my right forearm."

The blocked PAT was the difference in the game as LSU won its ninth

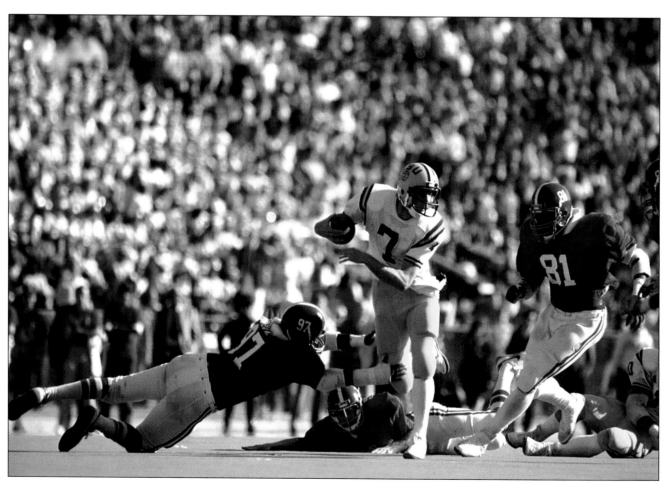

SLIDELL SLINGER — Alan Risher led the Tigers to a 20-10 victory over Alabama in 1982.

straight.

When McClendon was reminded of the letter afterward, he said, "I hope that prof is happy now."

LSU 20, ALABAMA 10
Birmingham, Ala.
Nov. 6, 1982

Bear Bryant took one last look at LSU — a program he thoroughly dominated throughout his legendary coaching career — and decided he had enough.

This could well have been the most lopsided 10-point victory in Tiger football history. LSU had less game domination against some opponents with the scores reaching astronomical proportions. It was a tribute to Alabama's tradition and courage that the difference between these teams even looked competitive.

The Crimson Tide, a 7-1-0 team Bryant was saying just days before the LSU clash, could be "the best bunch we've ever had," was by far the SEC's best offense, steamrolling behind the elusive option quarterback Walter Lewis

to 300.5 yards a game rushing and 446.2 total yards.

Coach Jerry Stovall's 6-0-1 Bayou Bengals, on the other hand, was the nation's stingiest defense — featuring tackle Leonard Marshall — coupled with a Kiddy-Korps, but very dangerous backfield. Freshman tailbacks Dalton Hilliard and Garry James, LSU's best runners since Charles Alexander in the late 1970s, scooted through holes created by an excellent offensive line dubbed "The Lunch Bunch."

Hilliard was only 5-foot-8, but tackle Clint Berry said, "That's OK. We open holes that are wide, not tall."

A slashing-type runner, Hilliard broke several tackles on a screen pass which went for 33 yards in the second quarter, setting up LSU's first touchdown. He then scored on a 16-yard run in which he broke through, and then outran, the Crimson Tide secondary.

When Hilliard went out shortly afterward with an injury, James set up a second LSU touchdown, which came on a three-

yard pass from Alan Risher to tight end Malcolm Scott.

When Bama's Craig Turner fumbled the ensuing kickoff, Juan Betanzos kicked a 23-yard field goal to give the Fightin' Tigers a 17-0 halftime lead.

At that point, with the LSU defense chasing down Tide runners and giving Lewis almost no room to even draw a breath, Alabama had a total of 32 yards — 10 yards rushing.

Defensive line coach Pete Jenkins knew it wasn't over. "I told our boys, 'Let's do our celebrating on the way home,' " he said.

Sure enough, Bama made a run on the scoreboard. Lewis drove the Tide to the Tiger five on its first second half drive. It ended with a field goal, cutting the score to 17-3. Then Hilliard, playing despite his injury, fumbled at the LSU 28, and Lewis hit Joey Jones for a touchdown. Alabama scored 10 points in 25 seconds, and made a game of it again.

But LSU allowed Bama only two more first downs — for a total of six — the rest of the way, and forced seven turnovers, including four lost fumbles. Lewis was followed like a fugitive, being brought down a half dozen times by inside linebackers Lawrence Williams and Al Richardson trying to run the option. "I have never been caught back there so many times," he mused later, almost disbelievingly.

It had been a no-quarter given butchering of an offense which had reigned football terror. Bama had managed only 45 yards rushing, and 119 yards in total offense. It was a sweet moment for LSU after 12 frustrating seasons of trying in vain to beat Bama.

"They ate our offense," growled the Bear. "I didn't think anybody could do that."

Bryant then said for the first time that maybe Alabama ought to think about a new coach. Bryant said the president of the university ought to be alerted "that we need to make some changes, and we need to start at the top."

At the end of the season, Bryant, perhaps the greatest coach in college football history, stepped down. A month later he

was dead.

LSU 13, TEXAS 0
Dallas, Texas
Jan. 1, 1963

They hit like two rams butting heads.

"You could hear it over to the sidelines," said former LSU coach Charlie McClendon.

Longhorn Ernie Koy took the opening kickoff, started to run before Tiger lineman Fred Miller came flying out of the sky to absolutely chill the Texas runner.

McClendon mused: "That kind of set the tone for the rest of the day."

Indeed. Texas would never get closer to the LSU goal than the Tiger 25. In other words, they never seriously threatened to score.

If ever there was a game of immovable objects, this was it.

In Texas' 9-0-1 season the Longhorns surrendered a total of 59 points. LSU, in its first season under McClendon, was a two-point favorite, in part because the Tigers led the nation in scoring defense, yielding 34 points in its 8-1-1 season.

Texas, which put together its first undefeated regular season since 1923, was by far the quickest team the Tigers had played. So the coaching staff put in a couple of new plays designed to make the Longhorns' quickness work to the Tigers' advantage. One looked like a sweep to one side, but wound up as an off-tackle play on the other side; the other had the appearance of a quarterback sprint-out which turned out to be a pass to an end cutting across the middle.

"They were our bread-and-butter," sighed Go Team quarterback Lynn Amedee, who turned out to be LSU's biggest weapon in its convincing victory. "Every time we needed something, we got it from those plays."

With time trickling away in the first half, and LSU playing a third-and-four at the Texas 34, Amedee sprinted to his right, stopped and speared tight end Billy Truax for a 22-yard gain. Two plays later, with eight seconds remaining in the half, Amedee somehow pushed a field goal through the goal-posts. A Longhorn got the tip of a finger on the ball, and it went over the crossbar in a circular motion instead of end over end.

Amedee kicked off to open the second half, and when Texas' Jerry Cook was hit at the 'Horns' 35 by Gene Sykes and Dennis Gaubatz, he fumbled. The ball bounced to Amedee at the 37. White Team quarterback Jimmy Field worked the Tigers down to the 22, then on a bootleg play, raced for the game's only touchdown.

"I was looking for Steve Ward," Field said, "but they had him well covered. For a minute, I was going to keep going to my right but when I looked and saw nothing to my left, I took off."

From then on, with 29 minutes left to play, LSU concentrated on not letting Texas hit a big play. The Tigers were successful. Two plays by the Chinese Bandits blunted a couple of drives, including one of the Longhorns' best. Texas drove to the LSU 25 — its deepest penetration of the day — when quarterback Johnny Genung faded for a pass to

end Charles Talbert.

"I was looking for the end to hook over the middle," said Bandit linebacker Ruffin Rodrigue. "The Texas quarterback was throwing right over my head at him . . . I leaped up and managed to get half my hand on the football." Rodrigue didn't hang on to the ball, but the 'Horns eventually attempted a field goal, which was short.

Buddy Hamic ripped the ball from a Texas runner with 10 minutes remaining at the Tiger 31. "He still had the ball under his arm," said Hamic, "but he didn't have a firm grip on it. I jerked it away from him, and then he tried to fight to get it back."

From there, the Go Team went in and Amedee ignited another long, time-consuming drive which resulted in another Tiger field goal, a 37-yard kick. "I never thought the ball would make the crossbar," said Amedee. "There was a little breeze blowing in from the end zone. . . . I don't believe I cleared it by more than two feet."

Accolades were heaped on the Tigers for their

masterful defensive performance. "It's the best team I ever played against in three varsity seasons," All-America linebacker Pat Culpepper said. Longhorn coach Darrell Royal said simply, "We were beaten by a great football team."

Royal, of course, knew what he was talking about. The next season the Longhorns, composed primarily of the troops who played against LSU, won the national championship.

LSU 7, AUBURN 6
Tiger Stadium
Oct. 8, 1988

"The Night the Tigers Shook the Earth" is how it will forevermore be remembered.

LSU's momentous comeback against mighty Auburn, as courageous a performance as any Tiger team ever turned in, produced a reaction which literally equalled a force of nature.

When Tommy Hodson hit Eddie Fuller on the back line of the end zone with 1:41 to play, such a thunder was unleashed

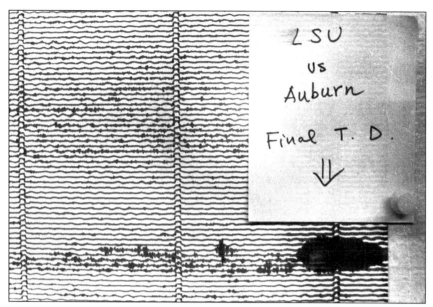

EARTHQUAKE — *When Eddie Fuller caught a game-winning TD pass from Tom Hodson against Auburn in 1988, the vibrations caused by the enthusiasm from the Tiger Stadium crowd registered on a seismograph in the Geology building across the LSU campus.*

from the full house at Tiger Stadium that the tremor caused by the vibrations registered on a seismograph in the LSU geology building, a half-mile from Tiger Stadium. The sound quake was recorded at 9:32 p.m., exactly the instant of the touchdown.

The Bayou Bengals, shackled all night by the SEC's best defense, lurched to life in the final minutes, made two memorable fourth-down plays — including the only touchdown of the evening — to stun the fourth-ranked Tigers of the Plains, Auburn's only defeat of the regular season.

LSU started the season like a team on fire, easily brushing aside Texas A&M (27-0) and Tennessee (34-9), and looking every bit the part of a national championship contender.

Then everything came apart, starting with a horrific fourth quarter at Ohio State when the Tigers unraveled and allowed two late Buckeye touchdowns in a 36-33 loss. Then LSU lost 19-6 at Florida, a game in which the Tiger coaching staff counted 35 offensive mistakes.

The suddenly shaky Tigers now had to go against lean, mean and mighty capable Auburn,

and an iron defense featuring Tracy Rocker and Craig Ogletree which had manhandled four straight opponents.

Auburn spent the night either sacking or pressuring Hodson and keeping the LSU running game in check. For three and a half quarters the Tigers couldn't penetrate the Auburn 23. Until six minutes remained, LSU's meager offensive statistics totalled 138 yards and eight first downs. The Tigers had already punted 11 times, and in the first half had 54 yards and two first downs.

And yet, the LSU defense played nearly as well in holding back the Auburn offense. Only two field goals by Auburn's Win Lyle were scored going into the final period. But it seemed more than enough. "I thought we'd win with three points," Auburn linebacker Quinton Riggins said ruefully afterward.

But after Lyle's 41-yard field goal with 10:18 to go made the score 6-0 — and it seemed like 60-0 — LSU, with no timeouts remaining, and starting at its 24, somehow found just enough in its offense to pull off a miracle.

Hodson hit Tony Moss for 19 yards, and tight end Willie Williams made a sideline catch for a 13-yard gain to the Auburn 45 — only the second time LSU crossed Auburn's side of the field — before being racked out of bounds.

Hodson worked the Tigers to the 21 with 3:33 left when he went to Fuller, the 5-foot-8 full-back, who dropped the ball at the goal line. A Hodson scramble netted one yard, and the third-down pass was incom-plete, setting up a clutch play which proved to be a precursor of things to come.

Hodson, on fourth-and-nine, found Williams in the flat. Williams was hit almost immediately but dived for three more yards to the 11, just making the first down with 2:45 to play.

"That was clutch," Hodson marveled at Williams' determination.

Hodson then speared Fuller at the back end of the end zone, but Fuller came down with one foot a millimeter out of

TOUCHDOWN!! — Eddie Fuller snags this TD pass from Tommy Hodson on fourth down to push LSU to a 7-6 victory over Auburn in 1988.

bounds. Two straight roll-out passes were incom-plete.

On fourth and 10, as they broke the huddle, Hodson said teasingly to his diminutive fullback, "Next time, catch it." Those words must have weighed on Fuller, who, after all, had just let two touchdown passes sail through his hands.

This time, on the same play LSU had run on first down, Hodson found an open Fuller in the north end zone, this time a com-fortable three yards shy of the end line.

The roar of the crowd was positively deafening.

"I knew he was going to be open," Hodson said.

"I saw the (line)backer lose him. . . . I was praying to God he'd catch the ball. I have confidence in everybody, but if there is one man I have confidence in it's Eddie Fuller. He'll make the big play."

He and Williams. Oh, and one other Tiger. Kicker David Browndyke, whose almost forgotten task was to kick the PAT — the deciding point. Browndyke hit the finger of holder Chris Moock, but the ball went through the uprights.

LSU had its improbable 7-6 victory.

And it was definitely improbable. The Tigers stayed in contention by playing grudging defense.

LSU yielded 316 yards to a team that had been averaging 510 yards.

Yet, 75 yards of LSU's 213-yard total came on its last drive; six of Hodson's 17 completions came on the last drive. The Tigers gained but 28 yards rushing, and Fuller was their leading rusher with 15 yards.

Assessed Hodson: "We didn't get a lot of first downs (13), a lot of completions (19 of 42) or a lot of yards rushing. But we got the most points."

**LSU 13,
NORTH CAROLINA 7
Tiger Stadium
Oct. 22, 1949**

North Carolina, with Charlie Justice at tailback, was one of the nation's hottest teams in 1949, riding a victory streak of 20-straight regular-season games.

It was left to over-achieving LSU, a 34-7 victim of the same Tar Heels in '48, to douse the Tar Heel flame. Stopping Justice — a tremendous runner, passer and kicker in the day when greatness in a back was measured by all three — was the obvi-

ous key.

"Coach Gaynell Tinsley and staff thought they'd have a better chance on a sloppy field," Bud Montet wrote in the *Baton Rouge Morning Advocate* the morning of the game, "and two days ago it looked as if they would have their wish." The day before he had suggested the Tigers were better "mudders" than most teams and said Tinsley's attitude was "let it rain."

"However, yesterday was a fine day," the column continued, "and the Bengal turf was in perfect shape, and if no further rain. . . 'Choo Choo' Justice will have as fine a field to run on as he's ever seen in his college career."

When the Tar Heels practiced the day before the game, they thought exactly the same thing, Justice recalled in a conversation with George Morris of the *Baton Rouge State-Times* in 1989. In fact, Justice said, North Carolina coach Carl Snavely commented on the excellence of the turf.

Something struck the Tar Heels as suspicious, though.

"We looked in the

stands and saw these fire hoses laying up there," Justice said. "We wondered what in the world they were going to do, and they told us they were going to wash the stands out the next day."

"All day Saturday it didn't rain a drop," Justice said. "I mean, it was sunshine hot, in fact. And we go out Saturday night and that field had two inches of water on it."

Justice exaggerated the amount of water, according to Tinsley, who said the incident was the result of an accident.

The custom of the day, Tinsley said, was for LSU to wet down the field on Friday nights after the visiting team finished practicing. There was no sprinkler system at the time, so hoses had to be used.

North Carolina practiced later than most opponents, Tinsley said, so he told the groundskeeper to go home and water the field the next morning. That, he said, is where the trouble started.

"Since he wasn't there, the managers took it on themselves to water the field, and the next morning when I get to the field the groundskeeper was back with the water turned on," Tinsley said. "I got him off as quick as I could, and we did everything we could to get the water off and that's all there was to it."

Wet field or not, North Carolina set the early tone. Tiger Kenny Konz put a second quarter punt out at the Tar Heel two, and North Carolina responded by driving 98 yards for the game's first touchdown.

LSU fought back. On the fifth play of the second half, Jim Roshto, normally a defensive back, went in on offense and took a pitchout, swung wide right, cut in and scored untouched from 27 yards out. The PAT was missed, and LSU still trailed, 7-6.

Carolina drove to the LSU 18, where the Tar Heels eventually faced a fourth-and-one. They went for it.

End Sam Lyle stuffed the play, and LSU then marched 82 yards and Zollie Toth scored the deciding touchdown from the one.

Toth and another Tiger, Billy Baggett, interestingly may have been the only

runners hurt by the wet field, both slipping on possible big gainers, according to accounts.

Justice disagreed. "I slipped and fell three times breaking in the clear," he said. Tinsley adamantly refuted that statement. "He's telling you a big lie," Tinsley said. "The only man who fell down on the field that I remember was Zollie Toth, our fullback, when he broke in the open one time."

Did the wet field have a direct bearing on the outcome? The jury is and always will be out on the question. North Carolina, which had scored 25.6 points a game, was held to one touchdown — but that would happen twice more that season.

Justice, who had averaged 80 rushing yards, was held to 58, but the wet turf didn't seem to affect the passing. The Tar Heels completed 14 of 22 passes.

Trainer Marty Broussard hinted Justice was looking for excuses. "We just laid the pine to Charlie Justice and beat his butt."

Tiger athletic director

T.P. "Red" Heard saw the complaints as an effort to diminish LSU's huge upset and would have none of it. "LSU would have beaten North Carolina Saturday night on a wet field, a snowed-in field or concrete. Some coaches, especially those who aren't used to losing, always have an alibi handy. . . If he had won, the officials would have been fine, the field would have been fine, the steaks would have been fine, the airplane would have been fine, everything would have been fine."

LSU 6, NEBRASKA 6
Tiger Stadium
Sept. 11, 1976

The No. 1-ranked Nebraska Cornhuskers came to Baton Rouge with preseason visions of an undefeated season dancing in their heads.

Nebraska was still undefeated when it left, but the numbing tie was treated as a defeat. "The loss," said 'Husker quarterback Vince Ferragamo in the silent Nebraska locker room, "will do us some good. Yeah, I know we didn't lose it . . . but we didn't win it either."

The mighty Cornhuskers showed every bit of their might on the game's first possession, pile-driving for a touchdown, achieved on a three-yard pass from Ferragamo to tight end Ken Spaeth. The PAT snap, though, was fumbled by holder Randy Garcia. It was a bobble which would change the complexion of the game for the rest of the night.

From then to the end of the half, the Tigers somehow held the 'Huskers at bay, even stopping them at the LSU 17.

Tiger stalwart tackles A.J. Duhe and Dan Alexander, linebackers Blake Whitlatch and Jon Street shackled the Nebraska running game, and the LSU secondary played Ferragamo superbly. The Cornhuskers gained yards, but for 56 minutes and one second after the opening possession denied points.

Nebraska controlled the ball for 20:13 of the first half, and rolled up 12 first downs and 176 total yards to LSU's four first downs and 67 yards.

The Bayou Bengal offense showed signs of life in the third quarter, and after stopping Nebraska on a fourth-and-three at the Tiger 36, quarterback Pat Lyons motored LSU into position for Mike Conway to kick a 35-yard field goal.

Nebraska countered with a 54-yard drive of its own, to the Tiger 21, where linebacker Rusty Domingue took the field goal attempt in the mid-section. LSU, behind the pounding of Charles Alexander and Terry Robiskie, inched its way to the Nebraska two, where Conway kicked the tying field goal amidst a chorus of boos from those who wanted McClendon to go for the touchdown. But with 7:08 to go, LSU had knotted the score.

In the remaining time, LSU got one last shot at victory. Conway lined up for a 44-yard field goal on the last play of the game. It veered two feet off at the last second, breaking a lot of Tiger hearts.

"I think our whole team," said Charlie McClendon, "played on sheer guts tonight."

BLOODY, BUT UNBOWED
12

L SU, like every college
football team, has
played superbly and
gallantly in some memorable
games but came up short. In
no particular order, these are
some of LSU's finest efforts.
In these instances, opponents
just happened to have more
points at the end than did
the Tigers.

TENNESSEE 14, LSU 13
Knoxville, Tennessee
Nov. 7, 1959

Billy Cannon took a
pitch at the three and
steamed toward the right
corner of the north end

zone of Tennessee's
Shields-Watkins Field.

Linebacker Charlie
Severance fired in from
linebacker, tackle Wayne
Grubb shot at Cannon's
knees and safety Bill
Majors went flying at the
ball-carrier over Grubb.

Cannon was churning
powerfully right at the
goal, and when the two-
point conversion attempt
was ruled dead he was in
the end zone. Then came
linesman Bob King's signal:
No good.

If successful, the play
would have extended a
Tigers' streak to 20 consecutive victories, and almost

certainly would have
ensured LSU — which had
only Mississippi State and
Tulane, both mediocre
teams, left to play — a second straight national
championship.

Falling short represent-
ed LSU's costliest defeat.
LSU dropped from No. 1 to
No. 3 in the polls, then got
caught in the crunch of
politics as the postseason
bowls began filling up.
Eventually, the Tigers
accepted a bid they didn't
want, a Sugar Bowl
rematch with Ole Miss, a
team LSU had already beat-
en. The Rebels not only
had all the incentives, they

caught the Tigers in their worst physical condition in two years, with Johnny Robinson and Warren Rabb severely limited by injury, and Wendell Harris out completely.

LSU would never have been placed in such a nothing-to-gain bowl game if Cannon had only made his way cleanly into the Tennessee end zone.

To this day Cannon says: "I'll go to my grave believing I was over." Johnny Majors, then the Vols' freshman coach, said Cannon's forward progress had been stopped. Majors said, "He damn sure didn't score."

LSU was 7-0-0 entering the game, with a defense that had not given up a touchdown in 40 quarters, dating to 1958. The Vols were 4-1-1 and already had broken Auburn's 24-game unbeaten streak earlier that season. But Tennessee "was not a very good team at all," according to Johnny Majors.

Amazingly, this incredible defeat came one week after one of LSU's greatest victories, 7-3 over Ole Miss on Cannon's legendary 89-yard punt return.

But there was no let-

down involved in this upset. On that brisk, 40 degree afternoon in the Smokies, the Bayou Bengals were clearly the superior team. LSU gained 334 yards to Tennessee's 112. Cannon (122) and Johnny Robinson (115) each rushed for more yards than the Vols gained as a team.

"Tennessee was only close to LSU in performance for about 15 seconds of the 60 minutes we played," LSU coach Paul Dietzel said.

"It was no contest," Majors conceded, "except on the scoreboard."

Which, of course, is all that counts.

LSU led only 7-0 at the half, despite 170 yards of offense to Tennessee's 38. Then, in the third quarter, Wendell Harris missed two field goal attempts, one from 22 yards in the third period.

That LSU attempted the second field goal went against Dietzel's philosophy. The Tigers had a fourth-and-two at the Tennessee five. If LSU went for it and failed, tendencies showed Vols coach Bowden Wyatt would punt on first down that close his goal.

But Dietzel felt a field goal would ice the game.

Tiger halfback Don Purvis said the kick went "smack dab over the upright." Veteran SEC ref Johnny Lynch ruled otherwise.

Said Johnny Majors, tongue-in-cheek, to the *Knoxville Sentinel-News'* Jimmy Hyams before the 30th anniversary of the game: "I forget those things. I was for Tennessee."

LSU came roaring back, with quarterback Warren Rabb hitting Cannon in the left flat for a 12-yard gain to the Tiger 41, before Cannon busted loose for a 16-yard gain.

Then Rabb called the same pass play, this time to Robinson in the right flat.

"I smelled it," said Tennessee defensive back Jim Cartwright, who cut in front of Robinson, picked off the pass, stepped out of Robinson's attempted diving tackle, and returned the interception 59 yards for the first touchdown scored against LSU in 10 games. "If we had been ahead 10-0," Dietzel said, "that pass never would have been thrown."

Sophomore Earl Gros of

the suddenly shaken Tigers then fumbled at the 26, and Tennessee recovered, then scored on a 14-yard run, and the Vols were on the verge of what Majors described as "one of the biggest upsets ever."

There was plenty of time remaining, 13:44, when Durel Matherne scored on a quarterback sneak in the fourth quarter, but Dietzel decided to go for the lead.

1959 was the first year college football had the option to run for two points after touchdowns. This was the first two-point conversion LSU ever attempted, and the first time Tennessee had ever defended a two-point conversion.

Dietzel sent in guard Mike Stupka, a Go Team lineman but one of his best pulling guards, and ordered Cannon off right tackle, which he knew wouldn't catch Tennessee off guard but was LSU's most consistent play. "It was our considered opinion that Cannon would be called off tackle," Wyatt said.

The controversial play followed.

And the game continued its bizarre path a few

moments later, Emile Fournet blocked a Vols' punt, and LSU's Bo Strange recovered at the Tennessee 26.

Matherne, normally the Go Team quarterback, was in with the White Team because Rabb injured a knee. Used to handing off to the much smaller Purvis, Matherne tried to give the ball to the bigger, faster Cannon on a sweep. Instead of getting the ball in the stomach, the ball hit Cannon on the hip — and bounced free. Tennessee got it.

Watching the play on film later was almost as bad as living through it. The blocking was perfect, and Cannon may well have scored, a scenario in which very few today would even remember the controversial two-point conversion.

Wyatt didn't seem certain his defense had stopped Cannon. "The movies will show that he got pretty close to those two points," he said right after the upset.

An obviously unhappy Dietzel said, "I told Bowden Wyatt that Cannon was in the end zone up to his waist, and he said, 'Probably.' "

SOUTHERN CAL 17, LSU 12
Baton Rouge, Louisiana
Sept. 29, 1979

Heart-breaking.

For 59 minutes, 28 seconds of searing, emotional football, LSU held the team of its worst nightmares at bay.

No. 1-ranked Southern California, perhaps the best team in terms of sheer talent ever to set cleats in Tiger Stadium - with future NFL standouts Brad Budde, Anthony Munoz, Keith Van Horn, Ronnie Lott, Hobie Brenner, Heisman Trophy recipient Charles White, and quarterback Paul McDonald and a half dozen more pro prospects — was everything everyone said about it. The Trojans were big, very big, with the average starting offensive lineman coming in at 6-foot-5, 252-pounds, which meant USC's line outweighed the New Orleans Saints' starting offensive line by an average of 22-pounds a man.

To put that USC team in individual terms: on some plays LSU's Benji Thibodeaux, at 6-foot-2, 242-pounds, would have

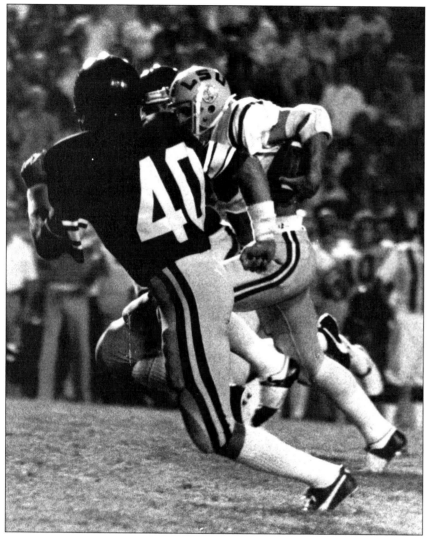

CLOSE CALL — No. 1-ranked Southern Cal barely escaped Death Valley as the Tigers fought hard in a 17-12 loss.

in others, and with no legitimate superstars to compare with the gifted behemoths of Troy. "LSU has only two players who, as they say, can make things happen: Wide receiver Carlos Carson and cornerback Chris Williams," assessed an NFL observer.

And yet Coach John Robinson was playing up the Tiger Stadium, saying the crowd could influence the officiating and so forth. Of course, he was planting psychological seeds for the split-crew of Pac-10 and SEC officials to ponder.

Mac was concerned about calls as well, though he kept his comments confined to his team. "I told my team all week even a five-yard penalty could be the difference. And I told them we were playing the holdingest team in football."

Tiger Stadium was rocking long before the kickoff, as raucous fans vented steam. They'd been waiting for a shot at ambushing USC ever since the game was announced several years before. Large crowds milled around under the creative signs hanging from the dormitory windows on

to take on both Budde and Van Horn, all 505 pounds of them.

"It's not just that they weigh so much," said Charlie McClendon. "It's also that they're so tall. They're like a basketball team. When they run that sweep, finding White will be like trying to find a sports car behind a lot of buses."

The Trojans, 3-0-0 and a 12-point favorite, were also fast and dangerous from any spot on the field, from either side of the ball.

Standing in their way was Charlie Mac's last band of Tigers, 2-0-0 and pretty fair in some areas, suspect

A VALIANT EFFORT — USC'S Ronnie Lott (42) closes in on LSU's Tracy Porter (21) as the top ranked Trojans hold on to a narrow 17-12 victory over the Tigers in 1979.

the outside of the arena for hours before kickoff.

Anticipation was building to a peak just before the teams came out to finally tee it up.

When the Trojans came on the field, the sound of the disapproving partisans was jarring. When the first glint of the flood lights on the gold helmets standing in the chute was spotted, the screams and yells started building. When the beloved Tigers finally rushed onto the field, the decibels were at shattering levels. From then to game's end, the quietest moment in the stadium was a low roar.

And the Tigers immediately stirred the crowd's adrenalin — and heart-strings — as LSU not only showed no early signs of playing the sacrificial lamb, despite an early USC field goal, but actually inched in front as quarterback Steve Ensminger put some second quarter sizzle in the Tiger attack. On a third and 13, Ensminger speared a galloping Tracy Porter for 15 yards, down to the 36. Jude Hernandez busted through the middle on a perfect call, a trap as the rover (Ronnie Lott)

charged into the backfield on a blitz.

The play netted 24 yards and two calls later Ensminger hit a wide-open LeRoid Jones (in the lineup because LSU's first two tailbacks, Hokie Gajan and Jude Hernandez were injured early), who was playing slot-left, in the middle of the end zone. The conversion was botched.

After White fumbled a few minutes later, LSU increased its lead to 9-3 on a 32-yard field goal by Don Barthels.

McDonald marshalled his mighty Trojans for one last gasp before the half, and got to the Tiger 11, where Eric Hipp missed a field goal as the horn sounded.

It was a testament to LSU's disciplined enthusiasm that the Tigers not only were actually in the hunt, but in front, and the denizens of Tiger Stadium were whipped into an emotional frenzy.

And the Tigers kept coming. Second-team quarterback David Woodley drove LSU to the USC two, but after a nine-yard loss, Barthels kicked another field goal and the place was

in bedlam.

Someone probably should have sensed what was coming though, because the Tigers were leaving too many points on the goal line, getting three-point field goals instead of seven point touchdowns.

On top of that, a golden opportunity slipped through LSU's fingers when McDonald, under a heavy rush on third-and-five from the USC 30, threw a pass in the flat. Chris Williams was there waiting, with clear sailing to the end zone. "I had it all the way," Williams said later. "Coach Mac always tells us never to take our eye off the ball. This time I did. The ball went right through my hands. If I catch it, I could have walked in."

But what happened was that, after dodging what could have been a fatal bullet, McDonald was able to pull together his troops in the fourth quarter. After a weak 30-yard Tiger punt to the USC 43, McDonald got the Trojans into the end zone in six plays when White went in from the four to score the first touchdown of the season against LSU, which still led 12-10.

Southern Cal took advantage of an opening. Then, when LSU had a chance to salt away the victory, it didn't. Marcus Allen fumbled at the USC 22, and LSU's George Atiyeh recovered. With a chance to shut the door on the Trojans, LSU unraveled.

On a dipsy-doodle incomplete pass LSU was assessed a 15-yard penalty for offensive interference; Woodley lost two yards and then the Tigers were called for delay of game before Woodley lost six more, and LSU finally punted from its own 44 yard line.

The sequence was crucial. Essentially staring at its last chance to get out with a victory, the Trojans started to drive. Three plays later, on third and nine from the USC 36 with three minutes to go, came the unkindest cut of all. McDonald called a pass play, but his line jumped before the snap. As Thibodeaux and Demetri Williams zeroed in on McDonald, he intentionally threw the ball away to avoid the very real possibility of a sack. A penalty flag fluttered to the Tiger Stadium turf and it seemed as if it were all over but the shouting.

Then, incredibly, umpire Neil Gareb of the Pac-10 signalled a penalty against LSU! Thibodeaux's hand had brushed McDonald's helmet as he made the tackle. "When I reached out to grab him," Thibodeaux said, "his head moved and my hand grazed his facemask." Never mind that the off-sides, and the intentional grounding infractions occurred before McDonald went down, meaning the very worst LSU could have expected was off-setting penalties.

You could almost see the Tigers sag. They were able to slow the Trojan express just enough to force another third down, at the LSU eight. McDonald hit 5-foot-8 jitterbug Kevin Williams slicing across the middle for the touchdown on that play. There were 32 seconds left.

And still Ensminger very nearly pulled off a miracle on the second-to-last play, arcing a 30-yard rainbow to a streaking Willie Turner in the end zone. The ball fell through Turner's hands as he tried to make the catch and stay in bounds at the end zone's backline.

Even in defeat, everyone in the stadium realized what kind of effort the Tigers had given. "L-S-U, L-S-U, we're proud of you," was the chant that echoed around the stadium from the student section long after the Tigers retired to lick their emotional wounds — and to wonder about one very questionable call. To this day, Tigers question Neil Gareb's football integrity.

And things never got better for LSU. It was as if college football was determined to give Charlie Mac a career full of showcase opponents to prepare for in his last season. Southern Cal wasn't the only No. 1 team to visit Tiger Stadium in 1979. Later that year, Alabama was ranked No. 1 and defeated LSU, 3-0. USC finished first in the UPI poll, Bama was first in the AP rankings.

Still, it's difficult to find a game when an LSU team played as much to its potential — maybe even beyond — than to the night when the outmanned Tigers held USC to a near standstill.

"When you look at our team compared to theirs," McClendon mused, "one-on-one, or even 11-on-11, the differences are obvious. But when you put a team before a crowd like tonight's, in a game like this, then that team must be measured from here," he said, pointing to his chest. "When a team plays with its heart, then the measuring stick between one team and another shortens."

NOTRE DAME 3, LSU 0
South Bend, Indiana
Nov. 21, 1970

"This place," Charlie McClendon said with a sweep of an arm that took in the 60,000 empty seats on the cold, misty morning the day before the first LSU-Notre Dame clash. "Too many teams come into this place and they've already lost the ball game before it starts.

"Not my kids. We're ready. They may not have enough sense to realize it up here, but we have a helluva football team. We're not going to be intimidated. We may get shellacked tomorrow. But that'll be tomorrow. Not today."

Charlie Mac knew his team well. The Tigers knew they had to perform extremely well in order to have any chance, but their adrenalin was pumping because of the circumstances of the Cotton Bowl fiasco the season before when Notre Dame played Texas after LSU thought it had an understanding. Oddsmakers, though, were giving LSU 14 points.

In a glorious defensive classic, the capacity crowd of 59,075 spent the afternoon with heads swiveling, as if at a tennis match, from one side to the other as the punters got workouts.

Two of the premier defenses in college football spent the afternoon in a see-saw battle. Wayne Dickinson booted 12 LSU punts away for a total of 455 yards; the Irish's Jim Yoder had 10 kicks for 426 total yards.

It was a little harder for LSU to hold back the Irish, with Joe Theismann at quarterback. The No. 2-ranked Irish were the nation's top-ranked offensive team, averaging 540 yards a game, and had scored 41 touchdowns. The Tiger defense, on the other hand, had gone 11 games without surrendering a rushing touchdown. And on this day, the Tiger defense — featuring Ronnie Estay, Mike Anderson and John Sage — was brilliant.

At the Tiger three, playing a first-and-goal, linebacker Richard Picou, a walk-on who turned into a quality starter, hit the ball-carrier and forced a fumble which he recovered.

Later, on third-and-one at midfield, tackle John Sage stopped the runner short. Irish coach Ara Parseghian, frustrated at the sticky going, went against his form and ordered his team to go for it. The Irish failed to gain the necessary inch.

Theismann couldn't find a method of moving his big offense against the comparative gnats that made up the Tiger defense. Notre Dame had trouble moving on the ground, and Tommy Casanova gave Tom Gatewood, the nation's No. 2 receiver, precious little breathing room. Gatewood, who later said Casanova was "playing in my jockstrap," caught four passes for 21 yards, none in the second half.

Of course, Notre Dame was also playing spectacular defense. LSU's best chance of denting the end zone came in the fourth quarter after Bill Norsworthy intercepted Theismann, a play that eventually gave the Tigers a shot at a field goal. But Mark Lumpkin's 34-yard attempt was blocked by end Bob Niedert.

The seeds of LSU's destruction were sown in Niedert's play.

After the Irish took over, on third-down from the Notre Dame 17, an "iffy" interference call gave them new life at midfield. The SEC official closest to the action waved the pass incomplete. The Big Ten official said Tiger defensive back John Nagel had interfered.

Notre Dame still couldn't budge LSU, but from this position, the next time the Irish punted, the ball went out at the one-yard line.

Quarterback Buddy Lee wiggled the Tigers out to the seven, before Dickinson came in to punt against a stiff wind. Clarence Ellis returned it

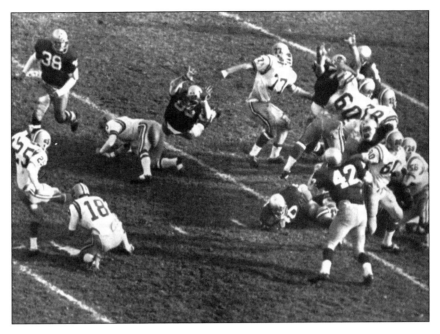

ONE-A — LSU's Mark Lumpkin (25) has his field goal attempt blocked at Notre Dame, 1970.

to the LSU 36. The Tigers yielded ground grudgingly, and on third down just missed their last opportunity to get out with at least a 0-0 tie. Theismann went for Gatewood in the end zone, and Casanova cut in front of the receiver, leaped, and got his hands on the ball. It was the kind of interception Casanova made a dozen times at LSU. But he dropped this one.

On the next play, fourth down, Scott Hempel went in to boot a 24-yard field goal. There was 2:54 remaining. The field goal was the difference.

How well did LSU perform? Well, Notre Dame was limited to 227 total yards, and the Irish rushing game, piling up an average of 304 yards before, managed 78 against the Tigers, only 30 when the game was on the line.

Afterward, Parsehigan paid tribute to the Tigers. "I feel LSU is probably the finest and quickest defensive team we have faced here at Notre Dame since I've been here."

Chicago Tribune sportswriter Dave Condon said it even more succinctly in print the next morning: "If Notre Dame is No. 1, then LSU is No. 1-A."

VANDERBILT 7, LSU 6
Nashville, Tennessee
Oct. 23, 1937

Jimmy Huggins, who called signals for Vanderbilt, leaned into the huddle and whispered the magic words: "Henry Frnka."

Seconds later, on the third play of the game, the entire LSU defense was chasing Dutch Reinschmidt, the Vandy quarterback, who was running around left end behind a wall of blockers.

The thing was, Reinschmidt did not have the football. When the Tigers realized they were after the wrong man, it was too late. Right guard Greer Ricketson was leading a one-man parade, steaming down the opposite sideline for a touchdown.

LSU had been victimized by what turned out to be one of the most famous plays — Vandy's 'Hidden Ball' — in the history of the Southeastern Conference.

The Tigers were 4-0-0, had wracked up 13 consecutive SEC victories, and had yet to yield a point in the '37 season. The Commodores were just as undefeated at 4-0-0. Still, Vandy coach Ray Morrison felt he'd need a surprise to puncture that formidable LSU defense.

Morrison's assistant, Henry Frnka (pronounced "Franka"), who had coached a Texas high school team to the 1932 state championship on a 'hidden ball' trick play, made a suggestion.

When Frnka drew up the play for Morrison, the Vandy coach decided it was so sensitive that only the starting team would be told. They called the play "Henry Frnka," and when the Commodores worked on the play during the week, Vanderbilt's starters moved out of sight of their teammates.

After two plays from scrimmage that chilly afternoon at Dudley Field, with the Commodores at midfield, the play was called.

Ricketson explained how it worked: "We lined up in the T and Reinschmidt took a direct snap from center. As soon as he got the ball, he laid it on the ground behind the left guard."

Left guard Bill Hays, with his forearms flat on the ground, hovered over the ball, while others screened him out.

"I had shifted from right tackle to right guard," Ricketson said. "I pulled out as if to join the interference. Faking possession beautifully, Reinschmidt swept wide to his left. Just as I got behind our left guard, I pretended to trip over him. After a three-count, I picked up the ball and ran down the right side of the field. I thought I'd be tackled any instant. I didn't learn until later that LSU had no idea where the ball was until it heard the roar of the crowd."

It was the forerunner of the play we know today as the "Fumblerooskie."

The stunned Tigers didn't score until the game's final minutes when Young Bussey hit Jabbo Stell on a 19-yard touchdown pass. A high pass from center, though, prevented Barry Booth's PAT attempt, and the score remained at 7-6, Vanderbilt — the only blot on LSU's regular-season record.

OLE MISS 26, LSU 23
Jackson, Mississippi
Nov. 1, 1969

Archie Manning broke Tiger hearts the same way LSU moved Ole Miss to tears in 1959, 1960, and 1961, by depriving them of a perfect season with dramatic heroics.

LSU was a finely-tuned football machine in '69, maybe the best team the school ever produced. A superb defensive team which led the nation in rushing defense at the end of the season, the Tiger offense also averaged more than 34 points a game. It was a team that could have looked any other in the eye and not blinked. LSU truly may have been the best football team in the country that year, but never got a chance to prove it — in large part because of Manning.

Of course, the Tigers should have been wary, despite Ole Miss' three losses. In 1968, when Manning was a sophomore, he rolled up 362 yards of offense in overcoming a 17-3 LSU lead for a 27-24 Rebel victory. Manning completed 24 of 40 passes,

including two for touchdowns — one a 65-yard pass in which two LSU defenders hit each other going for the ball, which the suddenly wide open Floyd Franks grabbed and ran in the end zone, the other a nine-yard pass to Steve Hindman with 55 seconds remaining. A drained Rebel coach Johnny Vaught said afterward: "Damndest thing I've ever seen."

Vaught hadn't seen anything yet.

A far better team in '69 than in '68, LSU was as complete a football aggregation as could be found in the college sport, and was 6-0 going into the Rebels' backyard in Jackson, yet fell victim to what amounted to a one-man team for a second consecutive year.

"You wouldn't think that, the way football is played today," said Tiger linebacker George Bevan when asked if Manning single-handedly ruined their season, "but he is the one who beat us. I thought we had him every time, but he can turn a 15-yard loss into a 25-yard gain. I thought the quarterback from Auburn (Pat Sullivan) was good, but he has only

one leg compared to Manning."

Quarterback Mike Hillman hit wide receiver Andy Hamilton with a 32-yard touchdown strike early in the third quarter to put LSU up, 23-12, as the legion of Tiger followers went into a purple-and-gold frenzy.

Right away Manning jump-started the Ole Miss offense and got the Rebels down to the Bayou Bengals' three, where he scrambled around right end and stepped untouched into the end zone to cut the score to 23-18.

An LSU fumble at the Tiger 23 put Manning in position for an Ole Miss lead and, just as the third quarter ended, he sneaked in from a foot away. Manning then ran in a two-point conversion to put the Rebels ahead by three at 26-23, obviously meaning LSU had to score a touchdown to win.

With time running out, the Tigers cranked it up one last time and drove to the Ole Miss 23 where safety Glenn Cannon made three sterling defensive plays.

The Tigers were in kicker Mark Lumpkin's range,

but on fourth down with time running out, Charlie McClendon elected to go for the yardage and possible victory rather than the tying field goal. "Yes, the field goal entered my mind," McClendon said, "but we had really put the sweat on 'em, and in this situation I felt we had a good chance for the first down."

The fourth down pass was batted down, and LSU sustained its first — and only — defeat of the 1969 season.

It was a setback of monumental proportions. LSU was all set to go to the Cotton Bowl, which had wined and dined the Tigers early on. But it was the year in which Notre Dame broke its long-standing bowl ban, and the Irish wanted a chance to play number one ranked Texas for the national championship. By the time all the backroom politics played out, LSU was stunned to find it didn't have the spot in the Cotton Bowl it had been led to believe was theirs.

Because LSU had already turned down feelers from the Sugar Bowl because of the Cotton

Bowl agreement, when it was time to make selections the Sugar took 7-3 Ole Miss over 9-1 LSU. The Tigers were so angry they voted not to go anywhere rather than a minor bowl.

Out of TV sight and out of mind, the dust of the bowl season settled with no one really remembering LSU, whose season ended a month before. The '69 Tigers — maybe the best ever at that school — finished in 10th place of the final Associated Press poll.

Had they found a way to overcome Manning, however, LSU would have been unbeaten at season's end and dealing with a lot more clout. If an unbeaten LSU wasn't playing Texas

for the national championship instead of Notre Dame, it surely would have been in the catbird's seat for the Orange or Sugar and calculating what opponent would bring LSU its highest possible ranking.

But that's what might have been.

What did happen was Archie Manning put on a dazzling show to defeat the Tigers again. It was almost too much for Frank J. Polozola, a huge LSU fan, to bear. Polozola, then a Baton Rouge attorney and later a judge, took the loss so hard that he filed suit in Federal District Court seeking an injunction to prevent Archie from "further harassment" of the Tigers.

IRISH EYES — This field goal gave No. 1 ranked Notre Dame a narrow 3-0 victory over LSU in 1970.

LSU's GREATEST TEAMS

13

The 10 greatest teams, arguably no doubt, in LSU football history:

■ **1969 (9-1-0):** An incredibly balanced team that averaged almost 35 points (34.9) a game offensively, and yielded a total of 384 rushing yards all season.

The tigerish defense — with a backbone of four All-Americans (linebacker George Bevan in '69; linebacker Mike Anderson, 1970; tackle Ronnie Estay, 1971; and safety Tommy Casanova, 1969-70-71) — held three opponents to minus rushing yardage.

A grand total of 87 yards on the ground was gained on LSU in its first four games. Only Kentucky, in the fifth game of the season, was able to gain as many as a hundred yards rushing on the Tigers. LSU beat the Wildcats, 37-10, despite fumbling the ball away four times in its first six possessions. "We have to have a great team to make the mistakes we do and still win," said Charlie McClendon afterward.

A late season loss to Ole Miss, and Notre Dame's breaking its long-standing policy of not playing in bowls, contributed to the '69 Tigers not playing in the post-season. LSU had a handshake agreement to play in the Cotton Bowl, but the Tigers were caught in the switches when the Irish decided late in the season they wanted to play No. 1 Texas for the national championship. Otherwise, this truly great, but overlooked team could have lined up against the Longhorns, a team whose strength was running the ball, against a more balanced offense and a defense whose strength was stuffing the run.

Who knows what might have happened?

■1961 (10-1-0): Upset by lowly Rice in its opening game, this team improved dramatically week-by-week, reaching higher levels each game to season's end, beating heavyweights Ole Miss (10-7) and Georgia Tech (10-0) in the process.

Fourth-ranked LSU slammed seventh-ranked Colorado (25-7) in the Orange Bowl, a victory that marked Paul Dietzel's final game as Tiger coach.

The '61 Tigers also were a team stocked with quality football beef. Three All-Americans — guard Roy Winston, 1961; halfback Jerry Stovall, 1962; and tight end Billy Truax, 1963 — were sprinkled throughout that lineup. Paul Dietzel said this team had more talent than his 1958 Tigers.

Though it's not always indicative of how good a college team is, it is interesting to note that 11 members of that squad went on to play professional football.

■1958 (11-0-0): Innovative, hungry and talented. Dietzel parlayed a liability into an asset when he designed a three-team system to keep his gifted front-line athletes (The White Team) fresh by splitting their playing time with two back-up units — one for offense (the Go Team), and one for defense (the Chinese Bandits) — and to combat the prevailing substitution rules.

The starting unit was probably as good a collection of starters as any in the country, with halfback Billy Cannon and center Max Fugler, both of whom would be All-Americans at season's end.

But the unexpected key to the season was how well the back-up units performed. They not only bought time for the rested White Team to overrun opponents late in games, but played well enough in some games to have been the ultimate deciding factor. In an era when points were at a premium, the '58 Tigers had only four games decided by 10 points or less.

■1908 (10-0-0): Scorched earth was left in the fiery wake of this Tiger team. "Great" may not be an adequate adjective to describe this turn-of-the-century club that rang up statistics that would raise eyebrows today.

The legendary Doc Fenton quarterbacked the Tigers to an astounding 442 points in the era of the five-point touchdown. If calculated by the modern scoring system, the 1908 Tigers would have averaged 50.8 points in its 10 games, just under 51 points a game, a gaudy figure even for the 1990s.

And they were just as imposing on defense. Only a single touchdown, and a total of 11 points, were scored on LSU, which had to be the most dominating team of its time.

■1936 (9-1-1): The first LSU team ever to be ranked No. 1 in the Deke Houlgate poll and Williamson System, these Tigers finished second to Minnesota in the first Associated Press poll. Gaynell Tinsley, LSU's end extraordinaire, was surrounded by an abundance of talented teammates good enough to lead the nation in scoring. They put up 295 points in 11 games (26.9 ppg), an eye-catching accomplishment at the time.

A grand total of 55 points (5.0 ppg), including those in a 21-14 defeat to Santa Clara in the Sugar

Bowl, were managed against the Tigers.

After LSU steamrolled Georgia, 47-7, Bulldog coach Harry Mehre said, "They're on a par with Alabama's 1934 club with better balance, more speed and more power. I've never seen a better looking squad."

Yet, the Tigers succumbed to aspiring West Coast power Santa Clara — and its deservedly heralded back Nello Falaschi — in a game LSU was never really a threat to win. The reason? The theory is that, for the second year in a row, LSU was disappointed in being passed over for the Rose Bowl.

■ **1946 (9-1-1):** John Ferguson, voice of the Tigers for the bulk of four decades, always insisted this was the best Tiger team ever to take the field, and he made a compelling case: "There was a quarterback named Y.A. Tittle, a punter named Rip Collins, who was the best in LSU, Ray Coates, an excellent back. That team, filled with returning war veterans was six deep everywhere."

Ferguson backs his argument by pointing to Joe Glamp, from Mount

Pleasant, Pennsylvania, who lettered in 1942 before going to war. When he rejoined the Tigers in '46, Glamp was soon unhappy about a lack of playing time and Coach Bernie Moore told him there just wasn't much opportunity for him at LSU, there were too many better backs ahead of him.

But Glamp later started for three seasons with the Pittsburgh Steelers.

Still, the 1946 Tigers lost to Georgia Tech, 26-7, though Ferguson said that was "just one of those games." In the infamous "Ice Bowl" against Arkansas, played in a blustery snowstorm in Dallas' Cotton Bowl, LSU ran up 15 first downs to the Razorbacks' one, and gained 271 yards to the Hogs' 54, but never did score in a 0-0 deadlock. "Believe me," Ferguson said, "pound for pound, as far as pure talent, this was the champion Tiger team."

■ **1959 (9-2-0):** An extension of the '58 Tigers, since the national champions were primarily a junior team, they were even more impressive statistically. They did not give up a touchdown until the eighth

game of the schedule and yielded a total of 29 points for the season.

Yet Dietzel always maintained this team suffered a bit from "senioritis," that they were not quite as intense as they were in '58. Still, LSU went 40 quarters without giving up a touchdown — and that came on an interception return. The season began unraveling in a fluky defeat to Tennessee, a game in which two Tiger backs each outgained the entire Volunteer team, but LSU still lost 14-13.

Interestingly, Dietzel may have sown the seeds for the downfall. Tommy Davis was one of the best place-kickers in the country in 1958, playing a crucial role in the national championship and directly responsible for two victories (Florida, 10-7 and Mississippi State, 7-6). Davis was older than his teammates, having served a hitch in the army, and had his own apartment. He didn't spend much of his off-time in the dorms or with his teammates. Davis basically did his job and went his own way.

At the end of the '58 season when he was drafted by the San Francisco

TITLE DRIVE — Billy Cannon crosses the goal-line for LSU's only touchdown in a narrow 10-7 victory over Florida, 1959.

PRODIGY — Mike Archer posted the best first-year record of any coach in LSU football history — 10-1-1 in 1987.

49ers, Dietzel advised Davis to forego his senior season and sign. So he wasn't there for the '59 Tigers against Tennessee when two short field goals were missed, giving the Volunteers their opening.

After that loss, with the postseason bowls filling up and without its No. 1 ranking as leverage, LSU was pressured into a Sugar Bowl rematch with Ole Miss, a team LSU beat during the regular season on Billy Cannon's famed Halloween night punt return. The Tigers not only didn't want to play a team with every psychological advantage, but by game-time was a battered football squad. Starting halfback Johnny Robinson had a broken arm, and starting quarterback Warren Rabb a knee injury. The result was a 21-0 defeat, almost as many points surrendered by the Tigers as they gave up all season.

■ **1987 (10-1-1):** Tommy Hodson and Wendell Davis were the premier passing combination in the nation, and they were protected by perhaps the finest offensive line ever assembled at LSU.

All-American center Nacho Albergamo anchored the line, and guard Eric Andolsek, considered one of the best linemen ever to put on a Tiger jersey, for one of the rare times in football history, showcased the intricacies of line play.

When Coach Mike Archer's Tigers weren't scoring touchdowns — and they totalled 365 points — they were getting field goals from David Browndyke, the kicker on LSU's Team of the Century.

Defense wasn't ignored, as it never is at LSU. The Tigers were solid with Eric Hill and Ron Sancho at linebacker, surrendering only 184 points in their 12 games, counting a 30-13 victory over South Carolina in the Gator Bowl. Matt

NACHO! — LSU offensive lineman Nacho Albergamo earned consensus All-America honors in 1987.

DeFrank was the All-SEC punter.

Oddly, considering their historical reputations, the blots on LSU's 1987 record came against Ohio State (13-13) and Alabama (10-22), the weakest offensive teams on the Tiger schedule that season. Hodson and All-SEC tight end Brian Kinchen were both out with injuries in the Bama defeat. LSU was clearly a legitimate national Top Five team that season, the last time it has been.

■1937 (9-2-0): Ken Kavanaugh, Young Bussey and Pinky Rohm (who Gaynell Tinsley maintains was the best back he ever saw at LSU), provided the firepower for a surprisingly potent sophomore-dominated team.

No one scored on the Tigers in their first four games, and when an opponent finally did penetrate the LSU goal line it was on Vanderbilt's infamous "hidden ball" trick that did the Tigers in, 7-6, LSU's only regular season loss. The Tigers yielded only two other touchdowns the remainder of the regular season while going on a touchdown binge themselves, and outscoring their last five opponents 174-13.

A Sugar Bowl rematch with Santa Clara, however, produced a dull LSU performance and a 6-0 defeat.

■1935 (9-2-0): Beaten by a strong Rice club, 10-7, in the season-opener — and in Coach Bernie Moore's first game as head coach — the Tigers developed into an uncommonly cohesive unit. Abe Mickal quarterbacked, and took snaps from All-America center Marvin "Moose" Stewart.

"Win them close, win them all" is an old football saying and LSU very nearly did just that. The Tigers had a string of relatively close victories (Texas, 18-6; Arkansas, 13-7; Vanderbilt, 7-2; Auburn, 6-0; and Georgia, 13-0) while still impressing observers. Georgia coach Harry Mehre said after LSU nudged his team in Athens, "LSU had the finest team that ever played on this field."

The season ended, though, with fate playing turnabout. On a muddy field in the Sugar Bowl, which affected the offenses of both teams, Texas Christian and "Slingin' Sammy" Baugh edged LSU, 3-2 — one field goal to one safety.

HOLD THAT TIGER

14

The stirring refrain in one of LSU's fight songs is: "Make Mike the Tiger stand right up and roar. ROAR!"

A Royal Bengal tiger has reigned, roared and presided over LSU athletics for more than a half century now, probably becoming the most famous mascot in college sports.

A regal 500-pound carnivore sitting and bellowing near the stadium entrance of the visiting team will normally get that team's attention, even if the beast is caged in a van painted and decorated in school colors.

LSU is named, of course, for a military unit, not the animal. But almost from the start in 1896 when the undefeated football team earned its stripes — and its sobriquet — the snarling and graceful feline has been its symbol. Early on there were flags and banners decorated with tiger heads at games, and later papier-maché replicas of tigers were designed and fixed onto Model-Ts for football excursions.

In 1922 Tulane carried several of its own imitation caged tigers to Baton Rouge on the special football train, obviously to tear apart and taunt the Tigers with at the game. A group of LSU cadets took action and went after the replicas. They captured one before superior Tulane numbers forced a retreat.

Later the hostilities were renewed in the street in front of the Istrouma Hotel, and the remainder of the papier-maché tigers were "rescued."

As for LSU's huge imitation tiger, a policy was adopted that whenever the Tigers played on the road it would be escorted by eight-to-10 heavyweight cadets.

The heated turn-of-the-century LSU-Tulane series

MIKE? — A paper mache tiger served as the forerunner to Mike the Tiger.

even gave the flimsy mascot its nickname. Tiger tackle Caddo Thielman is alleged to have bitten the ear of John T. Chambers, the Tulane captain in the 1905 game. Though Thielman vigorously denied guilt in the incident, from then on, in and around Baton Rouge tigers were referred to as "Little-Eat-Em-Ups."

"Little-Eat-Em-Up" was also the name of LSU's first live mascot. A bob-tailed South American cat was brought to several games in 1924, but LSU lost four of its last five games — which may have played a role in why no attachment to the animal seemed to develop.

On the other hand, Mike I was positively an LSU heart-throb even before he ever set a paw on

campus 12 years after "Little-Eat-Em-Up" quietly departed.

W.G. "Hickey" Higginbotham, LSU's swimming coach, author of one of LSU's fight songs and a former Tiger cheerleader, had the brainstorm that the Tigers should have a tiger — a live tiger — to call their own.

The suggestion was offered by Higginbotham at a student body convocation, with the proposal that the mascot be purchased strictly with student donations. The students enthusiastically embraced the idea. Ed Laborde, a student, agreed to head the fund-raising, and LSU's 250-pound athletic trainer, Mike Chambers, a man who once blocked for Red Grange at the University of

Illinois and one of the most popular figures on the Tiger campus, immediately began a nationwide search for an available animal at a reasonable price.

As it happened, a 6-foot-3 freshman football player by the name of Ken Kavanaugh — later an All-American and All-Pro end — gave Tiger tradition a huge assist by writing his mother back home in Little Rock, Ark. "I asked her to check out the Little Rock zoo to see if any tigers might be for sale," Kavanaugh said. "Sure enough, there were two, one priced at $500, another at $750."

Kavanaugh relayed the news to Chambers and, presto, there were signs posted all over the university, requesting each student to contribute 25 cents in the fund-raising drive that was strictly confined to the student body.

"In those days," Kavanaugh said 57 years later, "a quarter was enough to buy you dinner. It was a lot to ask of a student. But football fever was running so high — we were conference champions in '36 — contributions came to almost one thousand dollars. Which meant we had enough to buy the $750 tiger."

The tiger arrived November 21, 1936, and the students were practically giddy in anticipation.

"Reveille" for the cadets was sounded before sunup. It also was played outside the women's dorms, and at the home of President James Monroe Smith. The students went on a sit-down strike against classes. All roads leading onto the campus were barricaded, and automobiles with faculty members were barred. The band paraded through the campus avenues, and those few students with access to cars spent much of the morning in their automobiles pressing down on the horn. Motorcyclists raced around with reckless abandon.

"The students declared a holiday," Kavanaugh said. "They got the word out that all professors should stay home. Unless, of course, they wanted to be on hand when Mike showed up in Tiger Stadium."

Finally, around noon, word was given to head to the football stadium where in the back of an open

PREGAME — Driving Mike the Tiger around inside Tiger Stadium is a tradition which began with Mike I in 1937.

truck, was Mike Chambers and, amazingly, a wooden crate containing the LSU tiger cub.

The tiger's name was "Sheik," but as the animal was being showcased to the approximately 5,000 cheering students and townspeople, Glen Olds, the president of the student body association, suggested a name change to "Mike," in honor of Mike Chambers. It was loudly and instantly approved, though for the almost 21 years of his extraordinarily long life Mike always responded more readily to his original name, "Sheik."

President Smith, giving in to youthful excitement, declared the rest of the day a holiday, and that night there was a huge bonfire

MIKE — The man for whom Mike the Tiger is named: trainer Mike Chambers.

and a torch-light parade around town.

Mike spent his first months at the Baton Rouge City Zoo, where he was soon devouring 12 pounds of meat a day. President Smith, who had no such provisions in his budget, was concerned about this new expenditure. William Burch Lee, a 1905 alumnus, sent a check for ten dollars with the suggestion the money be used for an "LSU Alumni to Keep Mike in Food" fund. Smith said any contributions to the fund "would be happily accepted."

Governor Richard Leche eventually came up with several thousand dollars for a steam-heated home for Mike outside Tiger Stadium. It had all the modern conveniences, even a tree trunk on which Mike could sharpen his claws.

Mike I had an adventurous tenure overseeing LSU football games. He reigned at all home games, where he was circled around the stadium before kickoff, and where his cage was rattled to get him to roar, a sobering sound that was magnified by the public address system and echoed

throughout the arena, setting the stage for the gridiron wars that would follow.

(It should be noted the rattling and pounding of the tiger cage was objected to by animal lovers as excessive, and for years recorded growls were played for the fans. That practice was also discontinued, and today Mike participates in the pregame ceremonies without provocation.)

Mike I also traveled to away games once or twice a season, in his purple and gold caged trailer. That caused some problems.

Mike once had to spend several days in a Shreveport storage garage after his handlers made a vain attempt to get the tiger to the 1947 Cotton Bowl — the infamous "Ice Bowl" — after frigid weather, snow and ice made the highways to Dallas virtually impassible. Another time the trailer was overturned in an automobile accident. When the driver rushed to check the damage, he found the door of the cage wide open. It could have been a very dangerous situation. Hoping against hope, he peered into the dark of

the enclosure, but didn't see Mike. A frantic search was started, but ended quickly, when a low growl was heard from the black recesses of the cage.

The most famous, or infamous, incident occurred in the wee hours of December 2, 1950, when the cage, with Mike inside, was sitting in the parking lot of an Uptown New Orleans eatery.

Mike's keeper, David Melilli, was inside Ye Olde College Inn having a sandwich with a Newcombe coed, while another LSU student left in search of a tarpaulin with which to cover the cage. The departure did not escape the notice of four Tulane students, who also sat inside the restaurant.

"We noticed Mike was in the parking lot unattended," one of the Greenies recalled three decades later. "It seemed he was just sitting there."

The Tulane students decided Mike was lonely, and that the perfect cure would be a pleasant ride in an automobile. . . . one, preferably, with a trailer hitch.

"We just happened to have one we could use,"

one of the offenders remembered. "So we decided to pull him around. There was no malice of thought when it began."

And off into the early morning darkness they went. Mike got a grand tour of New Orleans — at least of Tulane's side of the tracks. Mike was quiet as a, well, a cat the entire trip.

The tour ended at an off-campus garage where Mike was put for the rest of the night.

The well-fed Melilli emerged from College Inn shortly before 2 a.m. to find Mike and his cage conspicuously absent.

The search began. When dawn arrived, the LSU posse became a bit discouraged and sent for the police.

"Yeah," they were informed by a gendarme at the Sixth District precinct, "we're looking for him. He's probably green by now."

Not quite. By 9:30 a.m. prowl cars were informed to be on the lookout for Mike and his cage, which by then had been slapped with olive green and blue paint and decorated with Tulane pennants.

Mike's temporary custo-

> *D*early beloved," the judge said, his voice bouncing off the concrete in the sparsely filled arena, beginning one of the most unique wedding ceremonies in the history of college sports. "We are gathered here today at the 50-yard line of Tiger Stadium . . ."
>
> Terry "Tony the Tiger" Friedman was the groom; Shirley Harris Walker was his bride; and the best man was LSU mascot Mike IV. They listened as Judge Dan LeBlanc's voice echoed through Tiger Stadium.
>
> Friedman, you must understand, follows LSU wherever the Tigers play, and owns a jeep with LSU tiger stripes. He also has an LSU Tiger suit — complete with head — and enough purple-and-gold clothing to outfit half the Golden Band from Tigerland.
>
> The kickoff for LSU's home opener of 1984 was still hours away, and there were just a few curious — and amused — onlookers in the stands as the couple tied the knot. At the end of the ceremony, Friedman whooped, "Goooooooooo, TIGERS!," then kissed the bride.
>
> To celebrate their first anniversary, the couple hosted a thousand of their closest friends and Tigers-in-arms in the southeast stadium parking lot.

dians also added what they considered a nice touch — a sign which read "Tulane 52, LSU 0," a hopeful forecast of that day's game.

Perhaps feeling heady with the success of their prank, the four headed for coffee at the University Center.

"A person who was our age and who held much influence over us came into the UC that Saturday morning," one said. "He had no idea what had

taken place."

He was informed shortly when the late Dr. John L. Stibbs, then dean of students, summoned him. Dean Stibbs suggested that the young man walk up to the office of Dr. Fred Cole, dean of Arts & Sciences.

"Look," Dean Cole said, "I know you know these young men. Let me tell you the problem we've got: the tiger's missing, and he's got to be back at a certain time. Otherwise, there won't be a ball game."

LSU threatened to pull out of the game if Mike was not returned.

Dr. Cole promised there would be no retribution for the guilty parties, and no names mentioned if the tiger was returned.

The student went back to the guilty four and said, "Listen, I'm going to get a cup of coffee and when I come back, I would like to have some indication of where the tiger is."

When he came back the table was empty, but leaning against the sugar container was a napkin on which the whereabouts of the tiger was written.

They found Mike safe and sound. He'd behaved the whole time like a nice kitty, although no one volunteered to open the cage and feed him. He was watered by one of the students, who gamely pointed a hose toward the cage.

With Mike back in tow, so to speak, Melilli and mascot arrived at Tulane Stadium safe and sound shortly before game time.

"And," one said, "everybody lived happily ever after."

Not quite. The desecrated green cage made the Tigers see red, and LSU played Tulane, which had won five in a row and was an imposing touchdown favorite, off its cleats. The Green Wave got a touchdown in the final two minutes to get out with a 14-14 standoff.

Despite those notable adventures, life as LSU's mascot certainly agreed with Mike. He lived for 20 years and nine months, the longest known lifespan of any tiger in captivity. Mike died of pneumonia during a six-game losing streak in 1956.

Jim Corbett, the LSU athletic director, told Pete Finney of the New Orleans States: "The 1956 season was so tough even Mike couldn't take it. I received a call early one morning that Mike had passed away. I decided to sit on it for awhile and put Mike on ice, figuring, if word got out, even the strong-hearted would give up hope. When we finally won a game, Mike's death was announced."

He was so well-known throughout the country that, upon news of his passing, a newspaper 400 miles away called Mike "the most famous tiger in the world."

There was genuine sadness throughout the college football world.

Benny Marshall, sports editor of the *Birmingham (Ala.) News* wrote, "Five generations of Louisiana State University men and women idolized his every growl. He saw more touchdowns scored than any tiger since the beginning of time, visited more football fields, traveled more miles, leered at more cheerleaders. And he knew all the words, the music and a dozen different arrangements to 'Hold That Tiger!'"

Bernie Moore, the Tiger football coach for most of Mike's tenure, but in 1956 the commissioner of the Southeastern Conference, reflected upon hearing the news. "Ole Mike, he had a great career. He just seemed to fit in with the tradition. . . . Or maybe he became the tradition. Maybe he made it what it was."

Marshall pondered the quote, and added, "What tiger ever had a better epitaph?"

Mike I is still at LSU, stuffed but appearing very lifelike, in a prominent display case in LSU's Museum of Natural History.

A replacement was immediately found in New Orleans' Audubon Park Zoo, but Mike II was an extremely nervous, skittish animal who never went into the outer cage area outside his shelter unless he was driven out by his trainers. He lived through one football season before succumbing to pneumonia, just as his predecessor.

Mike III was made of sterner stuff. Purchased from the Seattle Zoo for $1,500, again raised by the student body, he was shipped to LSU via Flying Tiger Airlines, a name made famous in China during World War II for the fighter squadron under Gen. Claire Chennault, a student at LSU in the early years of the century. Mike III got to LSU just in time to preside over the Tigers' national championship season of 1958.

He served with distinction for 18 years, but there must be something lethal to the feline system in witnessing namesakes falling short. Mike III died after the only sub .500 season of his reign, 1975, when the Tigers went 5-6-0.

MIKE II — Mike II served just one season, 1957.

Mike IV didn't have to die to lose his job, but was retired to the Baton Rouge Zoo after a 14-year reign. He was donated to LSU by August A. Busch III from the Dark Continent Amusement Park in Tampa, Florida in 1976. A 500-pound cat in his prime, Mike's age and health were determining factors in his retirement. His only hiatus from the LSU campus before moving to the Baton Rouge Zoo was the summer of 1981 which he spent at the Little Rock Zoo while his cage was being refurbished. Ironically, the Little Rock Zoo was the birthplace of the first Mike the Tiger.

The newest tiger mascot was donated by Dr. Thomas and Caroline Atchison of the Animal House Zoological Park in Moulten, Ala. Charles Becker, an avid Tiger fan, put Dr. Sheldon Bivin of the LSU School of Veterinary Medicine in touch with the Atchisons. Bivin traveled to Alabama and brought the cub back to LSU, where he has reigned since 1990.

Still, for all the fond memories of the tiger lineage there is also a frightening thought.

Just before a Tulane game in 1981, some misguided "pranksters," in the early morning hours, cut the locks to Mike IV's cage and he stepped out.

The tiger roamed around a short area between his shelter, the Pete Maravich Assembly Center and the nearby track and field stadium. School was out for Thanksgiving, which cut down on the number of people who might have happened by — with disastrous consequences. But Mike was just across the street from the married student apartments, meaning a potential calamity was just 50 yards away.

"Fortunately," said Paul Manasseh, the LSU sports information director at the time, "Mike was more frightened than anybody."

Campus police finally cornered Mike in the track stadium and tranquilized him.

But before they did, Mike playfully knocked down several small pine trees in the area. He crouched, then leaped onto the branches of one and . . . C-R-R-R-A-A-K-K-K, split it almost in half.

"That," said one of the shaken by-standers, "was the most awesome thing I ever saw."

THE BALD EAGLE

15

No one, but no one, ever fell quite so behind. Not in the LSU-Ole Miss series anyway.

Sure, it could be argued, anyone who could pass like Y.A. Tittle ought to be a football legend. But Tittle did it the hard way.

Bert Jones, Archie Manning, Billy Cannon, et al, it could be said, backed into their legends. Superhuman performances in the Tiger-Rebel series practically guarantees it. Tittle may be the only player in history to moon an opponent, in a losing cause, and still make the

Hall of Fame.

The 1947 game, one of the first of the heated LSU-Rebel bouts, featured Tittle at quarterback for the Tigers, Charley Conerly at quarterback for Ole Miss. They played for first place in the SEC standings.

LSU went ahead 6-0 before Conerly staked Johnny Vaught's first Rebel team to a 13-6 lead, and had 'em driving again just before the half.

Then Tittle stepped onto Olympus . . .

Conerly hung a pass up and Tittle, playing left corner on defense, timed his move and intercepted as

the Ole Miss receiver ran past. The intended receiver reached back, making a seemingly futile grab at Tittle's midriff before falling by the wayside.

Between that slight tug in one direction and Tittle's momentum to the other, however, something had to give. It turned out to be Tittle's belt buckle.

The end zone was 70 yards away, 40 of which were negotiated by a tippy-toeing Tittle running with one hand holding up his pants, the other cradling the ball.

Barney Poole, Ole Miss' all-time great end, recalled,

THE ARM — Strong-armed Y.A. Tittle led LSU to the 1947 Cotton Bowl.

"I was racing down the field after him laughing and laughing. I couldn't help it, it was just the funniest thing I ever saw in football."

Poole finally caught and hemmed Tittle in on the sideline and . . .

"I tried to stiff-arm him," Tittle said. When he did, his pants almost went down. They would have if he hadn't. "There I was on the 30 yard line," Tittle said, "and I've never been so alone in my life."

Forty-six thousand witnesses would probably have agreed.

Memories can fog memories, particularly decades after an incident. Tittle said he wasn't certain it was Conerly who threw the pass (it was), and Poole said he thought, but couldn't swear, that he made the tackle.

Both were clear about one thing, though. LSU didn't score at that point, and Vaught's team won the game, 20-18, and eventually his first SEC championship.

"I'm not sure if I could have scored or not," Tittle said, wondering what might have been had circumstances been different. "He was a good athlete, and he was wiggling all through us," Poole said. "He might have . . ."

Whatever. That night LSU was behind for good.

Tittle, of course, was one of the finest quarterbacks ever to play at LSU — ever to play anywhere for that matter. Interestingly, the Tigers landed him out of Marshall, Texas, in large part because of his older brother, who was an All-SEC player at Tulane.

"Every year," Tittle recalled, "we'd go see Jack play against LSU, and I was impressed even as a young kid with the enthusiasm, the tiger in the cage, the campus, just the whole LSU atmosphere. I was recruited by a number of schools, but I wanted LSU, and I signed a grant with LSU right after my senior season. But I got so much pressure from the people in Marshall about going to a Texas school that I finally agreed to visit the University of Texas. I went down there and after a week of, shall we say, good recruiting, I agreed to attend Texas."

Given a summer job in Austin, Tittle quickly became a bit disenchanted with the life-styles of some of the big-city Texas kids on campus, including his roommate, Bobby Layne. "He was so far ahead of me (socially), him being from Dallas," Tittle said with a cringe, "it wasn't even funny. At that point of my life I had never even had a taste of beer, and he was already playing no-limit poker and running around with all the gals in Austin and boozing it up, and having just a helluva good time. I guess I felt a bit inadequate. And every morning I had to listen to ol' Bobby's stories of conquest.

Three weeks after Tittle went to Austin, LSU assistant Red Swanson had breakfast with the 17-year-old, who had not yet actually enrolled at Texas. Swanson asked Y.A. if he'd like to change his mind. "I said I would, but I felt embarrassed about it," Tittle recalled. "But Swanson said it was okay as long as I called Coach (Dana) Bible and told him."

Swanson said he'd have no hand in taking the boy off campus without Bible's knowledge and that it was, after all, his own decision. The unhappy youngster went to a phone booth, faked a call, pretended to be talking, then walked out, and told Swanson, "Everything seems to be okay."

Swanson and Tittle made one stop at Houston to pick up another prospect, and the three sped straight to Baton Rouge. Four years later,

Y.A. left behind a fistful of records (including 2,717 yards passing and 21 touchdown passes, pretty gaudy stats for the era), most of his hair, and a lingering legend.

Known as the Bald Eagle throughout his notable professional career, Tittle began losing his hair at a young age. Trainer Herman Lang explained years later that in college Tittle felt his helmet had something to do with his receding hairline. "Y.A. always wanted to put something in his helmet. He was sure that was the reason he was losing his hair."

Tittle later thought an LSU tradition of shaving freshmen heads may have had an influence. "I had the ugliest-looking scalp, I'm not sure it didn't just stunt my hair growth because it sure never came back the right way."

His name was another sore spot aggravated by LSU. Publicist Jim Corbett recognized a good story angle. "Coach Bernie Moore," Corbett once said, "allowed me each day at the beginning of September practices to meet with a half dozen of

his football players for purposes of processing personnel data, and I vividly recall first meeting Y.A. I asked him to fill out his full name — initials were not enough.

"He responded with, 'That's my name, my full name.' Curiously enough, I checked the registrar's records and found that, indeed, his application carried the initials and not his first name. I was satisfied for the moment. For the next few days I saw him work at quarterback under the newly established T-formation. It was evident that here was a tremendous passer, if not a great quarterback, and the wheels of curiosity began to roll.

"I left the field and returned to my office and called the courthouse at his home in Marshall, Texas, and requested information on one Y.A. Tittle. There was no one by that name in the record book, the voice answered, but 'We do have a Yelberton Abraham Tittle.' The next day I called Y.A. in and asked him if he had ever seen this name before. He said, 'I'd appreciate it if you would lay off

HALL OF FAMERS — LSU Athletic Director Joe Dean welcomes LSU's Pro Football Hall of Famers: Steve Van Buren, Y.A. Tittle and Jimmy Taylor.

season. One was the infamous lost pants against Ole Miss. The other was after being knocked out against Vanderbilt, Tittle was revived with a whiff of ammonia. The team physician, however, cautioned against playing anymore that night. Swanson screeched, "WHY?"

"Well, the boy is hardly breathing," answered the physician logically.

"Hell, you're a doctor," the exasperated line coach snorted. "MAKE him breathe!"

He did, and Tittle guided LSU the rest of the way to a 19-13 victory.

Still, decades after their memorable night together, Poole said there was one thing that had never been cleared up. "Coach Vaught taught us a lot of football," Poole said. "But he never did teach us where to throw the head when tackling a man losing his pants."

using my name.' Instead I laid it on as football's most exciting name — and as it turned out at LSU — its greatest T-formation passer and quarterback."

Tittle gunned the Tigers to 7-2, 9-1, and 5-3-1 seasons. The first two propelled LSU into the national limelight for the first time since the 1930s. At the end of Y.A.'s junior season, LSU and Arkansas played the infamous "Ice Bowl" in Dallas. The Tigers ran up a 15-1 advantage in first downs in that Cotton Bowl, and accumulated 271 yards to the Razorbacks' 54. But the subfreezing temperatures under sheets of snow and rain prevented any scoring.

LSU was a monumental disappointment in 1947, but Tittle is probably best remembered in Baton Rouge because of two incidents that occurred that

KICKING GRASS
16

It was perhaps the classic case of sowing wild oats.

Spectators entering the old Sugar Bowl Stadium on November 19, 1949, had a peek at the future.

Splattered on ramps around the venerable old structure was the incredible prediction "LSU 21, TU 0."

And on the field, five inches high and 40 yards across the field, rye grass, clearly discernable from the regular turf was the lettering "LSU" in huge blocks.

Earlier in the week leading up to the LSU-Tulane game, a green flag had been run up on the Tiger campus with painted green footprints leading to the flagpole. The score of Tulane's winning 1948 victory, 46-0, was painted on the sides of several buildings. The culprits in both instances were the same.

As it turned out, it could be argued the vandalism highlighted the Greenies' most embarrassing football moment.

Tulane had already secured the Southeastern Conference championship, and in the offing, with a win over the Tigers, had received a Sugar Bowl invitation. Given the Green Wave's success, with a 7-1-1 record, coupled with the 1948 Wave rout of LSU — the biggest margin of a Tulane victory in the series — the Greenies were a solid touchdown favorite over the 7-2 Bengals.

Almost as if by divine design, the Tigers defeated Tulane by the predicted 21-0 score, knocked the Green Wave out of the Sugar Bowl, filled the berth themselves, and left the Greenies sputtering with rage.

That LSU students could actually break into the Wave sanctuary had Tulanians boiling. That the

Tigers could actually live up to the prediction had Tulanians sick.

"We didn't really mean any harm," Van (Putsy) Smith said in 1978. "But, God! You never saw people so angry . . ."

Smith, a couple of ex-Tigers, Dan Sandifer and Joe Leach, Bruce Lloyd and Doug Hull were the masterminds and the commandos who pulled it off. It was an act of love.

"We were losing enthusiasm for the LSU-Tulane game," said Leach, although Tulane was then at its football peak. Leach pointed out that, despite the lopsided '48 game, the Greenies hadn't really had extraordinary success against the Bayou Bengals. In the 10 games preceding 1949, LSU won six Tulane games, lost three and tied one.

"The football players and students were beginning to look to Ole Miss as their big game," Leach said. "Beating Barney Poole and Ray Poole and Charlie Conerly, well, that was just the thing to do.

"So, we just decided we had to do something about this!"

Several weeks before the game, in a bull session in the athletic dorm, someone came up with the idea. The group divided into teams. None were in agriculture so they took a cram course, talked to students and professors, and studied various grasses.

After figuring the growth time, Smith and Hull headed for New Orleans in a '32 Chevy loaded with 150 pounds of rye-seed sacks.

They spent a night monitoring the guard who patrolled the outer perimeter of the stadium. "That fence was about 10 feet high," Smith recalled, "and we realized we couldn't get the sacks ourselves. So we looked up the Sigma Alpha Epsilon fraternity, which was our fraternity, and went to their house at Tulane.

Borrowing three pledges from SAE, whose members thought the plan was hilarious, the unit prepared for its next step.

Under the cover of darkness, near the stadium perimeter, the five waited until the guard made his pass, then two went over the fence. Once over, the others hoisted the sacks over.

That done, one pledge was left to stand guard and the others were dismissed.

Smith and Hull started planting by midnight. "We already had it laid out by yard lines," Smith explained, "so all we had to do was follow that (guideline). Just get the oats sowed to the right grids."

The only thing that slowed matters was the sound of stadium rats knocking over bottles in the empty arena. "The hair on our necks stood straight up, I want you to know," Smith said with a laugh.

By 3 p.m. they were ready to come out. The pledge left outside to monitor the guard signalled when it was safe.

That was three weeks before the LSU-Tulane game. The rye started sprouting a few days beforehand. It couldn't be noticed from ground level at first, but a Tulane official looked down from one of the top levels and must have gagged.

Coach Henry Frnka was livid. He had his players try to cut and pick the offending grass, but to no avail. The stronger rye grass color still showed through.

Henry Threefoot, later a New Orleans physician, but then the sports editor of the Tulane student newspaper,

THE PROPHET — Kenny Konz returns this punt for a TD to lead LSU to an improbable 21-0 victory over Tulane in 1949.

said the attitude on campus was one of disgust. "The coach was angry," he said, "the players were angry and the students were angry."

Some measure of revenge was felt when the green flag, footprints and '48 score were painted on the LSU campus.

The same outfit — Smith, Sandifer, Hull, Lloyd and Leach — were responsible for that, too. "Remember, we were trying to get both schools worked up," Smith said.

When LSU did pull off the astonishing 21-0 upset, the story made the national wires. But only a handful of people ever learned the identities of the perpetrators. "They were so angry down there," Sandifer said, "I wasn't going to say anything. I went to the game in a big bearskin coat in that old car, and I giggled when I saw the result. But I didn't say anything."

There is an addendum to the story. Sandifer later attended Tulane graduate school where his next door neighbor was Threefoot, who for years got agitated about the subject every time it was brought up.

"All those years he was wondering how in the heck, and who in the heck, did it," Sandifer said. "He was still outraged that LSU just showed up right in the middle of their field before the game. Finally, I just had to tell him."

The reaction?

Threefoot answered for himself, and put it succinctly: "Disgust."

SOUR SUGAR

17

No one, as the saying goes, ever made an omelet without breaking eggs.

LSU reveled in devilish delight after its 1949 commando raid inside Tulane Stadium, lacing the field with rye grass and painting the ramps with the prophetic 21-0 upset score.

But there were plenty of eggshells to pay in the aftermath of LSU's merriment.

LSU was America's most publicized "David" in 1949. Coming off a horrendous 1948 in which the Bayou Bengals were 3-7, they lost two of their first four games before coming on to defeat three (Rice, 14-7; North Carolina, 13-7; and Tulane, 21-0) conference champions to finish 8-2.

The turnaround was so stunning that only a quick comparison with 1948 can correctly place it in focus. The Tigers were outscored 186-33 in five 1948 defeats (North Carolina, Ole Miss, Vanderbilt, Mississippi State and Tulane). In 1949, LSU outscored those same five teams 136-34 and defeated each.

Tulane took a double-whammy in losing to the Tigers because that was before the SEC-Sugar Bowl marriage, and the champion was not necessarily the team most attractive to the bowl. The Greenies already had a 46-7 loss to Notre Dame on its record, so LSU, hot and popular, looked like a godsend to the Sugar.

LSU's two early defeats, however, were to Kentucky and Georgia, and gave the Fightin' Tigers a .667 victory percentage in their six SEC games. The SEC rule, put in effect the previous year after LSU president H.W. Stoke made a long speech on the evils of bowl games, stipulated a conference school had to win at least 75 percent of its SEC games in order to be eligible for postseason play.

T.P. "Red" Heard, anticipating victory, began phoning around the SEC the day before the Tulane game and lobbying to rescind the rule. By 5 p.m. the next day, LSU had beaten the Greenies and the rule had been thrown out.

Fred Digby, the general manager of the Sugar Bowl, announced to newsmen, "LSU will play Oklahoma."

Gaynell Tinsley, one of LSU's all-time great players, coached the surprising Tigers and got as much from a team's ability with his 1949 LSU squad as any coach ever did. Even with as much fanfare as LSU received — beating high-quality opponents, gaining a No. 9 national ranking and earning a bowl berth — the disastrous record of 1948 resulted in no Tigers making the All-SEC first team.

Oklahoma was the nation's best rushing team (320.3 yards a game) and the nation's best defensive team against the rush (55.6), so Tinsley knew right off he was in trouble. "We just don't know very

much about them," he moaned two weeks before the Sugar Bowl. "We can't find out much either."

There were others curious about the Sooners, too. A resident glanced through a window toward the Biloxi, Mississippi, High School Stadium where Oklahoma was practicing, and noticed someone hiding on a platform in the rear of a house. Sooner officials shortly received a phone call with the information, and a suggestion that someone hide in the yard of the informer and observe the house that adjoined the stadium.

The next day a policeman, accompanied by a member of the Oklahoma athletic staff and John "Baby Grand" Scafide, a letterman on Tulane's 1932 Rose Bowl team, closed in on the spy, hidden behind a rigged blanket ringed with scratch pads and a pair of binoculars. Bill Dennis, a free lance Biloxi photographer shooting for *The New Orleans Times-Picayune*, got a picture as the three flushed out the suspect.

Although his identity wasn't then known, the man photographed was Walter "Piggy" Barnes, a

former LSU lineman then playing with the Philadelphia Eagles. There was also another person involved, Gustave Adolphus "Goober" Morse, a fan closely associated with the Tiger athletic department, and who had served in the Navy during World War II with Sooner coach Bud Wilkinson.

Barnes escaped the policeman's clutches and joined Morse on the garage roof, where he defied the growing police contingent to come and get him. The police, uncertain as to whether the pair was actually guilty of any illegality, or even who they were, hesitated. Eventually, Barnes and Morse, buoyed by the uncertainty, climbed down, walked through the police, got in their car and took off for New Orleans.

"God, they were fighting mad," Morse recalled. "That story just grew and grew (on the radio) all the time we drove to New Orleans until (when they arrived) it was front page. Man, we didn't stop until we reached the Roosevelt Hotel. We called Pappy (Art) Lewis (an assistant at Mississippi State about to be named head coach at

West Virginia) and asked what he thought we ought to do. 'Well,' he said, 'your name is M-o-r-s-e, and yours is B-a-r-n-e-s . . . tell 'em to make damn sure they don't leave the "r" out in the spelling.' He was a big help."

Morse insisted until the day he died almost 40 years later that he and Barnes were scouting prospects for Greasy Neale, the coach of the Eagles. "LSU didn't have a thing to do with it, which is true," Morse said. "We just thought it would be a good idea to look 'em over. We could've gone in the main gate, maybe. We didn't exactly scout like we were supposed to. Normally you walk through the gate and watch 'em work out. So, we didn't do it that way."

It's not a defense most lawyers would be eager to use.

"The coaches were furious, really angry," Darrell Royal, who was the Oklahoma quarterback, said three decades later. "That gave us additional impetus." Wilkinson shook his head and, with real rancor, said, "I can't believe LSU would do such a thing. I just can't believe

they'd do us this way."

At a meeting in New Orleans, Wilkinson refused at first to shake Tinsley's hand. LSU officials argued, before Barnes and Morse were identified, that it could have been done by Oklahoma to fire up a complacent team. "I naturally resented it when told that Coach Wilkinson questioned the character of our coaching staff and boys," Heard said. "And I told him to his face that the charges were untrue, and that I was surprised that the No. 1 coach of America had allowed himself to be worked up over what looks to me like a plan to steam up a football team."

Morse chuckled. "Later on, the Atlanta Touchdown Club gave Coach Wilkinson the Walter Barnes-Goober Morse Award, which was a pair of binoculars. Every time I see Coach Wilkinson we laugh about it now."

But Bud Wilkinson wasn't laughing on January 2, 1950.

Oklahoma jumped on LSU in the second quarter and from then on, never quit. The Sooners led 14-0 at the half, then put a lid

on the victory when fullback Leon Heath wheeled out of the Oklahoma split-T and blazed 86 yards for OU's third touchdown. Armand Kitto, then a 157-pound LSU player, recalled, "I chased Heath all the way. They say on a long run like that, a bear will jump on the runner's back. Well, I just kept waiting for the bear to jump on him, and instead he jumped on me. I carried that bear all the way down."

It was a frustrating day for the Tigers. Down 21-0, Kenny Konz intercepted Royal in the end zone and, with a chance at some face-saving, ran it out. He needed one block to go all the way, but didn't get it and was pulled down at the Tiger 32. From there LSU drove to the OU 29 where Buddy Jones intercepted Charley Pevey.

After Oklahoma built its lead to a humiliating 35-0, Mel Lyle took the ensuing kickoff and returned it for an apparent touchdown. It was called back to the LSU 45 for stepping out of bounds.

That score remains the biggest margin of victory in Sugar Bowl history. The headline in the *Dallas*

Morning News the next day read: "Oklahoma Overpowers Minor League LSU Team," a message which obviously ignored the fact that the Tigers had beaten both Rice and North Carolina, the Cotton Bowl participants.

Wilkinson was gracious. "If we played LSU a dozen times we'd never play that well against them again, or score that many points. They're too good a team."

Which is probably why he didn't take out his regulars until approximately three minutes remained in the game and the score stood at its final five touchdown difference.

DEATH VALLEY, U.S.A.

18

Encircling itself, high and in the air like a fortress abandoned during some particularly bloody age, towers the most ferocious address in Louisiana.

John Logue, an extraordinary writer, penned that description of Tiger Stadium, and added: "A college football game anywhere is a spectacle in the best sense of the word. In Tiger Stadium, a game is not merely seen. It is heard. The sound of it twists up the steel and concrete enclosure like a particularly sinister tornado. The parts are played out equally in the stands and on the field. . . . Writers in the press box, high over the crowd, find themselves unable to think when the noise stops. If it stops."

Tiger Stadium is one of the great football arenas of America, where night football was made popular; where, when two teams engage in gridiron combat, the air is heavy with the hot breath of bourbon. As recently as 1988, before the recent drop in LSU fortunes, Division 1-A coaches voted it the most dreaded road site in the nation.

The mossy old stadium, dubbed "Death Valley" by opponents, if it had to live up its reputation, would be lined with lye and its end zones would be bordered with skulls for pylons.

At its best, a night at Tiger Stadium can be likened to the devilish musical classic "Night on Bald Mountain," an experience which can stir demons, though *Sports Illustrated* once portrayed it as "A Vale of Tears."

It puts an icy fear in opponents, former LSU coach Charlie McClendon said of Tiger Stadium. A quintessential football snake pit, where unbridled emotion is fused with an unrelenting howl of 80,000 zealots that often stirs the home team into pigskin feeding frenzies. McClendon says the atmosphere can be shattering. "It's like an electric wire running from the stands to the field."

A 500-pound carnivore is showcased near the entrance of the visiting team, presumably as a not-so-subtle reminder of the night's expectations.

Football-crazed fans stand in steep rows that seem to hover straight over the stadium floor and crowd the sidelines, readily inclined to turn thumbs down on a tackled opponent.

"I stood in Tiger Stadium," said Ed Simonini, a former Texas A&M linebacker, "and I thought, 'This is what the Colosseum in Rome must have been like.'"

The late Bobby Dodd made the same analogy 15 years before. After a loss to LSU, he said it was as if his Georgia Tech Engineers had been thrown to the Tigers.

"It was like the Colosseum in Rome," Dodd said, "and we were the Christians."

Admittedly, it hasn't been quite the same since losses have mounted in recent years, or since television considerations have made day games as much the norm as the night, and it's no longer automatically filled to the rafters because of those same reasons: more defeats than LSU football is accustomed to, television, and day games.

And if playing LSU in Baton Rouge is like wrestling with demons in football hades for most opponents, the Bayou Bengals also are cursed with their own Tiger Stadium hex: Alabama. The Crimson Tide beats LSU in the Tiger lair at about the same rate (72.3) as LSU beats all other invaders.

At its best though, there is an atmosphere at the old colosseum unlike any football stadium anywhere. Practically everyone who ever covered a game in Baton Rouge has made the inevitable comparison with the ancient structure in Rome.

The sheer noise level is startling, and the roiled passions and unrepentant love which oozes like hot lava from the steep cliffs of the stadium onto the field

can be disarming. The intense level of noise — an almost tangible ingredient — cascades almost incessantly from the stadium peaks in a close game . Mike, the Royal Bengal tiger and cherished spiritual pet of all LSU zealots, roars from his cage. But these are almost inconsequential compared to the vilification LSU opposition may be subjected to by Tiger fanatics.

"Day in, day out," an SEC veteran once said, "LSU hates you more than anybody."

Southern Cal coach John Robinson, preparing for a 1979 game in Baton Rouge, opened the locker door and immediately found himself staring at a thousand wide-eyed bayou banshees.

"Tiger bait, Tiger bait, Tiger bait," went up the taunting chant as Robinson took his Southern Cal team onto the football field.

Robinson, in a quarter-century of coaching, had seen football fanaticism close-up many times, but never anything like this — at practice, the night before a game.

Brad Budde, Robinson's

115

ROLL 'EM– "Saturday Night Live" at Tiger Stadium.

All-American lineman who played in that game, later reflected on his visit to Baton Rouge and mused: "Unbelievable, crazy. That place makes Notre Dame seem like 'Romper Room.' "

Douglas S. Looney of *Sports Illustrated* described a Saturday night at the LSU arena thusly: "It makes a body tingle.

These folks go berserk when the band marches on the field. A huge roar is heard for the invocation, for heaven's sake. They not only know the words to the national anthem, they sing them, loudly. And when the Tigers win the toss . . . there are tears of ecstasy."

The Tigers, contrary to legend, are not invincible in Tiger Stadium, which

after all, was christened with a 1924 defeat to Tulane.

No one, though, has a home field that elevates the game like LSU. Over the almost 70 years the Bayou Bengals have played in Tiger Stadium, there have been many stirring performances that are attributed as much to the home field as to athletic performance.

"There's no question,

LET'S GO CRAZY — Tiger fans are among the most enthusiastic in the nation.

LSU has been a better team there than anywhere," McClendon said.

Billy Cannon once galloped through the fog and the night like a ghostly apparition to slay Ole Miss, a team Bert Jones later foiled as time ran out, to add to Tiger Stadium lore.

Choo-Choo Justice being slowed on a wet field; Notre Dame, called by Ara Parseghian before the game the best he'd ever coached, being derailed by the Tiger defense four times on fourth down and short; A fourth-quarter Texas A&M fumble at the goal in a one-point LSU victory; and Y.A. Tittle almost losing his pants — and the Tigers losing the game — sprinkled that much more luster on the legend.

Death Valley is where it once rained oranges, and where the strong scent of spirits can occasionally overwhelm the senses, but seldom the enthusiasm.

"It's a crazy place, a tough place to play," former New Orleans Saints tight end Hobie Brenner, who was a member of John Robinson's USC team that beat LSU in the final seconds in 1979, said. "It was the toughest place by far

REMEMBER WHEN — *The steamboat Ouachita rolls past the LSU campus and the newly-constructed Tiger Stadium, 1924.*

that I played in because of the crowd noise and how the fans get behind their team."

McClendon said that when his teams had the lead at the half, he always told them that now they would have to win it themselves. The fans, he said, were always "in" a Tiger Stadium game as long as LSU had a fight on its hands. Once LSU — or for that matter, an opponent — pulled away, the intensity level fell.

Bud Johnson, a former sports information director at LSU, specifically recalled instances when LSU football teams were somehow able to stay in games with superior opposition. "LSU was always good for a stunning upset at home," Johnson said. "In 1955, for example, during some lean times," Johnson pointed out, "LSU beat a well-thought-of Kentucky team (19-7), and played Georgia Tech (0-7) and Ole Miss (26-29), very good teams, to standstills in Tiger Stadium. That particular LSU team won three games.

"Still, you can't do it consistently without athletes."

The Tigers were sort of a vagabond team in LSU's early football days. Its first — and only — game of 1893 was played against Tulane in New Orleans. Not until Ole Miss visited Baton Rouge in 1894 did LSU need a local playing field, and that game was played at the north end of Third Street, just inside the gates of the old campus near what is now downtown Baton Rouge.

A few years later, sometime around 1901, increased interest called for moving a couple of blocks north to a site which remained the home of the Tigers until 1916 when they moved their home field across Third Street to a field running east and west, on the exact site where today's Louisiana State Capitol is located.

Eight years later another final transition was made.

It was deemed necessary for the physical growth of the university that the entire campus should be transported from its historic location, hemmed in by the city's burgeoning growth on one side and the Father of Waters on the other, to the vast expanse of plantation land south of Baton Rouge.

The first building erected was the Livestock Judging Pavilion, and the second was Tiger Stadium. The stadium was unique in that it was built not only as a football arena, but also became a men's dorm. The outer structure was filled in and compartmentalized with enough rooms for 1,500 men students. To this day, life in the Tiger Stadium dorms is a frequent feature when an LSU home game is televised.

Tiger Stadium capacity has increased four times, and when 24,000 seats were added by enclosing the north end in the mid-1930s it was the largest arena in the South with 46,000 seats. Capacity is now approximately 78,000, though there have been almost two dozen games with bigger crowds than that. No enlargement was more controversial, though, than the one in 1954 which closed the South end zone, gave LSU 67,500 seats, and made Tiger Stadium a bowl.

In 1950 LSU was seeking state revenues for its medical school in New Orleans and a new campus library. At the same time, there was a faction, at the behind-the-scenes urging of athletic director T.P.

SPECIAL TEAM — The 1924 Tigers were the first to play in Tiger Stadium.

"Red" Heard, wanting to expand the stadium seating capacity.

The state passed a bill granting $6 million for those projects and a gymnasium at Northeast Junior College, a school that was then governed by the LSU state-wide system. The gym was to cost no more than $300,000, leaving $5.7 million for the remaining projects. Heard got the bill's sponsors to have its priorities listed with expansion of the medical school first, the stadium second and the library third.

The med school expansion would cost $3.4 million. Steel became scarce because of the Korean Conflict, and the original estimate for the stadium

addition came to $1.5 million, leaving only $800,000 for the library which was expected to cost five times that total.

The hard-to-avoid impression was that LSU was more interested in the football stadium than the library.

After a series of political maneuverings over the next two years, the stadium project went for $1,242,342, and included in an $18 million building plan was $4 million for the new library.

In time Heard would pay dearly for his successful maneuvering. The academicians administering LSU didn't know how to play the political game as well as the athletic director, but they had priorities and

HORSESHOES?– A shot of the stadium before it became a bowl in 1954.

long memories. The South end zone expansion was a huge factor, maybe the overriding factor, when it was decided to clean house in the athletic department in 1954.

Four decades later, the South end zone is still referred to as "the library."

Don James, the gifted University of Washington coach, was intrigued by the mystique of Tiger Stadium. James said he always want-ed to coach a team there, and so he did. The Washington Huskies played LSU on a warm September night in 1983.

A drained James said afterward that Tiger Stadium was all he imag-ined, and more. In the midst of a howling din, and 82,390 LSU zealots, the Rose Bowl-bound Huskies were taken apart, 40-14.

In a similar setting in 1979, after No. 1-ranked USC was played off its col-lective cleats before scor-ing the winning touch-down with a half minute to play, Trojan quarterback Paul McDonald said, "The noise was deafening. One time I asked an official for help, but he said if I backed off it would only get worse."

LSU's fanatical fan sup-port, however, is a two-edged sword, according to McClendon. While the

Whether brain surgeon or bricklayer, teacher or truck driver, historian or haberdasher, the backers of LSU's Bayou Bengals are one in the flesh. They bleed purple and gold. They converge on Baton Rouge from all points. "They are sure to shuttle from Shreveport. Hustle from Houma. Convoy from Carencro," noted the Times-Picayune's John Jones before the season opener of 1985. "They are massed to march from Minden. Platoon from Plaquemine. Disembark from Delacroix.

"When dem Tigers play at home, dahlin', . . . all roads lead to Red Stick."

The recent downswing in LSU football, coupled with continued — and even increased — television exposure, has cut the Tiger Stadium crowds, though LSU averaged as many as 77,958 in a 78,000-seat stadium in 1984, which is an unnerving barometer of the intense state-wide interest when LSU football shows any sign of life. From 1957, the year the NCAA began keeping such records, through 1988, LSU was a fixture in the top 10 nationally in attendance, and even with sub-par teams has never been out of the top 20.

LSU was no better than a 5-5-0 team in '57, yet set what was then the Southeastern Conference attendance record (297,953 in eight home games, an average of 49,659). Since then more than 15 million fans have watched the Tigers at home. LSU was 2-9-0 in 1992, the worst season in Tiger history, yet ranked 13th nationally in attendance with an average crowd of 67,221. Texas A&M, by way of comparison, who defeated LSU in the season-opener and went on to win the Southwest Conference and play in the Cotton Bowl, didn't draw enough fans to finish in the top 20.

There is a reason for LSU's enormous popularity. The Tigers provide a reason for the unleashing of all that south Louisiana-Mediterranean emotion against a surrealistic backdrop of flood lights stabbing through the night onto the hallowed turf of Tiger Stadium. As Jones wrote, "It's the perfect setting for the excesses of devotion that characterize Tiger football fans, a species unique in the realm of sports fandom."

Southern Cal, Alabama, Ohio State have all bagged more national championships, but none can match the home field advantage of LSU when Tiger Stadium is roaring. The fans are truly the Tigers' 12th man.

After his appearance in Tiger Stadium in 1979, Southern Cal quarterback Paul McDonald wanted to know if all Cajuns were born with amplifiers in their voices.

"I was amazed at my first game at LSU in 1982," said former LSU athletic director Bob Brodhead. "There was more noise at Tiger Stadium than at any stadium I've ever been to, and I've been to 11 Super Bowls."

Tigers can get pumped up and play above their natural capabilities, so can opponents. The noise, emotion and taunts often elevate the other team's game as well.

Bear Bryant coached three schools — Kentucky, Texas A&M and Alabama — to victories in Tiger Stadium. "He used to walk real slow around the stadium before the game," McClendon said. "Not slow, real, real slow. He'd let them soak up all that 'Go to hell, Alabama' stuff for a long time, enough time where it began to make 'em mad. I told Coach Bryant, 'I know what you're doing: you're letting my fans do your job, getting your boys ready.' He laughed."

Bryant could afford to laugh. He retired with a 10-1-1 Tiger Stadium record, best by far of any LSU foe.

He didn't enjoy playing there, however. "Baton Rouge happens to be the worst place in the world to be a visiting team," Bryant said in his biography, *Bear*. He wrote, "It's a dugout arena, and you get all that noise. It's like being inside a drum. The officiating suffers because of it."

Bryant was right. Just as crowd conditions can lift an opponent, though, officiating can turn on a noisy, emotional home stadium. The Bear won two Tiger Stadium games on questionable calls. Texas A&M beat LSU 9-6 in 1956 on a late touchdown pass, and Bryant chuckled in his book that there was an ineligible receiver in the end zone when the touchdown pass was thrown.

Ken Stabler handed off to an Alabama back in 1967 and the ball bounced off the runner's chest into the end zone, where the fumble was recovered by LSU. Instead of a touch-

back, the play was called back and ruled no play. The ball was given back to Bama, which subsequently scored its only touchdown in a 7-6 victory.

Southern California, the first of two No. 1 teams LSU played at home in 1979, with a wealth of professional prospects, was hard-pressed to put down an average Tiger team, 17-12. Inside the final minute, on fourth down, USC jumped off-sides, then as the play unfolded, quarterback Paul McDonald, who was being severely pressured, intentionally grounded the ball. LSU fans, sitting on a 12-10 lead, were delirious.

When the Pac-10 official marked off the penalty, however, it was walked off against LSU — for brushing the facemask.

All LSU got for a truly heroic performance was a post-game finger from Heisman Trophy recipient Charles White.

Still, LSU doesn't get — or expect — sympathy from Ole Miss fans, who remain livid more than two decades after the Tigers got off two passes in five seconds to beat the Rebels, 17-16, after the horn

sounded in 1972, or from Mississippi State fans who were deprived of a crucial down in a 20-16 LSU victory in 1968.

What goes around comes around.

Tulane spoiled the 1924 Thanksgiving Day Tiger Stadium inaugural, a game that drew a huge-for-the-day crowd of 12,000 that might have been twice as large if the arena had been completed on time. A 1919 letterman, Buck Gladden, spent the afternoon walking up and down the sidelines, relaying the play-by-play through his microphone to a professor in the physics department.

The professor, in turn, relayed the first broadcast of a Southern football game to a network of several stations.

Tulane won, 13-0. Two years later, when LSU played its first game at the Greenies' new stadium, the Tigers prevailed, 7-0.

Johnny Vaught, who built Ole Miss into a football force in the 1950s and '60s, saw Tiger Stadium in full blaze. Two of his Rebel teams were knocked out of potential national championships after titanic defeats at LSU (7-3 in 1959 and

10-7 in 1961). The first is memorable because of Cannon's run and a last-minute goal-line stand, the second because LSU scored all its points the only two times it crossed midfield.

The noise level generated by Cannon's run is supposed to have brought people scurrying from their homes for miles around to see what happened, part of why the Tiger field was dubbed "Deaf Valley." The name "Death Valley" — which was used first at Clemson — was picked when the original term wasn't properly enunciated, and misunderstood.

It wasn't "Deaf Valley" the two years Florida's Steve Spurrier quieted the crowd. "Like a church," is the way one Gator coach put it.

But on the whole, Tiger Stadium is a noisy and emotional rush of LSU football. The stadium is one big goosebump each and every time the band tromps slowly onto the field, each second building to the near-climactic instant when the horns sound the opening notes of LSU's clarion call to arms, "Tiger Rag." The Tiger Stadium mystique begins

with that. Almost everything afterward is downhill. Everyone present, though, should be ready at that point. Anyone would have to be dead not to be.

"My eyes were this wide," said a former Texas A&M defensive back, holding his thumbs and index fingers together while remembering making a season-opening trip to Tiger Stadium with his 1968 teammates, defending Southwest Conference champions.

He recalled how the Aggies jumped out to a 12-0 lead before LSU asserted itself in the fourth quarter, inching ahead, 13-12. Just as if it had been scripted, the delirium turned to wild concern when the Aggies put together a last gasp drive inside the Tiger five. Then ball carrier Bob Long loped to within a foot of the goal-line when he was hit — and fumbled. The ball, almost as if by the will of the hordes, rolled all the way through the end zone, and out of bounds.

Victory in hand, LSU took over and ran the clock out.

"Oh, yeah, I knew all about Tiger Stadium before I ever got the job here,"

said Curley Hallman with a faraway look in his eye.

"There is nothing like standing in that chute, with everything building, then running on the field, with all that noise and feeling," former Tiger quarterback Steve Ensminger said. "We played three No. 1 teams (Nebraska in 1976, 6-6; and USC, 12-17, and Alabama, 0-3, both in 1979) in Tiger Stadium in the time I was at LSU, teams with talent we couldn't come close to, and we played them off their feet. That's part of the legacy of Tiger Stadium, of the LSU fans."

JIM TAYLOR
19

Paul Dietzel, in a way, owes his moment in the sun to one of his recruits — Jim Taylor.

Without Taylor, one of the greatest pro fullbacks in NFL history, but under-used in college, Dietzel may not have been around to coach the 1958 national champions.

And Dietzel, the man Taylor loved to call "The Great White Father," was plain lucky to even have him.

Taylor developed tremendous leg muscles with two paper routes — one in the morning, the other in the afternoon —

bicycling what he estimated to be "a million miles" for $3 a week to help his widowed mother. Those legs, and his awesome athletic ability, could have helped him to the top of many sports.

"Jim could have played anything and been good at it," Bat Gourrier, track and field coach at Baton Rouge High assessed. "If you stuck a tennis racket in his hand, he would have been great. If someone had bought him a set of clubs, he could outdo you in that, too. He was just natural as an athlete."

Basketball was Taylor's

first love, and he was a hellacious guard. "The first time I remember noticing Jimmy Taylor was when he played basketball," said Ted Castillo, the prep editor of the *Baton Rouge Morning Advocate.* "He was an outstanding player, and had a certain touch in his shooting."

In fact, Taylor didn't go out for the Baton Rouge High football team until he was a junior, when he stood 5-foot-9, and weighed 155 pounds. "I didn't like the game," Taylor candidly admitted. "I don't like anything unless I can do it real well."

He could play football real well, he found.

Taylor, 5-foot-10, 212-pounds, was the first athlete to play in both the Louisiana All-Star football and basketball games.

He had a raft of scholarship offers in both sports, but opted for LSU and football, a sport he was beginning to get the hang of. Clarence "Pop" Strange, who spent almost a half century on the Tiger campus, said Taylor was "probably the finest freshman athlete I've ever seen."

Everyone was panting to see Taylor with a ball under his arm for the varsity, but that was to be put on hold. Taylor ran into a defense he couldn't break away from: academics. Taylor was routed to Hinds (Mississippi) Junior College to make up his grades.

He did, and when he was eligible for major college competition again, Taylor was seriously tempted to accept a basketball grant-in-aid to Miami of Florida, Colorado, or Furman. But in the end, he decided his future was in football and at LSU.

Without benefit of spring practice, it took nearly half a season for Taylor to become acclimated to Dietzel's offense. Backfield coach Carl Maddox said LSU was simplifying its offense until Taylor became used to the new system. He played well defensively, but Taylor — the heart of the Tiger attack — scored eight points in LSU's first five games of 1956, all losses.

The remaining five games of the season, Taylor broke loose, scoring 51 points to lead the SEC, and LSU won three. If they hadn't, Dietzel might well have been just another footnote in LSU history books.

HARD-NOSED — LSU's Jim Taylor is one of the finest fullbacks ever to play the game.

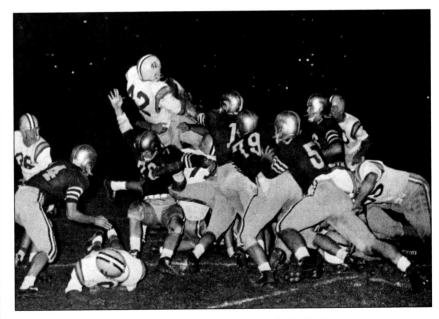

UP 'N OVER — Jim Taylor was known for diving over piles back-first.

Taylor triggered a 21-7 upset of Arkansas, setting up a huge game the following week with Tulane, a team also with only two victories to its name. "If I don't win this game," Dietzel confided to friends, "I'm through as a football coach."

The only LSU touchdown of the game was scored by Taylor, who also added the all-important PAT in a 7-6 Tiger victory, and LSU had gone from a winless season to 3-7, which isn't saying much unless it's seen from the vantage point of a potential 0-10 team. That effort may have saved Dietzel's bacon.

The following season, with all those talented sophomores like Johnny Robinson and Billy Cannon, the Tigers zoomed out to a 4-1 start before succumbing to youth and the Asian Flu, finishing 1-4. Still, Taylor led the SEC with 762 yards and 14 touchdowns — figures good enough to get him on several All-America teams.

Yet, Taylor never felt he was a complete football player until he got to the pros. "Until Coach (Vince) Lombardi came to Green Bay, I had only been a run-ning back for about 17 games. In high school I played mainly defense until I was a senior. At junior college I ran with the ball, but as a junior at LSU it took me half a season to become effective. And at LSU I didn't develop the skills necessary to become a pro running back. In college I was running only from tackle to tackle, did very little pass receiving and, really, very little blocking. I wasn't utilized that much."

He was utilized to the max, of course, under Lombardi as Green Bay won five NFL championships and the first Super Bowl.

Taylor, who probably saved Dietzel's job, meant a lot to Lombardi, too. He was the first of the Lombardi Packers to be enshrined in the NFL Hall of Fame.

"WE'RE NO. 1!"
20

Paul Dietzel blinked under the bright stadium lights of the Orange Bowl. Halfback Don Purvis had just snaked 51 yards through the Miami Hurricanes for the night's first touchdown.

"Good gravy," Dietzel, then the 34-year old coach of the LSU Tigers, recalled thinking to himself at that moment when his second string seized control of the game, "this team could really be something!"

Was it ever.

LSU, in the time when Ike was president and Elvis was king, was a dazzling football team that caught the fancy of the nation. The chant "We're No. 1," sung by fans of every team after every victory, had real meaning for the first — and only — time at LSU.

From the glory days of Doc Fenton, a turn-of-the-century football marvel and the heart of an undefeated Tiger team almost too good to be believed, the perennial cry of LSU optimists had been "1908 and next year."

The Fightin' Tigers playing a half-century later on that Friday night in Miami represented LSU's "Next Year" — its team for all seasons, a national champion.

The offensive speed and defensive pursuit of the Bayou Bengals that evening in the Orange Bowl had the much larger Hurricanes virtually grasping at the wind. The 41-0 victory, a month into the season, was the fourth of Dietzel's Grand Experiment of 1958.

"It was a golden moment," Dave McCarty, a tackle on that Tiger team, said of the 1958 season, "but, you know, a lot of things had to fall just right."

Dietzel was as much an alchemist as coach that year, mixing diverse ele-

CHAMPS — LSU's only national championship team: the 1958 Tigers.

ments into a potent football force.

He had recruited superior talent, including Billy Cannon, one of the country's premier runners. Cannon, who ran a 9.4 hundred and heaved the 16-pound shot more than 53 feet, was described by *Time* magazine as "a shattering, run-over-them power sprinter," and according to *Track & Field News* was "either the fastest shot-putter or the strongest sprinter in track annals."

There were other notable Tiger athletes, but LSU lacked depth, size and experience. LSU went into that season with 15 return-ing lettermen and three seniors from the 1957 Tigers, a 5-5 team that lost four of its last five. The biggest of Dietzel's linemen weighed 210 pounds, six pounds more than Cannon.

Three coaching decisions factored into LSU's only modern-day No. 1:

■ A switch from a power offense to the wing-T, a misdirection offense with constant breakaway potential for LSU's quick-draw backs — Cannon, Johnny Robinson and Purvis. The wing-T was being used successfully by Forest Evashevski at Iowa. Tubby Raymond, then an assistant at Delaware where the offense was created, helped Dietzel install it.

Evashevski, ironically, was a speaker at LSU's clinic in the spring. He took one look at the Tigers walking through wing-T plays and began to ungraciously mumble about "the scrawniest bunch of players I ever saw."

■ A three-team substitution system designed to keep everyone fresh and to counteract a new rules change. The NCAA decided that players could return to a game only once in each quarter. Coaches didn't know how to deal with that change, and Dietzel had been refining a substitution system to develop more depth.

There were only 16 Tigers the coaching staff believed could play both offense and defense. The best athletes were naturally placed on the first unit, the "White Team," so named for the color of their practice jerseys, which would play both ways for approximately half the game.

The White Team would be backed offensively by the Gold Team (named for the color of its practice jerseys but later shortened to "Go Team" because of a misunderstanding by a sportswriter). Second string backs and third string linemen made up the unit.

The Chinese Bandits were the defensive unit. The Bandits would become popularized as the "best third string in football," but they never truly were a third team. LSU's second team linemen and third string backs comprised the unit, which ended the season with a per-play-average yield of 0.9 yards.

■ The third change was switching Red Brodnax, a fine runner, from halfback to fullback to take advantage of his blocking skills and give LSU a first-team backfield of Cannon,

The year he was bitten with the bug was 1959. Al Bellott was a freshman at LSU, and he caught the worst case . . . no, wait, one of the worst cases of Tiger fever on record.

From the opening game that year through at least the 1992 season, as this is being penned, Bellot has been in attendance at every LSU football game played. Not just at home, every single one — from the City of Angels to the geritol playground, Miami.

Heading into the 1993 season, that's 385 consecutive football games — and counting! That streak, awesome as it seems, is even more impressive when it's pointed out that it includes all the games played in the years immediately after Bellott's graduation when he worked in Cape Kennedy, Florida and spent his falls driving to Baton Rouge, in that era before completed interstate highways crisscrossed the country, for the home games.

"I'd just get in my Volkswagen right after work Friday," Bellott said, "and I'd be in Tiger Stadium Saturday night."

Bellott admits this may not be completely normal behavior. "Some outgrow it," he said. "I think I've gotten worst. I'll never forget the day we were on our way to a game and a neighbor said, 'They must drug you all.'"

And, interestingly, that streak has spawned a streak of its own: Bellott has never seen LSU play live on television, though he now tapes every appearance and watches when he returns to his suburban New Orleans home. In his spare time, Bellott can listen to his collection of John Ferguson and Jim Hawthorne radio replays of Tiger games. Bellott can — and frequently does — hear the broadcast of any game LSU has played between in the 1970s and 1990s.

Robinson, quarterback Warren Rabb and Brodnax. At season's end, Cannon, Robinson and Rabb were the first-team All-SEC backs, the first time three of the four positions were

filled by one school.

But that was at season's end. In the preseason LSU was no more than a projected ninth-place team — not ninth in the nation, ninth in the SEC — and

MAD MAX — Max Fugler was part of LSU's awesome 1958 National Champs.

was an underdog in its first game against Rice.

If few others had any preseason faith in the 1958 Tigers, Cannon had enough for everybody. He startled backslappers who would ask how the team shaped up. "It'll be between us and Ole Miss," Cannon always answered matter-of-factly.

Cannon, then a junior, was so sure of his team that he took every cent he earned from his summer job at an electric company and, before school opened in the fall, bought almost a section of prime Tiger

Stadium seats for the Rebel game. He had almost the pick of the seats because LSU in 1958 had only 9,100 season-ticket holders.

LSU ran through a series of legends-in-the-making to open the '58 season, and didn't play to a home sellout until the seventh game of the season, the week the Tigers achieved their first No. 1 ranking.

■ LSU opened on the road against defending Southwest Conference champion Rice, and Jess Neely, a Hall of Fame coach. LSU won, 26-6.

■ Alabama, playing its first game under Bear Bryant, already respected for pre-eminent coaching performances at Kentucky and Texas A&M, was LSU's second opponent, at Mobile. LSU won, 13-3.

■ Hardin-Simmons, a pass-happy breather coached by the fabled old TCU and Redskins quarterback Sammy Baugh, was LSU's home opener, attended by 45,000 fans. LSU won, 20-6.

■ Miami, coached by the respected Andy Gustafson, represented LSU's fourth victory.

■ Kentucky, coached by

Blanton Collier, one of the finest tacticians in football history, was beaten 32-7 before a Tiger Stadium crowd of 65,000, just missing a sellout.

■ Bob Woodruff's Florida Gators, LSU's homecoming opponent, attracted 63,000 for a last minute 10-7 Tiger victory.

■ Ole Miss, an exciting, dominant Southeastern Conference and national challenger for a decade under Johnny Vaught, was the focal point of the Tiger season. Not only had LSU reached the No. 1 position in The Associated Press poll, and not only was the record of the sixth-ranked Rebels just as unblemished (6-0) as the Tigers', but Ole Miss represented a clear measure of how far LSU had come.

"We learned a lot from John Vaught," Dietzel reflected. "He was a fine fellow, and a great coach."

Dietzel had coached a couple of Vaught's players in an All-Star game after the 1956 season. Chatting after a practice, Dietzel asked about their superb conditioning. That came, the players said, as a result of twenty 50-yard dashes after each practice, sometimes more.

"No, you don't understand," Dietzel replied. "I meant every day, what kind of conditioning do you do every day?"

That was the daily regimen, the Rebels insisted.

Dietzel returned to Baton Rouge and promptly informed his team that from then on, each practice would end with a series of sprints — twenty one 50-yard dashes.

Ole Miss also taught Dietzel the value of quality depth. The Tigers led the Rebels 17-14 at the half of their 1956 game. "We played as well as we could play," Dietzel said, "but by the time we got to the dressing room we were worn out." The Rebels routed LSU in the second half, chalking up a 46-17 victory.

After that game Dietzel started tinkering with substitution plans that, two years later, were his acclaimed three-team system.

Dietzel learned well from Vaught, and together they produced not only unbeaten records going into their 1958 game, but the first Tiger Stadium sell-

out since the concrete structure was expanded to a seating capacity of 67,510 in 1954.

Cannon's preseason confidence in his team was well-rewarded. While the teams were warming up, Robinson walked past Cannon and asked if he were nervous. "No," Cannon replied, "my section is filling up."

Purvis, a Go Team back, remembered that night and the first Tiger Stadium sellout vividly. "It was an unbelievable setting," Purvis recalled, "the atmosphere was electric. There was tension in the air, emotion. Everything seemed so sharp. . . . It was as if all 68,000 people were concentrating on every play, every substitution. It was as if the crowd was out there with us, as if the crowd was saying, 'We're all playing this sucker.'"

The Tigers may have taken the collective heart out of the Rebels early in the second quarter when a goal-line stand denied Ole Miss any points after gaining a first down at LSU two, with three shots from a foot away.

Billy Brewer, the cur-

rent Rebel coach, later fumbled on the Ole Miss 21 and LSU recovered. On a fourth-and-goal from the four, with 25 seconds remaining until the half, Rabb rolled out. His receivers covered, Rabb cut toward the end zone and was hit at the two. As he was going down, another Rebel slammed into the falling bodies, sending Rabb across the goal.

Such are the ways national championships are won.

LSU passed its test against Ole Miss, 14-0.

"I've thought about that game many times in the years since we played it," Brewer said, "and I really believe that was the start of big-time football in the South. I'm proud we were a part of it. The spirit of those people in that stadium, then and now, is unmatched anywhere. It was a game to remember."

The Tigers breezed past Duke, 50-18; struggled in the mud and the rain with Mississippi State, 7-6; and soundly trounced Tulane, 62-0, after leading only 6-0 at the half.

Its national championship safely tucked away (since voting was done

SWEET AS SUGAR — LSU defeated Clemson, 7-0, to cap a national championship season.

after the regular season then), LSU played one more game, a 7-0 Sugar Bowl victory over Clemson. Rabb broke a hand on the game's second play, but Cannon threw a third quarter touchdown pass.

LSU was the overwhelming choice as the nation's No. 1 football team. Only one poll, the Football Writers of America, voted another team as college football's best. Evashevski's Iowa

Hawkeyes, the other dominant wing-T club, despite a loss and a tie, claimed that minor version of the national championship.

In retrospect, circumstance, as is frequently the case, played as much a role in LSU's 1958 fortunes as the design of Dietzel's Grand Experiment.

For one thing, LSU only had one serious injury throughout the season. Go Team guard Manson Nelson broke an arm in the season-opener

against Rice.

Also, the presence of Tommy Davis, punter, place-kicker and Go Team fullback, cannot be minimized.

Davis directly accounted for two victories, 10-7 over Florida and 7-6 over Mississippi State, with his place-kicking. He was also an excellent punter, with a 41-yard average. Davis may have put on the greatest punting exhibition in Tiger annals by averaging 55 yards on four kicks against Tulane, despite kicking twice into the end zone. In those years the 20-yard difference between the end zone and the point of the ensuing first down was deducted from a punters' total on a touchback.

"Tommy kicked two over the deep man's head that day," Purvis recalled. "He would've averaged 70 yards a kick under today's rules."

Davis was a 24-year-old junior in 1958. He had dropped out of school three years before to join the army, but did not formally resign from LSU, meaning all his grades that semester officially became "Fs." Before he could play college football again, those academic deficiencies had to be made up.

The task of getting Davis eligible fell to Joe May, a 1957 letterman and a 1958 graduate assistant. Davis moved in with May and the two zeroed in on the books. Two semesters later, Davis was eligible.

"When I think back on that team," May said, "I always come up with one conclusion: That I deserved one of those championship rings, too."

CLOSE CALL — Tommy Davis boots the winning extra point to push LSU past Mississippi State on the way to the 1958 National Championship.

CHINATOWN, LA 21

Shadows of the goal-posts stretched well beyond the line of scrimmage. Bear Bryant's Crimson Tide was camped at the LSU five.

It was there, in a 0-0 ballgame on a hot 1958 September night at Mobile's Ladd Memorial Stadium, the Chinese Bandits received their baptism of fire.

Bama's Duff Morrison pulled a Billy Cannon fumble out of mid-air and returned it 45 yards to put the Tide within easy reach of the lead — and the first touchdown of the Bryant era.

It was there Tiger coach Paul Dietzel waved in a revolutionary concept in college football — his defensive specialists, a back-up unit comprised of untested sophomores and 1957 redshirts and squadsmen. Gaynell Kinchen, who was the team manager the season before, led the "Chinese Bandits" as they trotted out to meet their football destiny.

At that time, many teams used two platoons, both of which played on offense and defense, that were obviously designed so the second string could keep the starters as fresh as possible.

But the substitution rules were changed before the '58 season. The new rule stipulated that if a player was in a game at the start of a quarter, he could be replaced and then return — but no more than once during that period.

It was a crucial rules change for Dietzel, who had quality front-line athletes, but questionable depth. His Bayou Bengals fired out to a 4-1 start in 1957, but a midseason flu epidemic took a toll on the team and the thin Tigers staggered in 1-4 down the stretch.

THE CHINESE BANDITS

Dietzel decided to divide his squad into three units: The White Team, which were his best athletes and who played both ways; The Go Team, offensive specialists; and the Chinese Bandits, the defensive team. The idea was for the White Team (named for the jerseys it wore in practice) to start and play approximately half of each quarter. The other half of the quarter ideally would be divided between the Go Team (originally the Gold Team, for their practice jerseys, but eventually changed in favor of its snazzy shortened name) and the Chinese Bandits.

Contrary to legend, the Bandits were never considered a "third team." LSU's second best linemen and third-string backs were on the defensive team. The Go Team was comprised of third-string linemen and second-string backs, meaning the two units were fairly even. And the Chinese Bandits had a modicum of basic offensive plays they could — and did — run when caught in a substitution dilemma. With the score tied at 6-6 against Duke, Bandit lineman Emile Fornet blocked a punt, and Kinchen recovered at the Blue Devil two. As a tip of the hat to his defensive specialists, Dietzel waved the Go Team back to the sidelines, and let the Chinese Bandits do the honors. Merle Schexnaildre, who had been in heated competition with J.W. Brodnax and Tommy Davis at fullback on one of the offensive teams until a knee injury settled matters, scored LSU's go-ahead touchdown.

The Go Team, Dietzel admits now, was virtually helpless on defense.

Besides, Bud Johnson, LSU's assistant sports information director in 1958, said, "No unit with a Mel Branch could ever be considered a third team."

Branch, an end, was one of Dietzel's finest lineman, a sterling athlete. He had, however, a defensive lineman's mentality — a charger — that limited him on offense. Right off, Branch was a quality commodity for the defensive specialists.

The Tigers had another defensive ace in its stripes with Kinchen, another end who entered LSU with the superb recruiting class of 1956. Kinchen injured a knee, though, and some believed his football career was over. He worked for his grant-in-aid in 1957 as a team manager. He was ready to return to football by '58, and was a factor in LSU's fortunes.

Unlike the White Team and Go Team, there was a colorful reason for the name of the defensive unit. "I got the idea for the Bandits in 1950 when I was a defensive coach under Sid Gillman at the University of Cincinnati," Dietzel recalled. Dietzel's favorite cartoon strip was "Terry and the Pirates," a military adventure set in the Orient. The Asian outlaws were led by a character named Chopsticks Joe, and one day he said "Chinese bandits are the most vicious people on earth."

The quote struck Dietzel. "So I took the cartoon and hung it in the dressing room," Dietzel said. "Our defensive unit (at Cincinnati) became known as the Chinese Bandits. But we were never big winners at Cincinnati, and nobody paid much attention to the Chinese Bandits then."

The Bandits played in LSU's first 1958 game against Rice, but undramatically in the Tigers' 26-6 victory. Nobody made reference to the name Dietzel had conferred on the unit, and it was mentioned only in passing as the "reserve platoon."

LSU football history would change when Dietzel took out his first team and replaced it with a raw and largely inexperienced cluster of reserves with Alabama at the Tiger five.

"I tell you, it took guts to try it the first time in game conditions," said Charlie McClendon, then Dietzel's first lieutenant and later his successor as head coach. "To take out Billy Cannon and your best players, and put in an entire team of substitutes!"

Kinchen said the athletes themselves didn't feel any particular pressure, or

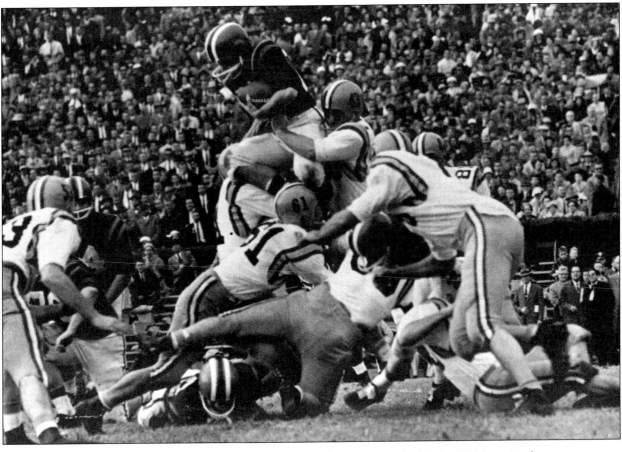

THE GREAT WALL OF CHINA— The Chinese Bandits pull down a Clemson running back in the 1959 Sugar Bowl.

even thought anything unusual about the situation. The only thing anyone agreed was out-of-the-ordinary was the several thousand spectators milling around the sidelines because a section of the stadium collapsed early in the game. No one was hurt, but some of those fans got a close-up view of a historical moment in Southern football.

Kinchen said, "We just went about our jobs."

And did their jobs pretty well.

In three plays, the pumped up Crimson Tide gained one yard. Alabama settled for a field goal. It was a milestone goal-line stand. LSU came back to defeat Bama, 13-3, and afterward Dietzel praised the stand and the unit. The name "Chinese Bandits" was used publicly for the first time, and picked up in the press.

"We were fortunate in

1958 that the first couple of times we put in the Bandits they managed to get the ball for us; then the thing started snowballing," McClendon said.

LSU's success — and Dietzel's imagination — fed off each other. It all caught the fancy of the college football world. The Chinese Bandits were quick and well-schooled in gang-tackling, and they exceeded expectations during their limited game time. "They really performed like a great team," Dietzel said. "On film you'd see nine gold helmets meeting at the ball-carrier. They were brilliant at gang-tackling."

In short order, there was a Chinese war chant, written by Memphis disc jockey Keith Huddleton, which was played whenever the Bandits took the field — not to mention incessantly, it seemed, throughout Louisiana at all other hours. Jack Sabin, who owned the Goalpost restaurant just off-campus, drove to New Orleans one day and picked up 1,400 coolie hats — which immediately became the rage at Tiger Stadium — to give away with meals. Frequently the biggest Saturday night roar at the mossy old arena would be when the P.A. announcer would shout — as he did for neither of the other units: "Here come the Chinese Bandits!"

It was a phenomena, not just in Louisiana or even just regionally. The Chinese Bandits became a national item, and the most celebrated reserve unit in the history of college football. When *Life* magazine did a spread on the Bayou Bengals, it didn't do stories on Cannon, or Dietzel. The Chinese Bandits were *Life's* focus.

The esprit de corps of the unit was powerful. Dietzel gave them a subtle mark of distinction, socks with red stripes at the top, and the identification bonded those back-up football players tightly.

When an injury caused Dietzel to juggle his lineups slightly, guard Tommy Lott was ticketed for a promotion to the White Team. When Lott was told, however, he gave Dietzel an indignant stare and said: "Okay, but as soon as possible I want to get back to the Bandits."

Dietzel reflected that being part of that unit "became a matter of real pride. They were terrific gang-tacklers, and they had speed. But they were also, remember, reserves. And there was a reason for that. But what they had more than anything was great hustle and enthusiasm. The greatest thrill I ever had in athletics was the opportunity to be associated with the Bandits," Dietzel said. "They showed me what football was really all about: heart and determination."

There was a little more.

From 1958 through 1961 LSU allowed a minuscule 4.57 points per game. The Chinese Bandits not only made winning easier at LSU, they did what was thought to be the impossible: They actually made defense popular with the fans.

Dietzel's theoretical three-team concept worked out perfectly in 1958. Over the course of the season the White Team averaged 35 minutes a game. The Go Team and Chinese Bandits divided the remaining 25 minutes of game time almost evenly. The back-up teams kept the front-line troops fresh enough to overrun all 11 opponents, and LSU was proclaimed the national champion.

And the Chinese Bandits, throughout that magical season, more than held up their end. In one of the most astounding statistics in sports that year, every time an opponent ran a play against them less than a yard (0.9) was gained against the Chinese Bandits.

"And we allowed only three touchdowns in our SEC schedule in 1958," McClendon reflected. "Imagine that."

THE ORIGINAL CHINESE BANDITS

Left end: Mel Branch (6-1, 210, Jr.)

Nose guard: Tommy Lott (5-9, 188, Jr.)

Right end: Gaynell Kinchen (6-3, 196, Soph.)

Left tackle: Emile Fournet (5-11, 195, Jr.)

Right tackle: Duane Leopard (6-3, 196, Soph.)

Linebacker: John Langan (6-3, 183, Jr.)

Linebacker: Merle Schexnaildre (5-9, 182, Jr.)

Left corner: Andy Bourgeois (5-10, 174, Soph.)

Right cornerback: Hart Bourque (5-8, 165, Soph.)

Safety: Darryl Jenkins (6-1, 163, Soph.)

Safety: Henry Lee Roberts (6-0, 172, Soph.)

EVERYBODY'S ALL-AMERICAN

22

Billy Cannon had to lunge to grab the Heisman Trophy. Vice President Richard Nixon, who was presenting Cannon the highest individual award in college football, misjudged the weight of the 50-pound bronze sculpture and almost dropped it.

Cannon saved the day — and the statue.

There was no question that in 1959, and perhaps for a season or two before that, Cannon was the nation's best collegiate football player.

He received 1,929 Heisman votes, more than tripling the total of the runner-up, Richie Lucas of Penn State, and Cannon's total was more than the combined vote of the next eight contenders.

As the leader of LSU's undefeated 1958 national championship team, Cannon was loved and revered in Louisiana. In LSU's illustrious 99-year football history, his No. 20 is the only jersey retired by the school.

But in 1983 all that changed when Cannon, an orthodontist in Baton Rouge, was caught in a counterfeiting scheme, embarrassing the people

THE WINNER — Billy Cannon accepts the Heisman Trophy from Richard Nixon, 1959.

who loved and admired him most.

More than a third of a century after accepting the

Heisman, and long after serving two and a half years in prison, Cannon has made a comeback at LSU. Just as he saved Nixon's fumble in 1959, Cannon may have recovered his self-respect in the 1990s.

He has been welcomed back into the Tiger family by football coach Curley Hallman and athletic director Joe Dean and, more importantly, has been forgiven by most, but definitely not all, LSU fans.

In his prime at LSU, Cannon may have been the most revered sports idol in Louisiana history. A frightening combination of strength and speed, Cannon was a 6-foot-1, 210-pound halfback with Olympic sprinter speed coupled with Olympic-competition strength.

People were amazed at LSU track meets in the late 1950s as Cannon ran the 100-yard dash in 9.4 seconds, then trotted across the track to throw

THE RUN — Billy Cannon is best known for his improbable 89-yard punt return-which beat Ole Miss, 7-3, in 1959.

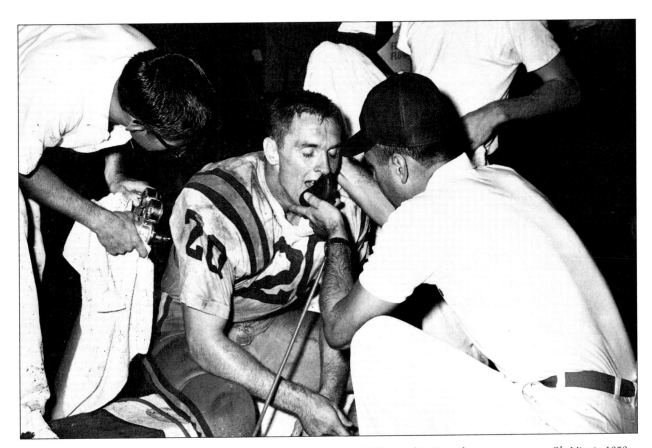

SUCK IT UP — Billy Cannon receives oxygen from trainer Marty Broussard following his 89-yard punt return versus Ole Miss in 1959.

LAST HOORAH — Billy Cannon darts for his final touchdown as a Tiger versus Tulane in 1959.

the 16-pound shot 54 feet. In that pre-steroid era, he could also bench-press at a level that was only 20 pounds off the gold medal effort for his weight class in the 1956 Olympics.

Full use of his abilities were made on the football field. In the second game of his collegiate career, Cannon hit Alabama with 53 and 73-yard touchdown runs. Against Texas Tech a week later, he grabbed a short pass, bounded over a defensive back and shot through the secondary for a 59-yard touchdown. Coolly, the Red Raiders marched right back to take a 14-13 lead, then kicked off — to Cannon. Eleven seconds and 97 yards later LSU was on top to stay.

"It's the only time," said Coach Paul Dietzel, "I ever saw one man single-handedly win a football game."

The biggest scare of the 1958 season may have come during a September practice. Lightning struck the field during a hot afternoon practice, sending players and coaches scurrying for cover. In the midst of the confusion, Coach Paul Dietzel stopped in his tracks, glanced wildly to his left, then right, looking for the key component in his football team, and began screaming, "Where's Cannon, WHERE'S CANNON?"

Dietzel said later, "I guess the thing I'll always remember about him was the way he took the bull by

the horns. There was one game when we were playing poorly in the first half. We came in at halftime and Billy went around the locker room and actually grabbed some of the big guys, the tackles and guards. He shook 'em up. He said something to the effect, 'If you guys don't start shaping up I'm going to whip all of you.' He was as fierce a competitor as I've ever seen. When the coin was flipped, he was always ready to play."

And Cannon's dramatic, herculean 89-yard punt return for a touchdown against Ole Miss on Halloween night 1959 is the most fabled single play in LSU football annals.

It's impossible to compare Cannon with the backs of today, though he had a career average of 5.7 yards per carry. It was a different game he played, and he couldn't carry the ball 25 times a game and amass the huge statistics that athletes are judged by now. Cannon had to be saved to play safety — or even linebacker on the goal-line — on defense too, in that era of two-way football. Carl Maddox, a coach and athletic director for 40 years, including service on the 1958 staff, put him in perspective, though, when he said, "Billy Cannon was the best defensive player I ever saw."

"There was nothing Billy couldn't do, it seemed," said Dave McCarty, a former teammate. "He was the ultimate hero."

So it seemed. Cannon was a huge name in Louisiana from 1955, when he gained 100 or more yards in 12 of Istrouma High School's 13 games, and scored 33 touchdowns as the Indians won the state championship, and Cannon became a prep All-America. Three years later he was a first-team college All-America and finished third in the Heisman Trophy balloting, which he won almost unanimously in 1959. In 1960 Cannon was an All-Pro halfback, and the MVP in the championship game as the Oilers won the AFL title. A year later he was again an All-Pro after leading the AFL in rushing with 948 yards, and in one stunning performance accounted for 331 total yards (115 receiving) and five touchdowns in a game against the New

York Titans. He again was the AFL championship game MVP as the Oilers won a second straight championship.

What seemed to be a golden career took a wicked twist, though, in 1962 when a linebacker came down knees-first on Cannon's back, and tore his back muscles loose. Never possessed with great lateral movement, when Cannon tried to come back three weeks later he had practically none.

Two years later Cannon was traded to the Raiders for three players, and played the 1964 season at flanker. Oakland coach Al Davis asked Cannon to move to tight end in '65, where he played primarily as a backup for two years. It seemed a sad way to end a potentially spectacular career.

But in 1967 Cannon caught fire – and footballs by the bushel — becoming a dangerous receiving threat in the Raiders' offensive scheme, with 32 catches, 10 for touchdowns as Oakland made its way to Super Bowl II. Cannon was again recognized as an All-Pro. "He was the classic case of too much too

soon," Davis said at the time. "Money, fame, buildup. It came close to ruining him. The wolves who love to see a hero fail couldn't wait to jump on him. But he took his beating and came back and made good at a new position, and now he's the best tight end in the business."

A knee injury in 1970 ended Cannon's playing career with Hank Stram's Kansas City Chiefs. He finished an 11-season career with 2,455 yards rushing, and 236 receptions for 3,656 yards, 1,882 yards in kick returns, and 392 points scored.

But the wolves who love to see a hero fail eventually had a feast on Cannon.

At his sentencing in 1983, the only LSU person on hand was former sports information director Paul Manasseh, who said he felt someone from LSU should be at Cannon's side.

"I made a tragic mistake, what else can I say," Cannon said reflectively a decade later. "I assume full responsibility. I paid my debt to society, but some people think I should pay more."

That number began to

dwindle as time went on. By the 1990s Cannon's voice was often heard again on Louisiana radio sports talk shows, and at halftime and after LSU games, often with analyst Doug Moreau, another former LSU All-American and Baton Rouge's district attorney.

And Cannon, who attends Tiger games in a pressbox-level suite, is purposely included in important LSU athletic functions.

Before he coached his first game at LSU, Hallman asked Cannon to fly with the team to Athens, Georgia, and talk to the players before that game.

Cannon at first refused, saying it would give people who didn't like him a reason to get at Hallman. But Hallman insisted, and Cannon finally agreed to go.

"We didn't live up to his talk," Hallman said, recalling the Tigers' 31-10 defeat, "but we were mighty proud he was with us."

Hallman vividly recalls fall Saturday nights of his adolescence, on the floor of his family's Northport, Alabama home. There, along with his sister, he was absorbed in the description of Tiger games, courtesy of New Orleans' WWL-radio's powerful 50,000 watts signal.

"I remember the names — 'Chinese Bandits,' 'Go Team,' " Hallman said. "And I remember the name Billy Cannon. There was a kind of excitement, a magic about it all."

Hallman was hooked. He became an LSU fan, and a Billy Cannon fan.

Never will Hallman ever forget the day when his older brother brought home a football magazine with Cannon on the cover.

"Here was that good-lookin' guy, with that great flat-top, the Heisman Trophy winner, and then I was reading of his great speed for a guy that big," Hallman remembered. "He was something, I'll tell you."

Throughout Cannon's career, Hallman followed the exploits of his idol. "I'd sit and watch on Sundays whenever his team was on TV," Hallman said. "He was a guy who was an excellent player at more than one position — a real football player."

Interestingly, Hallman coached Billy Cannon Jr. when he played in the secondary his first two seasons at Texas A&M. Hallman first met Cannon Sr. when he visited College Station to watch Billy Jr. play a baseball game.

"I sat by him and introduced myself. It was a great pleasure for me to meet the gentleman. I always tell people I had the honor of coaching the sons of two of my heroes, John David Crow's boy at Alabama and Billy Cannon Jr."

When he was hired at LSU, Hallman said he made a point of getting former players involved again with the program. And he said he wanted Cannon, despite the stain of the counterfeiting conviction, as much as anybody.

"There's a great tradition here, and a lot of wonderful football memories, Hallman said. "Billy Cannon contributed a lot to that great tradition and those great memories. He should be standing shoulder-to-shoulder with all Tigers."

Dean also made a special effort to bring Cannon back into the fold. "We like to think our people, LSU Tigers, are special," Dean said. "We all make mistakes, even those who like to point fingers at others. Billy Cannon is a special person. We want him here, with us."

Forgiving Cannon has been easier for some than others. A woman Dean attended a bible study class with for more than three decades was furious, Dean said, when she learned Cannon had been allowed to accompany the LSU team to Georgia.

That was before Dean wrote her a letter saying he was sure that somewhere in their Christian classes they had to have come across something about forgiveness and the casting of the first stone.

Cannon, on the other hand, said his love for LSU never wavered. "I've always wanted what was best for LSU, still do. For the most part, I try to keep a low profile. . . . But I'll always do what I can."

His usual self-deprecating sense of humor never left Cannon, normally a man with a warm, whimsical personality. During his trial he cracked to his lawyer, "Did you know you can tell it's a phony $100 bill if Ben Franklin has braces on his teeth?"

His time in prison though, was the worst of his life, Cannon admitted. "There was nothing good about it. I was away from my family, and that is the worst punishment of all. And I'm still trying to rebuild my (orthodontic) practice from more than two years of lost income. But there were some moments I'll remember fondly."

For example, Cannon received many letters from Louisiana and LSU people letting him know they were with him, understood that he had made a mistake and expressed confidence he would learn from it.

One of his best moments, he said, was receiving a perceptive and tender letter from someone who knew exactly what torment and personal second-guessing Cannon was living through.

"President Nixon," Cannon said quietly, perhaps recalling the day of his Heisman presentation, "wrote a wonderful, uplifting letter."

Yet there are those who are not nearly so magnanimous.

Because of his harsh criticism of former LSU coach Charlie McClendon,

Cannon had been persona non grata with many Tiger fans since the late 1970s. And they became further upset with him when Cannon's son, Billy Jr., signed a football grant-in-aid with Texas A&M.

Don Purvis, an LSU teammate of Cannon's and a former Tiger assistant coach under McClendon, said those people misinterpreted Cannon's motives.

"Billy just didn't want Billy Jr. to have to go 89 yards for a touchdown every time he touched the ball," Purvis said, referring to the kingsized expectations certain to await Cannon's son and namesake in Baton Rouge.

Still, among LSU fans there was a general feeling that Billy Cannon was no longer one of them, and he was resented.

So when he emerged from prison, Cannon was an inviting target for the more mean-spirited of his disappointed fans. On his first day back at his orthodontic practice, a woman's voice on Cannon's office intercom began screeching, "Jailbird, jailbird, jailbird." Cannon, who was in the embarrassed company of well-wishers at the time, recalled saying, "I wonder if she thinks I don't know I was in jail."

Cannon is well aware he is an easy public target, even on radio talk shows. Appearing on a preseason show as a guest analyst once, one caller began screaming, "Dr. Cannon, you're a disgrace to LSU and to the Heisman Trophy!"

Those who know him best say there always have been two distinct sides to Cannon's personality. A kid who grew up poor near the refineries and petro-chemical plants in the blue-collar North side of Baton Rouge, Cannon had run-ins with the law as a juvenile.

The late Gustave Adolphus 'Goober' Morse, an avid LSU fan and a friend of Cannon's, said that Cannon, while always a sweet, intelligent, and thoughtful person, could never quite shake the dust from the wrong side of the tracks from his shoes.

Yet, in college Cannon entered a difficult academic discipline — predentistry — and was a solid student, maintaining a B average. Tommy Neck, an LSU teammate of Cannon's and later a member of the

school's Board of Supervisors, recalled the thing he remembered most about Cannon: "One spring and summer he was having trouble with a particular class. So he locked himself in a room for a month to make the grades."

Cannon married his high school sweetheart as a freshman, and was, by all accounts, a loving husband and father of three by the time he left college for pro football.

Pete Rozelle, then the general manager of the NFL's Los Angeles Rams, originally — and illegally — signed Cannon a month before the 1960 Sugar Bowl. Then Cannon turned around and signed a contract with the Houston Oilers of the new American Football League, whose offer would make Cannon the sport's first six-figure athlete.

For the next nine years, in an era when many athletes lived off their names, Cannon played pro ball in the fall and worked at his academic pursuits in the off-season, earning dental degrees at the University of Tennessee and Loyola of Chicago.

After retiring Cannon

established a $300,000-a-year orthodontic practice in Baton Rouge, along with a reputation for treating children from families that couldn't always pay the cost of dental care.

"I think maybe the biggest thrill I ever had," Cannon said, "was receiving the high school graduation picture of a beautiful kid who used to be made fun of and called 'Fang,' but who now had a beautiful smile, with the words 'Thank you' written across it."

As he approached, then passed his half-century birthday, Cannon seemed to have come to grips with his personal failures and successes. He does not flinch when he is reminded of his errors.

"I know who I am, what I did, and what I have to live with," he said. "I have my past to live with, and I realize that.

"You know the old story: You join the church, you're reborn and your past is washed away. Well, that's not so. You live with your past. And I do."

Cannon said he is offended "by these guys who get thrown out of sports for drugs or whatever, who then come back and tell you how to live your life when they've screwed up theirs.

"It's the same analogy for me. I can't tell anybody anything."

Some who know him best disagree. Don Kennard, a close personal friend and a long-time state representative, said of Cannon: "Billy is the kind of person who has always learned from experience. He's had a bad experience. Billy was always a basically good person, and there's no question in my mind he'll be a better one now. He's resilient. He's very adaptable. He's going to stand tall. He's going to get his train back on track."

Bunnie Cannon, his youngest daughter who worked in the LSU press-box just a few feet from the suite where Cannon usually sees games, said, "People tell me all the time how much my father did for them."

To her at least, Billy Cannon "is a greater person in real life than he ever was on the football field — and on the football field he was one of the greatest ever."

THE SHRINE —The fruits of Billy Cannon's athletic feats.

THE ATHLETIC DIRECTORS

23

ake a football week-
end in Baton
Rouge, a Saturday
night in Tiger Stadium on
the campus of Louisiana
State University, and you
come to the conclusion
there is really nothing
quite so important in the
Cajun world."

Columnist Furman
Bisher passed those words
to his Atlanta audience in
his printed eulogy of former LSU athletic director
Jim Corbett.

Bisher painted a pic-
ture of a man who built a
solid program and a foot-
ball spectacle all in one
fell swoop.

When the Boston
Irishman was hired as
sports information director
at LSU in 1947, the school
had a 45,000-seat stadium
that attracted an average
attendance of 38,000. At
the time of his untimely
death in 1967, LSU had
35,000 season-ticket holders and a 67,500-seat stadium that was 98 percent
occupied every Saturday
night.

LSU has been fortunate
in that it has long had
visionaries at the helm.

T.P. "Red" Heard left an
indelible stamp on Tiger
football. When LSU presi-
dent James Smith proposed

a building expenditure of
$250,000 for men's dormi-
tories in 1928, Heard did
some fast-talking. He presented the idea of raising
the stands on both the East
and West sides of Tiger
Stadium, and extending
them to the end zones,
then filling in the outer
structure of the arena into
rooms and corridors. Thus,
LSU got its unique dorms
— and increased stadium
capacity by 10,000 seats.

Heard came up with the
notion of night football in
1931. An October 3, 1931
game with Spring Hill was
LSU's first under the lights,
but not the first in college

SATURDAY NIGHT LIVE — Night football at LSU is a tradition which started in 1931.

football. Illinois defeated Carlisle in an 1897 game played indoors at the Chicago Coliseum. Nowhere, however, did the "after dinner" games become more popular than in Baton Rouge.

It's said that Heard made the move because of competition for fans with Tulane and Loyola, both in New Orleans. That was not the case. Eighty percent of LSU's crowds came from within a 30-mile radius of Baton Rouge.

Heard was more con-cerned with the afternoon Louisiana heat in September (LSU, contrary to belief, frequently played day games in November and December when the weather was cooler until the McClendon regime), and making it easy for shift workers in Baton Rouge refineries to attend the games.

He also got LSU football on New Orleans' 50,000-watt clear channel station WWL in 1942, at a time when practically no one else played at night, making the Tigers a nationally known commodity. When Heard charted a plane ("The LSU Special") in 1939 to get the Tigers to Boston for a game with Holy Cross, the Tigers became the first Southern football team to fly to game sites.

"Gentleman Carl" Maddox, one of the finest figures in LSU history, was an AD of a different stripe than his predecessor, Corbett. Maddox was more of a builder, and under his administration LSU built the Pete Maravich Assembly Center, added a section to Tiger Stadium and put the Tiger program on solid business footing.

The only glitch on Maddox' record — and it was more a matter of circumstance than anything — was the failure of the 1969 Tigers to get a major bowl bid.

Maddox was a member of the Tiger coaching staff in 1959 when Paul Dietzel felt pressured by Corbett and Louisiana politicians into playing the Sugar Bowl rematch with Ole Miss. Maddox wanted his coach to have input in the decision. Charlie McClendon, on the other hand, was often out of the office with his team when bowl representatives called.

All that was exacerbated when Notre Dame, ranked No. 2, broke its 45-year bowl ban in order to play No. 1-ranked Texas in the Cotton Bowl — which is where LSU had been led to believe it was going to play.

Paul Dietzel returned to LSU as athletic director in 1978, hired by one chancellor (Paul Murrill) and, in essence, fired by another (James Wharton) in 1982.

Dietzel walked into a political ambush when he returned to LSU because his presence polarized some fans and hierarchy. A lot of people never forgave him for leaving for West Point in 1962.

Wharton, apparently intent on building a political base, found "a million dollar deficit" in the athletic department, though only $200,000 was ever in question, and Dietzel came up with recommendations to remedy the situation, including raising football ticket-prices by $1. Wharton refused the request, and soon had Dietzel walking the plank.

Bob Brodhead succeeded Dietzel, and soon put in place a program to generate new funds. Practically every aspect, including the raising of ticket prices by $1, was the same as Dietzel recommended. This time they were approved, and Brodhead hailed as a genius.

Brodhead was a charming, witty, intelligent man but in the wrong place at the wrong time. He came from the Miami Dolphins, had no feel for the school, the state or the people. Everything he and his hirelings found at LSU they found fault with: the uniform design, the tradition, the coaches, the SEC, etc. Brodhead shed WWL, saying, "Who listens to LSU games in Minnesota? Muskrats?" He dropped LSU's wrestling program after a nationally recognized recruiting harvest, when it was too late for the athletes to transfer without losing a year's eligibility.

The whole time

Brodhead was working, he said he had to answer 10 to 12 phone calls a day from Wharton, a chancellor who seemed to want to be the athletic director.

Brodhead did have a midas touch in hiring coaches. He brought Loren Seagrave, who started a run of national championships for the women's track team; Skip Bertman, who coached LSU to a raft of SEC — and two national — baseball championships; and Bill Arnsparger, who was two field goals short of three consecutive SEC football championships.

Brodhead, once described by former Governor John McKeithen as having "the touch of an elephant," seemed to have ended his own career by breaking federal eavesdropping laws in an attempt to listen to an NCAA investigator speaking to athletes. He pleaded guilty to federal charges, but surprisingly survived at LSU.

Then he took a trip with a newspaper publisher who owned the station on which "The Bob Brodhead Show" appeared weekly, a violation of the state Ethics Commission, but a weak violation even the commis-

sion said.

Brodhead was gone.

Joe Dean took over a very successful program, but found the price of Brodhead's success steep. Dean found the athletic department virtually bankrupt. He spent years nursing the self-sustaining Tiger athletic department back to health.

Of all the Ole War Skule's ADs, Corbett's influence was felt far beyond Louisiana's borders.

He was the NCAA coordinator for college football's first Game of the Week in 1953, and had an insight on how things were run at various schools across the country. Corbett knew who was doing things well and why — an invaluable tool as an athletic director. He was also NBC's coordinator of sports for a year. Corbett was an outspoken voice for restricted football on television to prevent oversaturation — a problem today.

His insights into the marriage of television and football created an unparalleled boom in the sport. Corbett was also one of the first college administrators to see marketing as a vehicle for universities. His

high-powered personality and network contacts helped usher in a golden age for LSU football.

Bud Montet, a former Baton Rouge sports editor, said Corbett "probably initiated the trend of selling a university that was never tried or thought of before."

Interestingly, LSU almost didn't get Corbett, a man who loved the school so much he once audited courses so he could say, "I attended LSU."

After Heard was released, the Board of Supervisors had the double-duty of searching for an athletic director and a coach. They found Paul Dietzel first and hired him. When Corbett was offered the AD's job, he turned it down, probably for two reasons: (1) He wasn't LSU's first choice. Biff Jones, the former Tiger coach who wouldn't let Huey Long talk to his team at halftime, was. (Jones declined but recommended a young Army assistant, Dietzel, for the head coaching position. Interestingly, the board received another recommendation for Dietzel from another source, LSU assistant Charlie McClendon). And

(2) Corbett wouldn't be able to hire his own coach.

Corbett eventually changed his mind, and he and Dietzel worked famously together. In their seven years together at LSU, there was only one real disagreement.

When LSU lost to Tennessee late in the 1959 season, and lost its number one ranking as leverage, most of the bowls had already been filled. At that point the Tigers, badly battered and without a real opportunity to regain its No. 1-ranking, would just as soon have stayed home. But LSU was pressured into the home state Sugar Bowl in a rematch with Ole Miss, whom the Tigers had previously defeated 7-3 on Billy Cannon's epic punt return, and put in a situation where the Tigers had nothing to gain. The result was a listless 21-0 defeat.

Two years later, after the 1961 Tigers completed their season ranked No. 4 with a 9-1-0 record, the Sugar Bowl again came calling. Dietzel, in a private meeting with Corbett, heatedly told his AD, "If this team plays in the Sugar Bowl, you're going

CORBETT — Athletic Director Jim Corbett helped raise LSU football to a higher level.

to have to coach them because I won't."

The Tigers beat Colorado in Miami's Orange Bowl in what turned out to be Dietzel's last LSU game anyway. He resigned to coach Army.

THE BABY-FACED ASSASSIN 24

George Bevan had a love affair with LSU athletics — or at least with the athletic director's daughter.

Bevan was a remarkable linebacker, one who made quickness more important than size (5-foot-11, 200-pounds) and proved it could be done in a memorable season in which, by his remarkable play, he convinced practically all the All-America selectors.

Tradition, the sense of playing for the state, whatever it is that usually attracts athletes to a particular school, was only a minor consideration in get-ting Bevan to the Tiger Den in the mid-1960s.

Ann Corbett, Bevan's high school sweetheart and the daughter of then AD Jim Corbett, knocked Tennessee and Alabama out of the running for Bevan's football services.

And LSU benefitted. Bevan was the anchor of the 1969 Tigers, possibly the finest team ever assem-bled in Baton Rouge. It was a team which won nine, lost one and scored a mod-ern school record 349 points.

But it was defense, where Bevan reigned, that was the teeth of that team.

With choirboy, cherubic good looks, Bevan was like a baby-faced assassin. LSU allowed only 38 yards a game rushing, a standard that hasn't been approached by any team anywhere since.

"I'd have to say playing on that 1969 team was the highlight of my playing career," Bevan, now a lawyer, said. "Football is often a blend of experience and talent, and that team was the perfect example because the talent level sure wasn't with the seniors. It was with the (Tommy) Casanovas, and (Ronnie) Estays, the juniors and sophomores.

"Those classes had great talent, but they never equalled what we had that season."

Bevan was considered too small to play line-backer for a major-college program, but he not only made a successful switch from fullback, but per-formed every bit as well as the heralded underclass-men. He made All-America, was a three-time Southeast Lineman of the Week, an Associated Press Lineman of the week, and a *Sports Illustrated* Lineman of the Week dur-ing that season. Bevan led LSU in tackles all three seasons he lettered.

Tommy Casanova, a three-time All-American and an All-Pro safety with the Cincinnati Bengals, said of Bevan, "George Bevan was the greatest football player I think I ever played with. Certainly he wasn't the biggest, the strongest or the fastest, but he was the most intense player I've ever seen. He had the whole team at the same level of intensity."

That intensity came to the fore perhaps most per-sonally in the 1969

Auburn game, a confronta-tion of dizzying propor-tions. That was the first season of the Pat Sullivan-Terry Beasley air show, but LSU scored on the first play from scrimmage on a halfback pass. The two teams traded body-blows the rest of the afternoon.

LSU was ahead 21-14 late when Auburn scored to cut the margin to 21-20. While everyone was won-dering if LSU had enough time to get back into field goal range, Auburn lined for the PAT. Then came the snap, and . . . THUMP! The attempt was blocked. Bevan sliced through to get a hand on it, the decid-ing play in a 21-20 LSU victory.

The low point was an earlier series of operations. "I had four operations on my Achilles tendon," Bevan said. "That makes you look kind of hard at what you're doing.

"But I had seen other guys, like (quarterbacks) Nelson Stokley and Pat Screen, work themselves back, and it made me work harder."

It paid off in one of LSU's greatest — yet one its most disappointing — football seasons. That was

the year the Tigers were wined and dined by the Cotton Bowl, only to be left at the altar when Notre Dame broke its bowl ban and most of the remaining bowls were filled up.

"The older I get the more disappointed I am in that," Bevan said reflective-ly. "There's no such thing as a 'minor' bowl, and I think had circumstances been different, we would have played somewhere, even in a non-New Year's Day game. We didn't feel we had to beg. So we voted to end the season. But if we had a definite place to go, then I think we would have played another game."

Bevan may have had a future in baseball had he pursued it. He had the genes. Two cousins, Hal Bevan and George Strickland, played in the major leagues.

But Bevan recalled the deciding factor in his selection of sport — and college — vividly.

"Ann and I had gone out since our senior season at Baton Rouge High. We had a date the night after we won the state champi-onship, and the night before I was supposed to

ALL-AMERICANS — Mike Anderson (45) and George Bevan (42) are two of LSU's greatest linebackers ever.

fly to Tennessee for a visit.

"Mr. Corbett was a warm, wonderful man, but he was waiting for us when I brought Ann to the door and the first thing he asked was where I was going to school.

"Well, I probably was going to go to LSU, but I told him I hadn't decided, but that I was visiting Tennessee in the morning. He told me to think it over, and that he wanted me to call him at seven in the morning.

"As it turned out, he called me — at five in the morning — and asked if I'd made up my mind. He and Ann came over to my house a few minutes later and I signed."

TRICK-OR-TREAT: LSU VS. OLE MISS

25

There's blood on the moon. Hidden in the night shadows cast by crones and covered by demonic shrieks is football played with a wooden stake. All Hallows Eve wakens the dead, and deadens the living.

LSU-Ole Miss. It comes with every flit of a witch in the breeze. College football with goose bumps. Take Transylvania and two.

There's nothing, Tulane and Mississippi State notwithstanding, like a Rebel yell or the Eye of the Tiger to turn blood to steam.

Flashback to 1964:

Doug Moreau kept his eyes on the ball as Tom Luke made a hellacious defensive play and tipped the pass with a finger.

Moreau's unbroken concentration allowed him to grab the tumbling ball and plant both feet six inches inside the sideline end zone boundary — the deciding two-point conversion in an 11-10 victory.

All eyes, 68,000 pairs, were riveted on Moreau, but had anyone glanced skyward they might have seen a silhouette against the October moon.

This is a series where the unexpected can be

expected, a series pocked with stunning upsets, dramatics and improbability.

"All I know," said Billy Brewer, who saw the series as a player and as a coach, "is anything can happen."

For a long time, the Tigers and Rebels contested what may have been the best rivalry anywhere. With natural rivals Tulane and Mississippi State in down cycles, and LSU and Ole Miss at the top of their games, they became each other's emotional outlet each season.

How intense can it be? Well, between 1959 and 1961 all that stood between

Ole Miss and three consecutive undefeated seasons — and conceivably three consecutive national championships — was LSU. The Rebels are still searching for their first No. 1 finish. On the other hand, Ole Miss prevented LSU from unbeaten seasons in 1962 and 1969, and smudged numerous other outstanding seasons.

The first time LSU ever met Ole Miss on Halloween was in 1953, a night when 5-1-0 Ole Miss used fourth quarter voodoo to overcome a 49-yard run by Jerry Marchand and an 85-yard interception return by Lou Deutschmann and brew a 27-16 defeat of LSU.

The second, of course, was the game which brought the series to its heated head, the foggy 1959 game when Billy Cannon bolted through the night to hand the Rebels their collective head.

Paul Dietzel, then the Tiger coach, described a strange circumstance that Halloween afternoon. His usual practice was to go to his office after lunch with the squad, get a book and read it until it was time to get ready for the game. "I never listened to or watched football games," he said, "and everyone knew I wanted to be alone." That day Dietzel heard a knock on the door. It was Athletic Director Jim Corbett, who intruded on Dietzel's pregame practice for the only time in their seven-year relationship.

He brought over a Colonel Rebel doll fixed like a voodoo figure with a blackened eye and tape all over. A sign on the doll read: "Hell, Coach, them Tigers are hell!" A smaller message from Corbett to Dietzel said, "Somehow, coach, I feel this is our night."

"Never before and never after that did Jim do anything like that," Dietzel said. "I thought it was kind of strange at the time."

Brewer found things strange, too. "I could have been the Billy Cannon of that night," he said. Brewer recovered two fumbles, one by Cannon which led to a 3-0 Ole Miss lead.

"In the third quarter," he added, "I knocked down a pass about our 18, but if I had played it for the interception, I think I could have brought it back a long way. I was heading for the Ole Miss bench, and there was nothing in front of me."

Dietzel reflected. "The whole week was unusual. "There was just something about it. . . . I remember Walter Stewart of the *Memphis Commercial Appeal* writing his prediction in the Tuesday or Wednesday paper. Walter pointed out Ole Miss was bigger, that LSU was quicker, but that both teams were so good they would nullify each other.

"He added that a game of this type usually turns out rather dull, but that somewhere, somehow, the superstar will do something to win it. Walter predicted that Billy Cannon will do that for LSU. It was about as clairvoyant a statement as I've seen."

Nobody was picking LSU a year later when the 1-4-0 Tigers invaded Oxford against the unbeaten Rebels, who needed a last-second field goal to get out with a 6-6 tie. A year after that, a great LSU team was able to penetrate Ole Miss' side of the field only twice, but scored both times in a 10-7 victory.

Charlie McClendon's ninth-ranked 1964 Tigers were nearly trapped by a 3-2-1 Rebel team that apparently had been caught reading its preseason clippings. Ole Miss scored the only two times it crossed midfield and held a seemingly insurmountable 10-3 fourth-quarter lead over an LSU that seemed leaderless.

Quarterback Pat Screen left the game with an injury, leaving the Tigers in the hands of untested back-up Billy Ezell.

The seven-point lead seemed to grow larger with each passing second. LSU invaded Rebel territory on nine of its 12 possessions, but could manage only a field goal, and Ezell threw the first two interceptions of the season.

Buster Brown stood on the Tiger goal-line to punt with seven minutes to go. Doug Cunningham took the ball at the Rebel 47 and it was there the gris-gris again took hold. Don Ellen, an LSU guard charging downfield, knocked a blocker into Cunningham, who fumbled.

Six plays later, LSU was on the Rebel 19 on second-and-10. Ezell called "flanker circle route" in the huddle, a play that required right end Billy Masters to run downfield and button-hook.

"I started running," Masters said, "but I got a sudden notion to keep going when the Ole Miss defensive man was running in. I guess he was looking for me to hook to the outside." Ezell dropped a soft pass into Masters' hands with no one within 10 yards. That brought the Tigers to 10-9, and a two-point conversion decision with 3:30 to play.

That set up Moreau's memorable heroics. Ezell called exactly the same play, with Masters hooking to the outside, deep. Moreau, a flanker, cut to the sidelines, and running back Gawain DiBetta went to the shallow area, all in the same zone.

Luke probably couldn't have made a better play — all for naught.

"I thought we had the thing under control," said Ole Miss coach Johnny Vaught. "It was a bit of an unusual game."

Moreau said later, "Before the game Pat (Screen) and I were talking about heaven. We were wondering what it would be like to have a vision. Now I have an idea. When I was coming off the field, with my eyes closed after those two points, I think I had one. . . . You might laugh, but nothing like it has ever happened to me before."

Archie Manning broke Tiger hearts with a stunning performance in which he almost single-handedly wrecked LSU's unbeaten 1969 team, 26-23, and three seasons after that Bert Jones took the Tigers the length of the field to beat the Rebels, 17-16, with no time left on the clock.

Even in years when nothing is at stake but the satisfaction of doing in a hated opponent, LSU-Ole Miss theatrics can be staggering. In 1977, the 6-5 Rebels jumped on LSU at the half, then watched the 8-3 Bayou Bengals come back for a 28-21 victory.

In 1979, sophomore quarterback John Fourcade led Ole Miss to a 17-0 lead just before the half. Then Fourcade, from New Orleans, turned to the LSU bench and waved his finger, as in "No. 1," at the Tigers, many of whom he knew and played against. LSU almost instantly came to life, and pulled off a 28-24 victory — one which was not assured until a last minute interception of Fourcade in the end zone.

A nail-biter which produced a 27-24 Ole Miss victory came in 1984, and the Rebels pulled off a numbing 21-19 victory at Tiger Stadium in 1986 against one of LSU's better teams. Still, as Curley Hallman struggled in his first season as Tiger coach in 1991, LSU was able

HAUL IT IN — Doug Moreau handles a two-point conversion pass from Billy Ezell which pushed LSU to an 11-10 victory over Ole Miss in 1964.

to pop Brewer's Johnny Rebs, 25-22.

"I'm not sure what it is," Brewer said, "but these schools go into an emotional frenzy at the sight of each other."

"There's just something magical about that series," McClendon added. "It's an electric happening. I think it's because the schools are so close. It's like rubbing elbows with a friend, but there's friction."

MIRACLE — Brad Davis ties the game with no time left on this TD reception in the 1972 LSU-Ole Miss clash.

AUTOMATIC — Rusty Jackson nails the game-winning PAT to give LSU a 17-16 win over Ole Miss in 1972.

CHARLIE MAC
26

Charlie McClendon reflected on his career at LSU and mused: "I'll probably be dead before the next man wins as many games as I have."

True enough.

McClendon coached the Tigers to 137 victories, nearly 30 percent of all LSU victories at the time of his retirement in 1979 and 70 percent of all games he coached. McClendon also:

■ Coached 17 All-Americans, more than all other LSU coaches combined in a century of Tiger football

■ Coached LSU in 13 bowl games

■ Coached the Tigers 18 years, longest tenure of any head coach in Tiger annals

■ Twice was named Southeastern Conference Coach of the Year and once National Coach of the Year

In short, McClendon was the most successful (137-59-7) football coach in Tiger history. The McClendon Era was, if not exactly the golden age of LSU football, then the gold-plated age, and the most successful long-term span in the program's history.

It was a time when McClendon's Tigers stood shoulder-to-shoulder with the legions of Parseghian, Royal, Broyles.

And yet he was forced out of his job, like some 3-7 football ragamuffin.

That is, in part, the fate of a Tiger coach who can't beat Alabama. Charlie Mac was just 2-14 against his old mentor Bear Bryant, and it ate at the guts of some Tigers, some of whom sat in end zone seats and some of whom sat in the seats of the school's Board of Supervisors.

Of course, there were some mighty good football teams around the South

SORRY, ARCHIE — LSU Head Coach Charles McClendon is carried off the field after LSU's 61-17 defeat of Archie Manning and Ole Miss in 1970.

that experienced the same problem. And a lot of them were healthy football teams. McClendon may have set an all-time NCAA record by going against Ole Miss (then at its football zenith, and LSU's most emotional opponent) and Alabama five consecutive years without his No. 1 quarterback.

"It's tough enough beating those people back-to-back with your number one quarterback," McClendon once reflected.

In those days it was always fashionable to believe that Mac didn't get the most out of his talent.

McClendon was appreciated far more in the real football world. All-America safety Tommy Casanova said, "We were just a bunch of small, slow kids that didn't realize (their shortcomings). We didn't grow as big as the kids in the Midwest or on the East Coast or West Coast, but we just got out there and scrapped with them for 60 minutes every game. I just think Coach Mac and the tradition of LSU football just brought it out of us."

Casanova said in a discussion on LSU with Cincinnati Bengals coach Paul Brown and some assistant coaches, "I said, 'Gosh knows, we should have won this and we should have won that.' They just

busted out laughing.

"He (Brown) said, overstating his point just a bit, 'You guys shouldn't win four games a year. Look at the amount of talent you put in the pros. You guys shouldn't win what you win.

"They just marveled at the record Coach Mac had year after year, winning 70 to 80 percent of his games. Brown said, 'You guys just don't have the talent to do what you do. We just can't believe it.'"

LSU football has been a roller coaster ride since McClendon left, sometimes very good, other times not so good. Casanova noticed it too. "I think when Coach Mac left, the program changed. The intensity was gone. That's what's missing, They have just never had that intensity (again)."

McClendon became head coach in the midst of controversy after Paul Dietzel broke Tiger hearts by accepting the head coaching job at Army after the January 1, 1962, Orange Bowl game with Colorado.

"I was the last to know," McClendon, then LSU's defensive coach, said of Dietzel's departure. "After

MILLER — LSU Head Coach Charles McClendon with All-America tackle Fred Miller.

CHOLLY MAC — *Charles McClendon gives Buddy Lee a few pointers.*

everybody else had heard it. It was public knowledge by the time of the bowl game. Paul didn't realize the people here were going to be mad and upset. I did realize this. Paul was going to recommend me for the job; to me, that would be the kiss of death. You know, you don't leave people upset and then make a recommendation. So, in all fairness to my family, I had to say that I didn't want the recommendation. Period.

Paul meant nothing but the best for me, but I knew I couldn't accept his recommendation."

The Tigers carried Mac off the Orange Bowl field, the moment he said was his greatest to that point. "I think this was their way of saying I had their recommendation, and that's the best. But it didn't fall that way.

"LSU didn't make a move for a while. And of all the places I ever wanted

to coach in my life — at LSU and my alma mater, Kentucky — both were offered to me at the same time. You talk about a real turmoil. My family left it strictly up to me. I knew I actually would have more pressure at LSU than at Kentucky, where they hadn't been winning. How do you compete with a team and a man (Dietzel) who have been national champions. I knew if I didn't keep the winning image LSU had I'd have everything to lose. What affected my decision to stay more than anything else were my personal ties. And we made it over the hump."

It wasn't easy. Just as Jim Corbett offered McClendon a four-year contract, Dietzel was informing the New York press that LSU was no longer a challenge, and how could anyone fail to win there.

In other words, the only way LSU could lose was if McClendon screwed up. "I'm sure Paul didn't mean it like it sounded. But it didn't read good, I'll put it that way," McClendon said.

McClendon recalled that one of the first questions asked of him by a member of the athletic board "was who I was going to be like: Dietzel, Bryant, or who? I told them I had better be Charlie McClendon. The one thing I felt I could do and be consistent in doing was to be honest with my football team, the people I worked with, and let the chips fall where they may. It might not be good copy, but as long as you can keep winning, your football

team makes interesting reading."

For the next 18 years he was Charlie Mac, his own man, a regular guy who said, "I guess I'm a little bit like Mae West. I never met a man I didn't like."

There was plenty of success in the early years, a memorable defeat of Texas in the 1963 Cotton Bowl, and a stunning upset in the '66 Cotton of an Arkansas team sniffing strongly at a national championship. McClendon coached the 1969 Tigers, perhaps the best football team in school history. From '69 through '73, for five consecutive years, the Bayou Bengals won nine games a season.

Somehow, it never seemed to measure up to what was expected — which, of course, was undefeated seasons.

Two things mixed to ensure McClendon's departure long before he was ready to hang up his whistle: the first was the frustrating inability to beat Alabama (the Ole Miss dilemma had been solved); and the second was an 1971 offer to coach Texas A&M.

WE DID IT!! — Charles McClendon celebrates with Jim Corbett following LSU's 14-7 upset victory over Arkansas in the 1966 Cotton Bowl.

When McClendon took his '71 Tigers to El Paso to play Iowa State in the Sun Bowl, a story broke, out of all places Nashville, saying he had been offered the A&M job and was seriously considering it. The board, moving with uncommon haste, ended that notion in a hurry, giving McClendon a new five-year rollover contract. In other words, at the end of each year, the contract was still in effect for five years, giving McClendon security.

Years later it was learned that the A&M offer was not an official overture, but more of a "feeler."

165

The disclosure really steamed some members of the board.

When the program slipped (and the word "slipped" is used advisedly because it never exactly became a sinking ship; 5-6 in 1975 was McClendon's worst record), the board kept McClendon sitting in a car for hours during a rainstorm at the University of New Orleans, an LSU satellite campus, while they debated his future.

What they came up with was either allow the board to buy out his contract, or let him coach for two more seasons then step aside. Because his assistants' lives were affected, McClendon accepted the latter. He later got a third season when Paul Dietzel was named athletic director.

"You know, I'm somebody everywhere but Baton Rouge," McClendon said in 1979. "Hell, I can go to New York, Chicago, Los Angeles, anywhere and be at the top. But Baton Rouge . . . it's a little bit different. Sometimes I think a man needs to be a horse's back end to grab the attention.

"Some say if I had politicked a little things might have been different. But if it made a difference I didn't want any part of it. I have been proud to say I've done whatever is best for LSU, not what is best for Charlie McClendon. And so, therefore, I don't have any apology to make. Disappointment, but no bitterness."

It made for a vicious cycle. McClendon beat three previously undefeated teams in bowls in his first six years, and the Bayou Bengals were a feared opponent to the nation's football elite — Notre Dame, Texas, Southern Cal — under McClendon. But all the back-biting and subterfuge by those who claimed "undying love" of LSU eventually took a toll.

After a while the cry that "Mac can't win the big one" became a self-fulfilling prophecy as some blue-chippers were scared off to other programs. None of his last eight teams finished in the Top 20.

Carl Maddox, who was athletic director during most of McClendon's tenure, once said knowingly, "Mac is like the biblical prophet without honor in his own country. I think some of these fans may realize what he's accomplished after he's gone."

They realize it now.

The predicament was odd in that McClendon was recognized as a superior coach by the press nationwide. Taking the formula of a proven winner and man of integrity, which LSU said it would use to chose its next coach, the universal feeling was the man it wanted was already on the job.

Before the 1979 season, at a press gathering where McClendon was scheduled to give a run-down of his team before LSU's opener with Colorado, John Logue of *Southern Living* took the forum and said, "We've always known LSU was a special place and endowed with a special spirit." Logue had spent 30 minutes that afternoon composing a poem of that Tiger spirit and Charlie McClendon entitled "Final Call." Logue read:

Mac, how do we stand?
Alone.
Well, we've done that before.
Yes.
In Dallas that day and Arkansas unbeaten.

Labruzzo, remember him from Cutoff? And Corbett, afterward, shouting in your ear, "We stuck it up their a—es."

No. Not many were with us. The best of us are gone. Winston, Stovall, Truax, Moreau, Bevan, Casanova. And Casanova under the ball in the air and nothing all of Mississippi could do.

Casanova's not here?

No.

Where are Cantrelle, Jones, Capone, and Estay?

Jones grew up, and left with the best we had.

Alexander the Great?

The best of the best. He would be here if he could.

Who do we have?

Us.

Where do we stand?

Here.

Alone?

No. I can hear them who were with us in the pit at Notre Dame.

And tomorrow at Colorado?

We fight!

It was all Charlie McClendon could do to keep from weeping.

THE RUSTON RIFLE
27

He was a consolation prize, a gawky blue-eyed kid with mussed fawn-colored hair and a big-toothed grin. And he would become the biggest basement bargain in Louisiana college football annals.

Bert Jones walked onto the Louisiana State University campus in 1969 as the unheralded afterthought of a recruiting TKO. He quarterbacked in 27 LSU victories in a 36-game career, would stamp his signature throughout the school's offensive record book, and would be considered by panting profes-

SIGN HIM UP — Bert Jones signs with LSU, 1969, witnessed by his parents and LSU Head Coach Charles McClendon.

sionals as the rightful heir to Johnny Unitas.

From such deeds are ugly ducklings transformed.

There was never any doubt in Jones' mind that he was a supreme talent. Almost everyone else was dazzled by the polished poise of another north Louisiana quarterback — Joe Ferguson.

Ferguson, of

Shreveport-Woodlawn, amassed awesome statistics directing a pro-style offense while Jones, still growing into his 6-foot-3 frame, labored for Ruston High, which ran a conservative offense. Every coach in the South — and even beyond — wanted Ferguson. Louisiana Tech, Tulane and Grambling showed the most interest in Jones.

Grambling coach Eddie Robinson, who noted that Bert's father Dub had played and coached at Cleveland and that Bert's youth was spent pestering Frank Ryan and Jim Ninowski for football tips, asked: "How could he miss? He was watching films of his dad running passing routes when other kids were watching cartoons."

RUSTON RIFLE — Bert Jones is LSU's only All-American at quarterback.

While Gov. John McKeithen and Y.A. Tittle were trying to woo Ferguson to LSU, the Tigers also made a cursory offer of a grant-in-aid to Jones, projecting him as a backup, no doubt. Intelligent and realistic, Jones realized that no school would have room for both and waited for Ferguson to make his choice. When Ferguson opted for Arkansas, Jones signed with LSU.

"Shucks," Robinson said, "I wanted Bert to play for us. We're right down the road, you know, and I've known the family for years. I'll tell you, he would have made me a helluva better football coach."

Jones had an interesting pedigree. His grandfather on his mother's side lettered in football and baseball at Tulane in the early 1900s and later played both sports professionally. "I can remember him holding me on his knee teaching me to throw the knuckler," Bert said. "When he was in college, he'd pitch doubleheaders, the first game right-handed, the second left-handed."

Dub Jones, Bert's father, had a been a jitterbug runner during the World War II years, and was the only man

SACKED – LSU's Ronnie Estay (78) sacks Auburn's Pat Sullivan for a safety in 1970.

to play for LSU when it defeated Tulane, and for Tulane when it defeated LSU. A 1942 freshman, the 6-foot-2, 158-pound Dub was a third-string tailback behind Sulcer Harris and Alvin Dark in a single wing offense that had Steve Van Buren at blocking back. That season the Tigers whipped the Green Wave, 18-6. The following season, because of the Navy's V-12 program, the 6-foot-4, 190-pound Dub spearheaded a 27-0 victory over Orange Bowl-bound LSU. He went on to a distinguished career as a receiver for the Cleveland Browns, where he coached after retiring as a player.

Dub's son always wanted to follow his dad in football.

"When I was in first grade," Bert reminisced, "my teacher asked me what I wanted to be when I grew up. She expected me to say a policeman or fireman or something like that. I told her I wanted to be a professional football player. She said, 'Suppose you can't. Then what? I told her I didn't want to be anything else."

The teacher, Mrs. Ball, who taught both Bert and Dub, may have wanted to

provided the boy with a shelter. An attack of rickets at age two left Bert an awkward-looking child. "It left him bowlegged and pigeon-toed," Dub said during Bert's college years. "He had to wear braces for two years. Actually, the disease hurt his appearance more than his ability. To some, he might still look a little awkward. That's deceiving. He can stand flat-footed today and clear six feet."

What Bert and Dub both knew, but what others had to be shown when he reported to LSU as a freshman, became quickly apparent on the Tiger practice field — this young prospect could hurl thunderbolts. He had the confidence of a champion, which his teammates loved, and he was headstrong, which bothered his coaches.

Jones' size, speed (4.7 seconds in the 40) and that slingshot arm quickly had LSU fans beside themselves with anticipation. The Baby Bengal quarterback, it was plain, was the school's best passing talent since Tittle. It made for an itchy situation: even though the 1969 Fightin' Tigers, possibly the best of Coach Charlie McClendon's career, won

nine of 10 games, fans were drooling at the thought of all that raw ability that was quarterbacking the freshman team at the steering wheel of the varsity offense.

But Jones didn't figure to play as a sophomore either. Two experienced quarterbacks were returning, and Jones was projected to spend the 1970 season as a redshirt. A preseason tragedy changed all that. Butch Duhe', LSU's No. 2 quarterback, died of a brain ailment. The "Ruston Rifle," as Jones was being called, moved up and played 40 percent of the time in McClendon's two-QB system.

However, Jones was as headstrong as he was talented, and it was clear he thought he knew more about offensive football than his coaches. Bert spent a lot of time in McClendon's doghouse.

A knee operation in January, and another during spring practice, shoved Jones behind converted cornerback Paul Lyons. Lyons was 5-foot-10, 190-pounds, and possessed nothing close to Jones' natural ability. He did run the option very well, no small inducement in McClendon's rush-oriented offense, and the team responded to Lyons.

"He (Jones) knew the game all right," confided one of Jones' teammates, "but not as thoroughly as he thought he did. He didn't accept advice easily. I think it was pretty hard on him, especially when he saw how the team reacted to Paul Lyons. What made it hard was — Bert realized as everyone else did — there was no comparison between his athletic ability and Paul's. This was college, not the pros."

No one knew it at the time, but the unhappy Jones was contemplating a transfer, a situation that would come out years later when Jones was asked what was the highlight of his collegiate career. "Getting out," he retorted.

McClendon, Jones said, never fully utilized his talents. "I probably threw more third-down passes than any man in history . . . but never a first-down pass. So, I'd say my ability was not fully utilized at LSU, especially considering the receiving crew we had."

Acknowledging that McClendon also had excellent qualities as a coach, Jones said that the "getting

out" quote was misinterpreted but that "there were just some things that, all things being equal, I would have done differently."

But he decided against transferring.

Lyons was McClendon's starting quarterback for nine 1971 games. Then Notre Dame, with an exceptional defense, came to Baton Rouge. A verbal ripple fluttered through the crowd as Jones — unquestionably still the Tigers' best pure pitcher — trotted out with the starting unit. When it was over, the Irish defense down in flames, no one ever considered Jones a No. 2 quarterback again. In an extraordinary display, LSU utterly destroyed Notre Dame, 28-8, at the time Ara Parseghian's worst Irish defeat.

Jones had the Bayou Bengals ahead 7-0 in fewer than three minutes. He ended the evening with two touchdown passes and another rushing. Jones' cousin, wide receiver Andy Hamilton, caught three scoring passes and the Tiger defense, all on fourth downs, threw the Irish back from an inch from the LSU goal, from the 10, and from the three.

In the season's final three games, including a Sun Bowl appearance, starter Jones threw eight touchdown passes and completed 30-of-46 attempts.

McClendon had a better-than-average team coming back for 1972, one that would win nine games, although in retrospect it was a team Jones carried to an extra victory or two. After the Auburn game, in which Jones passed for 240 yards and three touchdowns, McClendon said, "Bert is now a disciplined quarterback. He's not just throwing the ball to put it in the air . . . . If it's a short pass, fine. If it's a long one, that's okay, too. I can't say it was always that way when he hit campus, but he's picked it up and it's making a difference."

Jones added: "Passing is a never-ending job of trying to beat perfection. I'm always trying to do that."

Perfection is an overused jock term, but Jones put some meat on it against ancient rival Ole Miss, at least in the final three minutes. The loose Rebels, playing only for pride in a disappointing season, turned the Tigers every which way but out for 57 minutes. A missed field goal that would have given Ole Miss an insurmountable 19-10 lead with three minutes to go allowed Jones to breathe life into the listless Bayou Bengals.

"We were in a position where we had to throw," Jones mused, "and we did."

He certainly did, in a memorable, frenzied race against the clock, Jones jockeyed his team steadily upfield on a series of short and medium darters to his backs, taking whatever the defense would yield until 70 of the necessary 80 yards were made up.

The drive appeared to die at the Rebel 10 when a fourth down pass fell incomplete. Ole Miss was guilty of interference, however, and Jones got off a controversial two passes in the final four seconds. The horn went off with the snap on the game's last play. Jones swung a pass to running back Brad Davis, who wheeled into the end zone. Rusty Jackson's conversion was delayed several minutes because of the pandemonium, but he finally kicked it and LSU was a 17-16 victor.

> *The Rev. Stanley Ott strolled out of raucous Tiger Stadium the night of November 20, 1971, after LSU massacred Notre Dame, 28-8, and passed a group of deliriously happy students — high on the victory.*
>
> *Their chants, yells and laughter quieted, however, as the priest's Roman collar was noticed. "We're sorry your team lost, Father," one said awkwardly but politely as the bishop of Baton Rouge went by. Bishop Ott laughed, and said with a wide smile, "No, you don't understand. My team won. GEAUX, TIGERS!"*
>
> *Bishop Ott grew up in Gretna, across the Mississippi River from New Orleans, and said he was "a committed Tulane follower" from boyhood through young adulthood. The second most important happening in his life was being sent to LSU as student chaplain. "I so enjoyed it there with those wonderful kids and so many wonderful experiences. Let's just say, I underwent a major conversion."*

"You know what he did?" asked the amazed McClendon when queried about a conference he held with Jones just prior to the touchdown. "He winked at me! Can you believe that? He winked at me."

LSU ended the season in the Bluebonnet Bowl as Jones was being called the finest pure passer in college football. No one was more appreciative of his accomplishments than McClendon. "Bert came to LSU with a strong arm and strong convictions," the coach said. "He had been exposed to the pro game, and was pretty set in his ideas. What I'm saying is he wasn't the most coachable boy we've ever had. But now he's more aware of the facts of life, aware of the overall picture. He's always been highly intelligent. Maturity is what did it."

Joe Thomas, the general manager of the Baltimore Colts, was also appreciative of Jones' talents; he wanted them for his organization. Thomas was a veritable prophet without football honor in his own city after stripping the Colts of a legion of heroes, including the legendary Johnny Unitas. He started trying to

16 OLE MISS [0:0] LSU 10
3 TIME OUTS LEFT 0
2 DOWN 10 TO GO YD LN 10 QTR 4

Bert Jones' pass that beat Ole Miss in 1972 with no time remaining.

reassemble the team by obtaining Bert Jones with the second pick of the 1973 draft.

Thomas told *Sports Illustrated*, "The kid I wanted in the 1973 draft was Bert Jones. He had a Koufax arm and a great football background. Well, Houston had the No. 1 pick and New Orleans the No. 2, and the way I saw it, they were both fixed with young quarterbacks. Houston wanted to draft a big defensive lineman, not a quarterback. So I went around the back door and gave the Saints (defensive end) Billy Newsome and a fourth-round pick for their No. 2 in the first round. Houston drafted John Matuszak, just as I figured, and I got Bert Jones." Who turned out to be one of the best pro quarterbacks of his era.

Bert fulfilled his dream, and followed his father into the NFL — just as he told his first grade teacher.

RACING WITH THE MOON

28

There was Bert Jones, lashing the Tigers across the moonlit field, like Ben Hur and his chargers in the chariot races of ancient Rome, in a frenzied gallop to the finish line.

It was the night some say time literally stood still.

When it came to a stop, 00:1 burned brightly from the Tiger Stadium scoreboard through the Louisiana darkness, and into the souls of the Ole Miss Rebels.

It was the night of LSU's most improbable — and maybe most memo-rable — victory, 17-16 over the University of Mississippi.

Rebel faithful angrily insist more than two decades later it was an impossible feat.

Jones, with one second, or less, to play, and LSU at the Rebel 10, swung a pass out to tail-back Brad Davis at the flag who juggled the ball but dove into the end zone to tie the game. The ensuing PAT gave LSU the victory that November 4, 1972, evening.

In the game's last 3:02, LSU had made up 80 yards, and overcame two fourth down situations in a do-or-die drive against the Rebels, who clearly outplayed the Tigers most of the night, to keep alive the nation's longest victory streak at 11 straight. "It seemed like time — apart from the clock — stopped," Norris Weese, then the Ole Miss quarter-back, recalled, "and the stadium just exploded. In slow motion, everyone seemed to jump 10 feet out of their seats. It was a memorable moment, but it wasn't a pleasant moment." Harry Harrison, who hit Davis as the Tiger back went over the goal line pylon, argues now that Davis never had control of the ball, and that he frequently dreams about that play, except that in his dreams he intercepts and runs for 95-yard touchdown.

Rebel proponents from that day to this argue that LSU benefitted from faulty time-keeping, citing the impossibility of getting off three plays in the final 10 seconds.

Actually, the controversy centers on one play, not three. With 10 seconds left, interference was called on Ole Miss, stopping the clock with four seconds to play and putting the Tigers at the Rebel 10.

After a pass over the middle and into the end zone was broken up, the one disputed second remained. The time remaining on LSU's last play, the touchdown, was inconsequential because obviously a game cannot end while a play is in progress.

Whether the game should have ended on the second-to-last play is the crux of the matter.

There's almost no argument the pass took more than four seconds, but because the electric clock runs on tenths of a second, LSU may have been working with a hair under five seconds, not four.

James W. Campbell Jr. of Memphis was the electric clock operator that night, and he admits the last few plays of that series were handled differently than usual. The clock operator usually stands at the line of scrimmage where he activates a stopped clock at the snap of the ball. But for some reason, perhaps someone was standing on the wire, the cord did not reach the line of scrimmage on the last few plays. Campbell said he was trying to see through the feet of the quarterback and center to catch the precise instant of the snap, but couldn't. He started the clock at the first movement of the quarterback.

SEC commissioner Boyd McWhorter was in attendance and said he didn't realize there was a controversy until he returned to Birmingham the next day. "I didn't question it at the time," McWhorter said. "I was like everyone else, caught up in the excitement of a thrilling game."

Former Rebel coach Billy Kinard, 20 years later a high school coach in Alabama, brusquely refused to discuss the issue, but in Lawrence Wells' book "Ole Miss Football," Kinard was quoted as saying, "In my opinion, it ain't no human way for them to do that."

There was a difference of opinion. Southeastern Conference officials were then headquartered in Atlanta, and George Gardner, the supervisor of SEC officials, took the film to Georgia Tech and broke it down frame by frame. The SEC could not find fault with Campbell.

New Orleans sportscaster Buddy Diliberto, with a reputation of being an independent journalist, responding to pleas by Ole Miss fans, had his WVUE-TV engineers break down the film, too. Diliberto also could not find Campbell wrong in what was obviously a hairline call.

Stan Torgerson, the Ole Miss announcer and a respected and honest observer of college athletics, said he was stunned.

"I've timed that film 30 times since then," Torgerson said, "and not once was it even close (that the second-to-last play took less than four seconds). In my mind it is not possible. I am convinced the official was in serious error."

Campbell was found guilty of one misdeed by his fellow officials, but it had nothing to do with the correctness of his performance in Tiger Stadium. Referees now say he broke an unspoken rule by allowing the second on the clock whether it was the right time or not. No one will argue if the second runs out, the theory goes, but leaving it on only opens the refs up to controversy. Bobby Gaston, now the SEC supervisor of officials and the head linesman in the 1972 LSU-Ole Miss game, pointed out that had the same sequence occurred at another point, in other words, not at game's end, nothing probably would have ever been said.

The only controversy Jones was aware of when he looked up and saw one second remaining was that he had another chance after another pass interference penalty was not called. "They interfered again," Jones said, "and got away with it." Former LSU coach Charlie McClendon remembered Jones "rubbing his hands in a towel like he was going to bore a hole in it." During a timeout called by Ole Miss, McClendon said he told his quarterback, "Bert, this is what you came to LSU for." Jones winked, and trotted back out to pull off his most memorable feat as a Tiger.

That defeat still burns, though, in the collective pit of the Rebels. Weese, who grew up in Chalmette, Louisiana, outside New Orleans, said he remembers that game more than any he played, high school, college or pro, because of the circumstances. "Two plays in four seconds?" he asks rhetorically. "It just doesn't happen."

On the other hand, when Davis, a dentist in Opelousas, Louisiana, needs an emotional lift, he watches a tape of that last second play. "When I'm down," Davis said, "it picks me up."

Days after the LSU-Ole Miss game, a sign went up on the Louisiana-Mississippi border with the inscription: "Entering Louisiana, set your clocks back four seconds."

And the next year, the score in the Rebel football brochure read: Ole Miss 16, LSU 10 plus 7.

The Tigers got even a year later, after a 51-14 waxing of the Rebels. The *Daily Reveille*, the LSU school paper, ran the score as Ole Miss 14, LSU 10 plus 7 plus 7 plus 7, plus 7, plus 7, plus 6.

But it's always small events that set great events in motion. In this case, a torn jersey may well have determined the controversial outcome. Davis was in the game to catch Jones' touchdown pass because starting tailback Chris Dantin, the leading Tiger rusher in the game with 60 yards and who picked up a critical first down with less than a minute to play, gaining six yards to the Rebel 24 on fourth and one, had his jersey ripped on that play.

An official warned Dantin about it. After the interference call which gave LSU its first and goal at the

10 with four seconds to play, the official told Dantin, "You gotta go. They can't see your number in the pressbox." Dantin told Glenn Guilbeau of the Alexandria Town Talk, "I was arguing with the ref, but there wasn't enough time and we didn't have any more timeouts."

So Dantin went out and in the confusion didn't get back in for the game's last two plays — which turned out to be a good thing. Dantin said had he been in the game he's sure he would have talked Jones or McClendon out of the play LSU used to score — which was the Tigers' two-point conversion play.

"You don't run a two-point play from the 10-yard line," he said with some exasperation even after all these years. "It was designed to go (only) three yards."

On this particular night, though, LSU was master of time and space.

PRIME TIME — *Fireworks explode on an LSU Saturday Night.*

"HEY, FIGHTIN' TIGERS"

29

Bob Brodhead, then the athletic director at LSU, watched as "The Golden Band from Tigerland" tromped onto the field before a game, sounding the clarion call of all Tigers: The spine-tingling opening notes of "Tiger Rag."

"If I could ever get LSU football to the level of the LSU band," mused Brodhead, moved, like everyone else in the stadium, by the syncopation, color, brass and precision of the marching musical Tigers, "I wouldn't have any worries."

Brodhead was making

that comparison with a nine-victory football squad, and knew it.

The Golden Band from Tigerland was conceived, like so many things LSU, in the fertile mind of Huey Long. An 85-member military band was sponsored by LSU in 1934. Seymour Weiss, a close friend and confidant of Long's, and the manager of New Orleans' opulent Roosevelt Hotel, kept a suite available for the senator whenever he was in the city.

Castro Carazo was the Roosevelt's director of music and orchestra leader at the time, and Long

enjoyed his arrangements. Carazo, a small man who was a native of Costa Rica, was once summoned to Baton Rouge. He arrived at Long's Heidelberg Hotel at 11:30 p.m., and the senator was asleep, so Carazo fluffed up a pillow himself and fell asleep in the living room. Two or three hours later Long roused Carazo and told him the reason he was called: Long needed a new campaign song. Carazo wrote "Every Man a King" in a half-hour, Long put the words to it by 5 a.m., and it was played on a state-wide radio show that evening.

Long could barely stand

CADET BAND — *The forerunner to the Tiger Band — the Cadet Band, 1896.*

Castro Carazo directing the Tiger band in a special appearance in the 1970s.

listening to the wide breadth of Carazo's popular music because the mental comparison he always made to the martial marches of his beloved LSU was maddening. Long and Carazo ran into each at the Roosevelt one day, with the band leader on his way to a concert for school children.

The words spilled out of Long's mouth, with no apparent thought of contradiction that Weiss had fired Carazo, and that Long was giving him a job as the band director at LSU. It was settled.

Carazo transformed LSU's military band into a colorful, crack marching unit of 240 members which pioneered the glittering halftime shows which have mesmerized generations of Tiger Stadium crowds, and he and Long collaborated on "Fight for LSU," and "Touchdown for LSU," two of the school's most popular fight songs.

Almost three decades later the Tiger athletic director was Jim Corbett, who was in New York on NCAA television business in 1962 when he took in the Broadway musical "Wildcat," with Lucille Ball, and was smitten with the

SPEEDY — LSU tailback Garry James and Mike the Tiger celebrate an LSU victory.

catchy show tune "Hey, Look Me Over."

He returned to his hotel room unable to get "Hey, Look Me Over" out of his head. Corbett, who once said he would trade two All-SEC tackles for a song like Georgia Tech's "Rambling Wreck," decided to try and get the "Wildcat" song for LSU.

Entering considerable negotiations, Corbett finally received permission to use the music with exclu-

sive rights to it on the college and university level. Song writer Gene Quaw was hired to compose new words for LSU.

Corbett's friends Bill LeBlanc and F.T. Bordelon heard the first version on a family fishing trip to Grand Isle. Corbett was quite pleased with it, and got the kids of all three families to sing it. It was fun, but his buddies thought it needed a little work.

Corbett didn't change it, and "Hey, Fightin' Tigers" began to grow on them. On LSU, too — except for one man.

Band director Bill Swor was adamantly opposed to the new fight song. "To the rest of the world," Swor argued, "that song will always be "Hey, Look Me Over." Corbett retorted, "The rest of the world isn't coming to LSU football games."

PRE-GAME PANDEMONIUM — The Golden Band from Tigerland's pre-game performance is a vital component of all Tiger football games

"Hey, Fightin' Tigers" has since become the most played and popular of LSU fight songs.

FIGHT FOR LSU
(LSU Fight Song)

Like Knights of old,
Let's fight to hold
The glory of the Purple Gold

Let's carry through, Let's die or do
To win the game for dear old LSU

Keep trying for that high score;
Come on and fight,
We want some more, some more.
Come on you tigers.
Fight! Fight! Fight!
for dear old LSU.
RAH!

HEY, FIGHTIN' TIGERS

(Adapted from the original composition "Hey, Look Me Over" from the Broadway production "Wildcat."

Hey, Fightin' Tigers,
Fight all the way
Play Fightin' Tigers, win the game today.
You've got the know how, you're doing fine,

There are fans, and there are fans. Men like "Big Jawn" McKeithen, James "Big Red" Braswell, Dr. Jack Andonie, Augie Cross and Terry Friedman are fans of the highest order.

McKeithen, governor of Louisiana in the 1960s, often had prospects to the mansion for breakfast and often put on a jump suit and left state business waiting while he went out to catch an afternoon practice.

McKeithen, a forceful personality, is called "the greatest Tiger of them all" by Cross, who should know.

"Baton Rouge is the greatest football town in America, my fren'," McKeithen once exclaimed during a game while he was governor. "Columbus, Ohio, don't even come close to the spirit we got right heah in this li'l ol' country town. Football is the social season and politics don't even come close. When you see football at LSU you see a spectacle, my fren'. A real spectacle."

Braswell holds the unofficial world record for nonstop cheering of the LSU taunt, "Tigerbait." Braswell was a fixture at Tiger athletic events for more than two decades — much to the amusement of some and much to the chagrin of others. Denied a practice field pass in the 1960s, Big Red showed his support for the Tigers by standing outside the practice field fence and yelling nonstop until practice was over. He began doing it day after day, and incessantly through any and all LSU games, to the point where other Tiger fans wanted him to shut up. He never did.

Andonie, a member of the LSU board and an LSU med-school grad, is a chip off George Kalil. He feels he owes LSU for his success in life. Andonie holds a special spot among upscale Tiger fans with his Tiger room, a private collection of memorabilia on display in the den of his lakefront home in Metairie, a suburb of New Orleans. With purple carpeting, gold walls and everything displayed from Tiger jerseys to toilet seats, the Tiger room is a mini-hall of LSU history.

Cross was a founder of the New Orleans-based Year Round Tiger Booster Club, a viable booster organization which sponsored many LSU functions before disbanding after 20 years because NCAA rules changed, making the presence of players at their get-togethers a violation. Cross never misses an LSU game and frequently attends practices in Baton Rouge. He mobilizes a mass of LSU support and can be counted on to phone radio call-in shows whenever an LSU opinion is required.

Sometimes you might think there are no limits to what a Tiger fan, with all that love pent up inside, might do.

Hang on to the ball as you hit the wall
And smash right through the line.

You've got to go for a touchdown,
Run up the score.

Make Mike the Tiger stand right up and roar
ROAR!

Give it all of your might as you fight tonight
and keep the goal in view:

Victory for L-S-U!

TIGER RAG
(Hold That Tiger)

Long ago, way down in the jungle
Someone got an inspira-

tion for a tune,
    And that jingle brought from the jungle
    Became famous mighty soon
    Thrills and chills it sends thru you!
    Hot! So hot, it burns you too!

    Tho' it's just the growl of the tiger
    It was written in a syncopated way,
    More and more they howl for the "Tiger"
    Ev'ry where you go today
    They're shoutin'

    Where's that Tiger!
Where's that Tiger!
    Where's that Tiger!
Where's that Tiger!
    Hold that Tiger! Hold that Tiger
    Hold that Tiger!

TOUCHDOWN FOR LSU

    Tigers! Tigers! They've come to town,
    They fight! They fight! Call a first down,
    Just look them over, and how they can go,
    Smashing the line with runs and passes high and low.

    Touchdown!

DAZZLING — LSU's Golden Girls add a certain zip to the LSU experience.

Touchdown! It's Tigers' score.
Give them hell and a little bit more.
Come on you Tigers,
Fight them, you Tigers,
Touchdown for LSU.
Rah! U. Rah!

LSU ALMA MATER

Where Stately oaks and broad magnolias
shade inspiring halls,
There stands our dear Alma Mater
who to us recalls
Fond memories that waken in our hearts
a tender glow,
And make us happy for the love
that we have learned to know.

All hail to thee our Alma Mater,
May greater glory, love unending
be forever thine.
Our worth in life will be thy worth
we pray to keep it true,
And thy spirit dwell in us forever . . . LSU.

CASTRO — LSU band director Castro Carazo collaborated with Huey Long to write "Touchdown for LSU" in 1935.

ALEXANDER THE GREAT

30

St. Mark wrote: "One came running."

That was gospel at LSU in the mid-1970s, the memorable years of Charles Alexander in the Tiger backfield.

He wasn't from Macedonia. He came out of Galveston, Texas. But at LSU he was Alexander the Great, a runner who left nine SEC records and 27 LSU records in his wake.

Alexander ranks with the very best who ever carried a ball at LSU — Doc Fenton, Steve Van Buren, Jim Taylor, Billy Cannon, Jerry Stovall, Dalton Hilliard. "He looks good in a hotel lobby," Dallas Cowboys player personnel director Gil Brandt sighed.

As a junior in 1977, Alexander was the nation's best all-purpose runner, with 1,686 yards on 311 attempts, a 5.4 average and 17 touchdowns. He caught 12 passes for 80 yards and, for good measure, was one-for-one passing for 17 yards.

Alexander left LSU not only as the Tigers' all-time leading rusher (4,035 yards), but also that of the SEC. He was still second in the LSU record book, behind Dalton Hilliard, and fourth in the SEC, behind Herschel Walker, Bo Jackson, and Hilliard through 1992.

Yet, no one had to come from so far behind to make a dent on the charts. To say Alexander had an inauspicious start would be understating the obvious. In his first two varsity games, as the back-up tailback to Terry Robiskie, Alexander had a net gain of one yard in 16 carries against Nebraska and Texas A&M.

By comparison, Alexander's teammate Robiskie, at the same point of his Tiger career, had 77 rushing yards. Billy

Cannon had 211, Art Cantrelle, 103, Brad Davis 55. By the end of the 1975 season, however, Alexander had made inroads, slight though they may have seemed at the time. An 81-yard game against Tulane in the finale gave Alexander 301 yards on 108 carries as a freshman.

Charlie McClendon recalled: "Against Nebraska he carried the ball eight times for a minus two yards. In the dressing room I patted him on the back and said, 'Charlie, things are going to get better.' He just looked at me and didn't say a word. Then came that real fine Texas A&M bunch and he carried eight times for a plus three (yards). So here's a total of 16 carries for one yard. I kept patting him on the back and saying, 'Things are going to get better.' Now we can laugh, look back and say that things really did get better."

That they did. Alexander's first 100-yard plus performance came against Vanderbilt (152) in the fifth game of his sophomore year. A 138-yard game against Ole

SWEETS– Charles Alexander still ranks second on LSU's all-time rushing charts with 4,035 yards and 42 TDs.

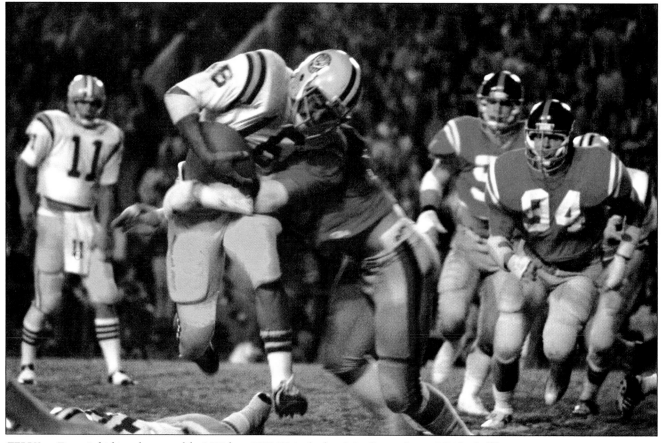

TERRY — Terry Robiskie, who starred for LSU from 1973-76, is the fourth-leading rusher in LSU football history.

Miss and 141 against Utah filled out the muscular Texan's seasonal stats to 876 yards on 155 carries as the Tigers began to depend more on their hammerin' reserve tailback.

Flashes of immense potential began to show as Alexander spelled Robiskie. If he ever learned to run under control, observers said, Alexander could develop into more than just a good back. He blossomed just when LSU needed it most.

LSU opened the 1977 season with a solid offensive line, but with Robiskie's graduation, only one real threat in the backfield. A solid corps of receivers returned, but the young Tiger quarterbacks were erratic. Defenses could — and did — tee off on Alexander and take their chances with the rest of the LSU offense.

To compound matters, the 1977 Tiger defense bore little resemblance to the brick walls McClendon's reputation was built on. Possession, buying time for the defense, became as much the responsibility of the offense as scoring.

"The Root Hogs," the offensive line composed of men who were far more students than athletes (including tackle Robert Dugas, now an M.D.; tackle Chris Rich, also an M.D.; center Jay Whitley, a dentist; and novelist John Ed Bradley, who backed up

Whitley), vowed to burrow as many traffic lanes for Alexander as possible. Alexander was clearly the linchpin of this team, and the Root Hogs were going to give him every opportunity to lead them to victory. It became a joke around Broussard Hall, the athletic dormitory, that Alexander wouldn't go into his room unless the door was opened by Dugas.

The battering ram onslaught left tattered and bruised defenses in its wake. Statisticians, however, may have had the most difficult task of 1977 — keeping up with Charlie Alexander.

He set school records for: most yards in a single game (237); touchdowns in a single game (4); carries in a single game (41); carries for a season (311); touchdowns in a season (17); and yards rushing in a season (1,686).

Southeastern Conference records included: rushes in a single game; average rushes per game (28.3); carries in a season and average rushing yards (153.3). And Alexander fumbled only

ROOT HOGS — Robert Dugas was part of the offensive line which paved the way for Charles Alexander.

three times.

The 1,686 total yards came principally from tackle to tackle, in the pit, and was accomplished with only one run as much as 43 yards.

"That's the incredible thing about him," said Vic Eumont, then a Tulane assistant. "I've seen backs I felt were better break-away threats. But not many who can take the pounding Charlie Alexander takes 20, 30, 40 times a game and still come back ready to do it again.

"I don't think I was really all that impressed with him (in 1976) until we started seeing film on him. He runs high, so he really takes some shots. But he doesn't fumble and he doesn't get hurt."

Eumont's sentiment must have been reinforced in the LSU-Green Wave game. Alexander carried 41 times for 231 yards and three touchdowns in a 20-17 victory.

At Galveston's Ball High School, track seemed to be Alexander's sport, even though he was named to Texas' football Super Team as a senior, an impressive accomplishment considering he was basically a second-string blocking back on a mediocre team throughout his prep career. In track, though, Alexander was a champion and listed as his biggest thrill on the questionnaire he returned to the LSU athletic department as "Running a 9.5 hundred."

"I have more love of football," he said matter-of-factly, "but track was my biggest thrill." Specifically, that thrill entailed winning two state championship events (the 100-yard dash and 220-yard relay) in 1973. That kind of success eluded Alexander in football.

Insisting he was not misused in high school, Alexander said he was simply a late bloomer. Actually, circumstances beyond his control may have had as much to do with his high school role as anything.

Ball High was also the alma mater of Kerry Jackson, a talented quarterback who signed a grant-in-aid with the University of Oklahoma. Some time after his first varsity season with the Sooners it was discovered Jackson's grade transcripts had been altered by a Ball assistant coach.

After the responsible parties had been dealt with, the Galveston school system began playing musical chairs with Ball. Alexander played for three coaches in three years.

Kermit Courville, who coached Ball to three state track championships in five years and served as a football assistant until the Jackson incident, said, "Charlie had potential all right, but each coach would come in with different systems and different ideas, and that hurt the kid. But Charlie had good games running as a second-teamer. He was sup-posed to move up as a senior, but then we changed coaches again, and the new man came in with a dead three-back offense and half the time nobody knew what they were doing back there. Shuffling them in and out like that, nobody touched the ball more than three or four times a game.

"There were times when Charlie would have 90 or 95 yards at the half, and never had his number called again."

Jerry Stovall, who recruited east Texas for LSU, recalled attending a Ball football game in which Alexander had a spectacular three-carry half. Stovall went to the press box to talk to Courville, who was the stadium announcer, and commented to the effect that he expected fireworks in the second half. Courville shrugged and answered, "He may not even see the ball again."

Alexander didn't have another carry that night.

Stovall had seen enough, however. Feeling Alexander was an untapped talent, Stovall sold McClendon on the prospect. Others —

Baylor, Houston, UCLA — also saw the potential.

A Baylor scout may have talked the Bears right out of the picture. UCLA, which would have afforded Charlie proximity to his dad, was really only luke-warm on him, and besides, Alexander preferred the Baton Rouge campus. LSU had a couple of pluses the others lacked.

Courville, who was like a second father to Alexander, explained: "Charlie Walker (former assistant LSU track coach) was really the first to try to recruit Charlie. Two of my blue chippers had run track at LSU and one, Greg Edmund, a good friend to Charlie, was there when he was being recruited. Greg told Charlie what he liked about the school and what he didn't, without pulling punches.

And then?

"Charlie and I got together and we decided if he was going to be the kind of football player he wanted to be, he was going to have to go somewhere that employed the I-formation, because that's what (type runner) he

really was. Now the schools around here, in the Southwest Conference and the SWAC, were all going to veer-type offenses. LSU wasn't. We wanted him to go somewhere that would depend on him. This is the main thing that got Charlie to LSU."

The result? LSU learned to depend on Alexander in a big way. Alexander still holds LSU records for most yards in a single game (237 yards versus Oregon, 1977); most yards gained in a single season (1,686 yards, 1977); most rushes in a single game (43 versus Wyoming, 1977); most yards averaged in a season (153.3, 1977).

McClendon said of Alexander: "Make sure to capitalize the 'G' on great, because that's exactly what he was for us."

JERRY STOVALL
31

Jerry Stovall blanched. He couldn't believe his ears. "I think I'd build a mantle to put it on, then build a house around it to get the perfect setting," the incredulous Stovall said.

The topic of discussion was the Heisman Trophy. Then an assistant on Charlie McClendon's staff, Stovall was preparing for a game with Oregon State. Fourteen years before, in what was then the closest ballot of the Heisman, Stovall finished second to Terry Baker of Oregon State.

Baker, an enterprising newspaper reporter found out, put his Heisman in a closet and kept it there. "Unbelievable," said Stovall, who tallied 618 points to Baker's 707 in 1962.

The Heisman was the only symbol of football achievement Stovall ever missed out on. Stovall was so good that he was a two-time All-American on offense and an All-Pro on defense. And he probably played with more expectations than any Tiger in history. Stovall was the man who replaced Billy Cannon as the arrowhead of the

LSU offense.

Despite his stature of 6-foot-2, and a lean 195-pounds, Stovall didn't look the part of a superstar running back. He was mild-mannered and bespectacled, with a demeanor more fitting the library than the football field.

That all changed in his very first appearance in a Tiger uniform, although Stovall didn't score a point.

Locked in a tight defensive battle with Texas A&M, Stovall got off a rainmaker of a punt. An Aggie return man escaped the Tiger rush, picked up a wall of blockers and began

MIAMI BOUND — Head Coach Jerry Stovall led the Fighting Tigers to a 55-21 romp over Florida State in foggy Tiger Stadium, a victory which vaulted LSU into the 1983 Orange Bowl.

steaming toward the LSU goal. As he hit the East sideline at midfield, only the punter was left in the runner's path.

Stovall backpeddled all the way to the 20, fighting off a blocker the whole way without letting the runner get past him. Finally, Stovall pinned both against the sideline and was able to make the tackle — and prevent a certain touchdown in what turned into a 9-0 LSU victory.

Tiger coach Paul Dietzel sighed afterward, "Stovall's debut was as impressive as any I've seen by a sophomore."

There was more to come. Much more.

Stovall scored the touchdown against undefeated Ole Miss in 1960 that caused the Rebels to have to kick a last-play field goal that allowed them to get out with a 6-6 tie.

A year later, Stovall dramatically ran the second-half kickoff back 98 yards to defeat Georgia Tech, 10-0, in Atlanta. It was a far

SHINING MOMENT — LSU Head Coach Jerry Stovall meets Alabama's Paul "Bear" Bryant at midfield following LSU's 20-10 win over the Crimson Tide in 1982.

more dramatic play than people in the stands realized. "In the second quarter," said Dr. Marty Broussard, then the trainer, "Jerry gets hit really hard. He comes to the sidelines and we look at him and could feel he had a cracked rib. We put a pad on it and kept him out six or seven minutes."

After Stovall ran back the kickoff, he played the rest of the game on offense and defense.

In a struggle of SEC giants later that season, one in which LSU could penetrate Ole Miss' side of the field only twice, Stovall's 57-yard run put the Tigers in position to defeat the mighty Rebels, 10-7.

Against Florida in 1962,

he ran and caught passes for 65 yards of a 77-yard drive, caught a 16-yard touchdown pass, and scored on a six-yard bruising run. Stovall's blocking and tackling in that game was "the most vicious this season by one of our backs," said coach Charlie Mclendon.

That season Stovall gained 368 yards on 89 carries, and gained another 203 yards receiving, an average of 22.6 yards per catch — impressive credentials for an athlete whose forte was defense.

About the only thing that ever slowed Stovall was church. A devout man, he spent every Sunday in church. After checking in with the LSU trainer early

in the morning, Stovall and his wife, Judy, would attend 9 a.m. services at the campus Baptist student center. They would return home for 11:30 to catch the televised pro games, then return to the Baptist Training Union and recreation, which usually lasted until 9:30 p.m.

Stovall left LSU as a two-time All-American, with a 4.8 yards per carry career average, twice was LSU's leading receiver, and an indelible memory for fans as one of the Tigers' all-time greats.

The one job Stovall ever really wanted was head coach of the Tigers, and he got it only through the ill-fated plane crash of Bo Rein. After four seasons of either very good or disappointing teams, Stovall was released.

But perhaps the most incisive description of Jerry Stovall came from ex-teammate Tommy Neck, then serving on the LSU Board of Supervisors at the time of the Rein tragedy: "I've seen Jerry Stovall, in the fourth quarter, when you're so tired you can hardly move, and you're lungs are burning, suck it up more than anyone else I've ever seen."

LITTLE BIG MAN 32

No one could believe it — or would believe it — in the fall of 1982.

After the heated recruiting battle for ultra-talented running back Garry James of New Orleans, the first depth chart at that position read:

Dalton Hilliard
Garry James
Gene Lang
Karl Bernard

Dalton who? This had to be a psychological ploy by Coach Jerry Stovall.

The fans weren't the only ones perplexed. Before that chart was released, backfield coach Darrell Moody had to tell his boss, "We've got a problem. Our third-string back is better than anyone we have."

Moody was speaking of the little known Hilliard, a back who seemed to glide into a hole, and then change speed and direction as if he weren't governed by the laws of physics. Still, only a few knew of Hilliard. LSU had to beat the rest of the college football world for James, 6-foot-2, 200-pounds. Only Tulane was in the running for Hilliard, who came out of a small, southwest Louisiana town.

Even some of the Tiger coaches questioned playing a man so small, until LSU linebacker coach Buddy Nix, who first spotted Hilliard, reminded them all, "An offensive line opens holes that are wide, not high."

Stovall, nobody's fool, told Moody to keep the chart in the order of productivity, and nothing else.

Hilliard turned out to be a dazzling, exciting runner. At 5-foot-8, 185-pounds, but with thigh muscles that appeared at

THE PHENOM — Dalton Hilliard gained national attention as a freshman in 1982 when he befuddled a staunch Florida defense, rushing for 127 yards on 26 attempts.

first glance to be the size of most male waists, Hilliard, a prospect from little Patterson, Louisiana, became the first freshman running back in modern Tiger history to draw a starting assignment in a season-opening game. He gained 133 yards and scored three touchdowns in that game against Oregon State, and the job was Hilliard's from then on, although James also started in a backfield known in LSU lore as the "Dalton-James Gang."

Hilliard, clearly LSU's "Little Big Man," left college four seasons later as the best running back statistically in LSU annals — one of only two Tigers to rush for more than 4,000 yards. Two games later, in a 24-13 upset of Florida that propelled Hilliard into national consciousness, Hilliard gained 127 yards. There was more in those figures than most people realized.

Moody kept two game charts, one listed the yards a back gained, the other listed yardage gained after being hit or after the ball-carrier made a defender miss a tackle. Against the Gators, Moody said, Hilliard shouldn't have gotten more than half the net yardage he was credited with. Of the 127 yards he picked up, 73 yards came after he been hit or after making a defender miss a tackle.

"He runs with his eyes as well as his feet," Stovall said.

Indeed. Consider this, Hilliard was not only LSU's all-time leading rusher in 1993, LSU's football centennial, but was also the Tigers' ninth all-time receiver with 1,133 yards on 119 catches, and LSU's leading scorer with 302 points.

Surely that fulfills the promise Nix first saw in him.

Nix, who recruited James Brooks for Auburn, practically lived in Patterson for two years. "When I saw Dalton in the spring of his (high school) junior year, I said to myself, 'Well, here's another one,' " Nix said of the quick-footed back wearing No. 21. "He's even wearing Brooks' number. I told Darrell (Moody), 'I've found another Brooks.'

"People were wondering if Dalton was big enough to take the punishment," Nix chuckled after Hilliard set an NCAA freshman record when he scored 16 touchdowns and 96 points. "Hell, nobody's had a clean tackle on him yet."

That is part of the reason Hilliard was such a devastating runner: seldom does a defender get a clear shot at the gliding ghost, but when they did, they hit legs as sturdy as pillars. Hilliard's leg muscles protrude like that of a body-builder.

When he was injured in high school, Jo Ann Landry, the assistant principal at Patterson, drove Hilliard to a Napoleonville physician. She recalled: "We'd gotten to the doc-

tor's office and the nurse put Dalton on the examining table. All of a sudden the doctor yelled, 'Jo Ann! Come see!' I thought something was really wrong with Dalton.' " The doctor asked Hilliard to flex the thigh muscles in his healthy leg. When he did, bands of muscle ballooned under the skin and the physician's eyes widened. "He said he'd never seen muscles like that . . . even in medical school," Landry chuckled.

Hilliard gained 901 yards as a freshman, dropped to 747 yards as injuries slowed him in '83, then ripped off 1,268 as a junior and 1,134 yards as a senior, joining Charles Alexander and Terry Robiskie as the only Tigers to put together two thousand yard seasons.

But it wasn't easy passing Alexander as LSU's leading rusher. Alexander said beforehand: "I didn't think my record would last forever. But I did think it would last a little longer than it did."

Hilliard went into the Tigers' last regular-season game of 1985 against East Carolina needing 156 yards to pass Alexander

PANCAKE — A record Tiger Stadium crowd of 82,390 watched LSU smother the Washington Huskies, 40-14, in 1983.

the Great. Hilliard gained 70 yards in the first half, and 73 in the third quarter.

He was still 13 yards shy of the record in the fourth quarter when he reversed his field on second-and-seven at the Tiger 23, breaking containment of the East Carolina defense and streaking 24 yards for the all-time Tiger record — and a first down with 12:08 remaining in the game.

It marked the 20th 100-yard game of Hilliard's career.

Afterward, a surprisingly low-key Hilliard said simply: "I'd like to give credit to God, my family, and my offensive line."

On the other side of the stadium, the East Carolina team was profuse in their evaluation of LSU's "Little Big Man." Pirate cornerback Kevin Walker said: "Hilliard, pound-for-pound, is better than (Auburn's Bo) Jackson," an ECU opponent a month before. "It's not his speed that beats you; it's his moves. He's one of the best backs we've ever seen."

TOMMY CASANOVA
33

N o one who ever saw him play would agree, but Tommy Casanova said there were no real highlights of his football career.

A three-time All-America defensive back at LSU and an All-Pro safety with the Cincinnati Bengals, Casanova was one of the most complete athletes ever to play in Louisiana.

A pro scout said after watching Tommy Casanova at practice at LSU: "My wife could scout Tommy and put him down as a first-round draft choice."

To put Casanova, who was recruited by only three universities, into the context of LSU football, when fans were asked to vote on a modern-era LSU team, Casanova received more votes than any other Tiger. "Aw, that's ridiculous," Casanova said.

But is it?

In the modern era of specialization, Casanova was so good that Tiger coaches weren't quite sure what to do with him. As a sophomore and junior, Casanova played both offense and defense. The dark-haired Casanova, with looks to match his name, gained 302 yards rushing in spot duty on offense, returned punts for 491 yards, returned kickoffs for 334 yards, intercepted seven passes and shut down numerous receivers — almost always taking the ace of the opponent's team.

An athlete of infinite grace, on the gridiron Casanova was reminiscent of a dancer on stage. "He was tremendously gifted," said Charlie McClendon, who coached Casanova, "one of the most gifted athletes I ever had. There's no question he could have

CAZZ — Some Tiger fans call him the most graceful LSU gridder ever — Tommy Casanova.

been an All-America running back, and really could've jazzed up our offense. But I needed him more on defense."

In part because of his presence, by diverting opponents' passing schemes to other parts of the field, and in part because of the presence of All-America tackle Ronnie

Estay on the line, McClendon's defense led the nation in 1970 by yielding the minuscule scoring average of 8.7 points a game.

Casanova said he really would have enjoyed a shot at wide receiver, but has no regrets.

As a sprinter on the LSU track team, he turned

in several 9.7 hundreds, and against Ole Miss in 1970, Casanova tied an NCAA record by returning two punts for touchdowns, one a run of 61 yards, the other for 73 yards.

It was that type of performance that caught the eye of *Sports Illustrated*, which made Casanova its

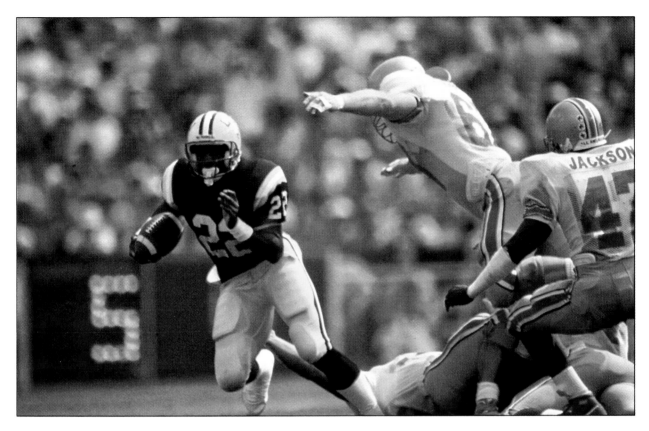

HEMPSTEAD FLASH — Harvey Williams is the third-leading rusher in LSU history with 2,780 yards and 27 TDs.

coverboy for the 1971 college football issue, and proclaimed Casanova the nation's most complete football player.

"I really don't look back and think of 'highpoints' per se," Casanova, now an ophthalmologist in Crowley, Louisiana, his hometown, said. "Most of my games sort of blend together. The Auburn game (a 21-20 LSU victory) my sophomore year would rank with my most vivid memories. Auburn had (quarterback Pat)

Sullivan and (receiver Terry) Beasley, and they were definitely a Top Ten team."

In that game, Casanova made a brilliant tackle behind the line on a fourth down play inside the LSU five. He dismisses the play "because we knew what was coming. Auburn was very well scouted. Too much was made of that tackle."

But not to anyone at the game, or to the national television audience looking in.

None of that compares to the most difficult thing Casanova ever had to overcome — combining medical school with his pro career in Cincinnati. "That really became rough," he said. "I wouldn't want to do that again. In fact, if I had to do it all over again now I don't think I'd try it. I'd chose one over the other, but I'm not sure which one it would be."

A PASSING FANCY

34

It's funny how life turns out. Wendell Davis caught 183 passes in his LSU career, led the nation in receiving once with 80 catches, and the same season led the nation in touchdown receptions.

Every one of those — and his school record 19 career touchdown catches — may have been caused by irregular yard lining in Tiger Stadium.

Until 1985 there was almost no running room outside the north end zone. A player ran out of the north end zone directly into a fence. The south end zone, on the other hand, had several yards of cushion between the end marker and fence.

On such miscalculations are All-Americans created.

The field was altered in 1985, with the north end zone being moved out five yards. But before it was done, Glenn Holt, an up-and-coming LSU receiver, shot into the north end zone during spring training to make a catch. He made the reception near the end marker and, moving at full speed, couldn't stop himself from slamming into the fence.

Holt put out his hand to break his momentum. He also broke his hand.

The Tiger Stadium dimensions were adjusted shortly afterward, but the north end zone had claimed a victim. A bad break for Holt turned into the break of a lifetime for Davis.

Davis, Holt's best friend and a second-string flanker who caught exactly zero passes as a freshman, was switched to split end. Holt never could win back his job, took ill and flunked out of school. Davis caught 31 passes as a sophomore, 80 as a junior and 72 as a senior, and was a consensus All-American his last two

TOMMY GUN — Tom Hodson led the Tigers to a 30-13 victory over South Carolina in the 1987 Gator Bowl.

seasons.

Whenever the Tigers needed a clutch play during their 9-3-0 Southeastern Conference championship season of 1986, Tommy Hodson, the precocious redshirt freshman quarterback, invariably went to Davis. That, looking back, Hodson said, surprised him as much as it surprised opposing secondaries.

Davis was given the last available grant-in-aid in the recruiting class of 1984.

Hodson was the number one recruiting prize of 1985, a passer so pure he was thought of as a candidate for LSU canonization before he ever arrived on campus. Before he ever threw a pass for the Tigers, however, Hodson suddenly lost all feeling in his right arm. An injury in a high school all-star game resulted in a frayed nerve, and threatened Hodson's career before it ever started.

Hodson and Davis started working out together. Hodson, an accomplished passer couldn't quite believe that Davis, who couldn't run under Hodson's long throws and couldn't hang on to his short ones either, was actually a major-college athlete.

SURE THING — Clutch receiver Wendell Davis is tops on the LSU receiving charts with 2, 708 yards and 19 touchdowns.

"I was not overly impressed," Hodson said diplomatically with a smile, "nothing exceptional."

Davis did have a strong work ethic, though. He practiced tirelessly, and ran precise, disciplined routes. He worked on his hand-eye coordination, and eventually began making routine catches routinely. "The patterns," he said, "came before the hands." Then difficult catches began sticking in Davis' hands. His speed in the 40-yard dash improved from 5.0 seconds to 4.6.

"My father is the person I thank for that," Davis said. The work ethic was instilled in Wendell throughout his adolescence. No matter what outside interests Wendell had, they were to be enjoyed only after family chores were completed.

"I had to do things around the house — cut the grass, empty the trash, you know, odd jobs," Davis said of his youth. "But I had to do them. Football and other things came after my duties at home. My parents taught me discipline."

Davis' father, a crew chief in a Shreveport water district, may have been responsible for some of the most precise pass routes ever run in the SEC. Wendell thought so.

When Jackie Sherrill, then the head coach at Texas A&M, met Davis at an NCAA track meet held at LSU in the spring of 1987, he thought on first impression that the 6-foot-0, 186-pound self-made receiver was a veteran pro athlete.

"I thought he was a 28, 29-year-old pro player back for the weekend. He's an impressive person. I don't think anyone has stopped him."

No one did. When Hodson recovered and took over the No. 1 quarterback duties as a redshirt freshman, he had a ready-made, polished target to throw to: Davis.

Hodson passed for 2,261 yards and 19 touchdowns in 1986, the season his primary receiver, Davis, led the NCAA in total receptions and touchdown receptions. The pair was football's equivalent of the Dynamic Duo as LSU again won the SEC. There was more of the same in 1987 when the Tigers, clearly one of the nation's best teams, went 10-1-1.

"Those first two seasons were storybook seasons," Hodson said. "We had really great personnel and won a lot of games."

Davis left LSU as the SEC's most productive receiver (2,708 yards), and the No. 1 draft choice of the Chicago Bears. Hodson left two years later, after chalking up another league title, as the SEC's most productive passer. A case could be logically made that any school all-star team should include Hodson on its starting unit. No one ever quarterbacked LSU to as many victories (31), passed for as many yards (9,115), threw as many completions (674), or as many touchdown passes (69).

He once split his tongue open in a game at Kentucky, then came back to steer LSU to victory. Against Georgia in 1987, Hodson took a vicious cheap shot five yards out of bounds and had to be replaced. Former LSU coach Bill Arnsparger, who had coached some of the best defenses in NFL memory at Miami, was then the athletic director at the University of Florida and watching the televised Tiger-Bulldog donnybrook.

"Don't worry about him," Arnsparger commented of Hodson. "That's the toughest kid I've ever been around." Hodson came back in to throw the winning touchdown pass in a 26-23 Bayou Bengal victory.

Davis and Hodson, though they only played together two seasons, will forever be linked in LSU's collective memory bank.

But, interestingly, while Davis became the object of multiple coverage — and media coverage as a hot story — Glenn Holt faded from LSU memory. During the spring of 1987, two years after Holt's ill-fated crash into the north end zone fence, Davis turned a corner in Orlando, Florida — and ran right into his old buddy.

"We were both shocked," Davis said. "Neither of us could believe it for a minute." Holt was then an athlete at Western Kentucky and on his way to a track meet. Davis was on his way to a photo session with the preseason Playboy All-America team.

They made small talk. Holt congratulated Davis, and then the friends said goodbye.

ALL-AMERICAN — With this catch versus Kentucky in 1987, Wendell Davis broke Eric Martin's career receptions mark with his 153rd catch.

NOT THIS TIME — LSU noseguard Darrell Phillips (62) blocks a Buckeye field goal attempt in a classic clash with Ohio State in 1987.

"IT MIGHT HAVE BEEN" 35

For of all sad words of tongue or pen," John Whittier wrote in 1856, "the saddest are these: 'It might have been.' "

Indeed. And you really have to wonder how much football history would have been changed if Jesse Myles hadn't fumbled at midfield just before the half in the seventh game of LSU's 1979 season, Charlie McClendon's last as head coach of the Fightin' Tigers.

Jimmy Jordan took immediate advantage of the sudden opportunity and hit a streaking Hardis Johnson for a touchdown and a 14-13 Florida State halftime

lead over LSU in an eventual 24-19 Seminole victory.

Both of FSU's first half touchdowns came after Tiger fumbles, but if Fate could take that touchdown away from Florida State, or give it to LSU, which seemed to be moving with an air of authority at that point, then the complexion of Deep South football — as well as the national elite — for the next decade and a half could have been changed.

Bobby Bowden, the roly-poly football mastermind who reshaped Florida State from a rag-tag team into one of the country's

strongest programs, had made up his mind he was going to be the next LSU coach if his best Seminole team to that point, unbeaten in six games, couldn't beat the 4-2 Bayou Bengals.

Then-Tiger athletic director Paul Dietzel had assured the LSU faithful he was going after "the best coach available" to replace McClendon. The best coach available was Bowden, and Bowden was more than interested.

"I always kind of lusted after LSU," he said more than a decade later. "That's one of those real good-lookin' jobs that catches

HANK — Henry Thomas is one of the greatest defensive lineman in SEC history.

everybody's eye, and Coach Dietzel kind of let me know it was mine if I wanted it."

Bowden talked of how he hitchhiked from Birmingham to Baton Rouge as a boy in 1946 to see LSU and Y.A. Tittle take on Alabama and Harry Gilmer. "I think I kind of fell in love with LSU then," Bowden said. "It's a beautiful campus, with those moss-covered trees and those lovely lakes. And the stadium, and all those excited fans. I loved everything about LSU. It was an unforgettable setting for an impressionable boy watching two of his idols. And

Baton Rouge is really a lot like Tallahassee in that both are state capitals and college towns, and both towns have sort of grown up with the schools."

Thirty-three years after the gridiron duel of Tittle and Gilmer, a 31-21 Tiger victory, Bowden made up his mind he was going to succeed McClendon if the Seminoles came up short against LSU. "My thinking was, with the best team Florida State ever had up to that time, if we couldn't beat just a pretty good LSU team, then we never would. I'd have to consider going where I felt could win con-

sistently."

Myles' fumble paved the way for the Florida State victory — considered at the time the biggest in school history, and one Bowden said showed him "what we could do at Florida State."

The Monday after the game, Bowden, who felt he had to kill all the speculation that he might leave, signed a new five-year contract with the Seminoles. Since then, of course, Florida State has soared to the very heights of college football.

Think of how that one 1979 fumble, or one more LSU touchdown might have changed history:

■Dietzel (now retired), assuming Bowden enjoyed any degree of success approximating that of Florida State, would have been hailed as an administrative genius and probably would have retired from LSU around 1990 with accolades and warm and sentimental regards. Instead, he hired Bo Rein, who was killed in a plane crash 42 days after he was announced as LSU's new coach, setting into motion a whole new series of events. Dietzel, vulnerable after not getting a "name" coach and after a couple of so-so seasons under Jerry Stovall, was bushwacked by a politically motivated chancellor and board.

■And we might never have heard of Bob Brodhead (now an administrator for a Louisiana horse race track), who had a controversial reign as athletic director at LSU that played to mixed reviews. Controversy was Brodhead's hallmark, and, as one LSU board member said, he had "the touch of an elephant." But, to be fair, he also hired uncommonly qualified coaches and lifted the overall performance of

THE GENERAL — Bill Arnsparger led LSU to two Sugar Bowls and one Liberty Bowl appearance in his three seasons as LSU head coach.

LSU athletics. The question was how long could LSU have enjoyed those year-round championship results before the athletic department went bankrupt?

■Bo Rein (deceased), the coach Dietzel did eventually hire from North Carolina State, would never have taken that flight into eternity, a recruiting trip that ended with a crash in the Atlantic Ocean. Rein probably still would be alive and coaching at Ohio State, his alma mater.

■Jerry Stovall (athletic director at Louisiana Tech), who succeeded Rein and had a roller-coaster tenure as LSU coach — extremely good teams in some years and poor teams in others — likely would be an LSU

SPOILS OF VICTORY — LSU Head Coach Mike Archer led the Tigers to a Gator Bowl victory over South Carolina in 1987.

might also be a Dolphins' assistant and waiting for a shot to be a head coach.

A lot of things can turn on a card — or a football.

How much LSU football might have been different if Butch Duhe, an extremely talented junior quarterback, hadn't tragically died just before the 1970 season? Bert Jones, then a true sophomore, would have been redshirted and LSU would have had a much more mature quarterback when he took his turn at the Tiger helm.

'Miracle Mike' Miley, who was also to die tragically at a young age, left school for a professional baseball contract after McClendon, not believing the handwriting on the wall, put in an entire new offense called the Veer, specifically to take advantage of Miley's running talents.

Those two developments completely changed his two-quarterback system. Never again did McClendon have the solid, seasoned vet as the starter, and the eager young talent panting to learn as his backup.

But then, on the other hand, there is the case of

athletic department administrator, raising money and secretly bemoaning the fact that he never realized his lifelong dream: coaching at LSU. Of course, he wouldn't have been publicly executed by Brodhead either.

■ Bill Arnsparger (defensive coordinator of the San Diego Chargers) likely still would be Don Shula's defensive coordinator with the Miami Dolphins, sitting in the dark studying game film and seething about his one and only head coaching stint, with the New York Giants.

■ Mike Archer (linebackers coach at Kentucky), who caught Arnsparger's eye early and who succeeded him at LSU,

T.P. "Red" Heard, the former athletic director who outsnookered the academic administrators when he got the south end zone of Tiger Stadium built over their preferred projects — specifically a new library.

Heard knew how to play the game with the politicians, and the academicians didn't. The library was built in short order, but the administrators have long memories and from then on Heard was living on borrowed time.

Heard was fired, along with Coach Gaynell Tinsley, in a 1954 "housecleaning."

If Heard had not bullied his way to the stadium expansion, chances are he would have survived. Tinsley, with a couple of fair teams, might have made it too. That issue erected an us-versus-them atmosphere at LSU, and at the first opportunity the most visible athletic department heads were lopped off.

But think about this: that action brought in the dynamic duo of Coach Paul Dietzel and athletic director Jim Corbett — which meant the library skirmish was the first block in building the national championship of 1958.

CRAZY 'BOUT CURLEY — Curley Hallman leads LSU into its second century of football.

A

AARON, John (RG)
Natchitoches, La., 1963-64-65
ABEL, Leo (FB)
Baton Rouge, La., 1990-91
ABNEY, Wilbert (E)
Sildell, La., 1945
ABRAMSON, Louis J. (Luke) (HB)
Shreveport, La., 1923
ABY, Hulette F. (Red) (T)
Natchez, Miss, 1898-99
ADAMS, Jeff (E)
Memphis, Tenn., 1946-47-48
ADAMS, John Aubrey (DE)
DeRidder, La., 1976-77-78-79
ADAMS, Ray (CB)
Jasper, Tex., 1989-90-91-92
ADDISON, Don (S)
Springhill, La., 1968-69-70
ADDY, Ken (FB)
Baton Rouge, La., 1972-73
ADSIT, John Jr.
Decatur, Ga., 1943-44
ALBERGAMO, Nacho (C)
Marrero, La., 1984-85-86-87
ALBRIGHT, John G. (Jonnie) (QB)
Memphis, Tenn., 1908-09
ALEXANDER, Arnold (RE)
Bear Creek, Ala., 1954-55
ALEXANDER, Charles (TB)
Galveston, Tex., 1975-76-77-78
ALEXANDER, Dan (DT)
Houston, Tex., 1974-75-76
ALEXANDER, Glenn (T)
Rayville, La., 1969-70
ALEXANDER, Ricky (ILB)
Pascagoula, Miss., 1990-91
ALFORD, Andrew (Andy) (LG)
Bogalusa, La., 1952-53
ALLEN, Byron (FB)
Lafayette, La., 1992
ALLEN, Tommy (Trigger) (TB)
DeRidder, La., 1966-67-68
ALLEN, W. D. (Bill) (T)
McComb, Miss., 1929-30-31
ALMOKARY, Joe (HB)
Oil City, La., 1930-31-32
ALSTON, Francis H. (Frank) (HB)
Logansport, La., 1927-28
AMEDEE, Lynn (QB)
Baton Rouge, La., 1960-61-62
ANASTASIO, Charles (HB)
White Castle, La., 1938-39-40
ANDERSON, Mike (LB)
Baton Rouge, La., 1968-69-70
ANDERSON, Roy Joe (FB)
Shreveport, La., 1937-38-39
ANDING, Aubrey (E)
Tyler, Tex., 1944
ANDOLSEK, Eric (OG)
Thibodaux, La., 1984-85-86-87
ANDREAS, Herman (C)
El Paso, Tex., 1930
ANDREWS, Charles P.
Mer Rouge, La., 1893
ANDREWS, Mitchell D. (TE)
Houma, La., 1982-83-84-85
ARRIGHI, J. H. (Hughes) (T)
Natchez, Miss., 1894-95-96
ATIYEH, George (DT-NG)
Allentown, Pa., 1977-78-79-80
ATKINSON, James S. (QB)
Ruston, La., 1896
AUCOIN, Alvin (LT)
Houma, La., 1955-56-57
AUSBERRY, Verge (ILB)
New Iberia, La., 1986-87-88-89

B

BABERS, Bertram (Bert) (T-G)
Baton Rouge, La., 1926-27
BAGGETT, Billy (RHB)
Beaumont, Tex., 1948-49-50
BAILEY, Robert L. (Bunkie) (HB)
Bunkie, La., 1926-27
BAILEY, Scott (ILB)
LaPlace, La., 1983-84-86
BAIRD, Albert W. (Dub) (QB)
Shreveport, La., 1916
BAIRD, Joe Garnett (Red) (T)
Shreveport, La., 1946-47-48-49
BALDWIN, Bob (C)
Fort Worth, Tex., 1955

BALDWIN, Harry (G)
Albion, Mich., 1907
BALDWIN, Marvin (T)
Lake Charles, La., 1934-35-36
BALLARD, Shelton (C)
Bogalusa, La., 1946-47
BAME, Abie A. (T)
Toledo, Ohio, 1922
BANKER, Eddie (LG)
Jennings, La., 1964-65-66
BANNISTER, Bobby (T)
Bogalusa, La., 1931-32
BARBAY, Roland A. (DT)
Chalmette, La., 1982-83-85-86
BARBER, Ronald J. (Ronnie) (S)
Oil City, La., 1974-75-76
BARBIN, A. T.
Marksville, La., 1896
BARHAM, Garnett E. (Joe) (HB)
Oak Ridge, La., 1925
BARNES, Walter (Piggy) (T)
Parkersburg, W. Va., 1940-46-47
BARNEY, Charles (C)
Shreveport, La., 1943
BARRETT, Jack (T)
Houston, Tex., 1940
BARRETT, W. Jeff (E)
Houston, Tex., 1933-34-35
BARRETT, Woodrow (C)
San Antonio, Tex., 1940
BARRILLEAUX, Jim (LG)
Amite, La., 1968
BARROW, Edward R.
Baton Rouge, La., 1899
BARTHEL, Donald R. (KS)
Rayville, La., 1979-80
BARTON, James (Jim) (LHB)
Marshall, Tex., 1949-50-51
BARTRAM, Dave (G)
Laurel, Miss., 1937-38-39
BASS, Aaron (OLB)
Carencro, La., 1989
BASS, William (Bill) (C-LB)
Lafayette, La., 1963-64-65
BATEMAN, Joel B. (G)
Franklin, La., 1895-1898
BATES, Oran P. (E)
Cairo, Ill., 1903
BATES, William C. (RE)
Baton Rouge, La.
BAUER, Charles C. (HB)
Winnfield, La., 1907
BAUER, F. Ogden (E)
Cairo, Ill., 1937-38-39
BAZILE, Sterling (DT)
Mt. Airy, La., 1979
BEALE, L. S. (Rusty) (HB)
Baton Rouge, La., 1919-21
BEARD, James (RHB)
Lake Providence, La., 1893-94
BECH, Brett (WR)
Slidell, La., 1992
BECKHAM, Odell (TB)
Marshall, Texas, 1990-91-92
BEGUE, Dale (S)
Baton Rouge, La., 1983
BENGLIS, Jim (FB)
Lake Charles, La., 1970-71-72
BENNETT, Reldon (T)
Lake Village, Ark., 1941
BENOIT, Robert L (Rabbit) (QB)
Shreveport, La., 1917-19-20
BENTLEY, Granville D. (QB)
New Orleans, La., 1903
BERGERON, Carroll (T)
Houma, La., 1958
BERNHARD, James (T)
Baton Rouge, La., 1943-44-45
BERNSTEIN, Dave (T)
New Orleans, La., 1939-40
BERNSTEIN, Joe (FB)
Elmira, N.Y., 1915-16-19
BERON, Phil Jr. (LG)
New Orleans, La., 1952-54
BERRY, Clint (OT)
Opelousas, La., 1981-82-83
BERTUCCI, Gerald (G)
New Orleans, La., 1944-45
BESSELMAN, Tom (OT)
New Orleans, La., 1970
BETANZOS, Juan Carlos (KS)
Mexico City, Mex., 1982-83-84
BEVAN, George (LB)
Baton Rouge, La., 1966-67-69
BICE, Jamie (S)
Lake Charles, La., 1985-86-87-88

BIENVENU, Greg (C)
Lafayette, La., 1973-74-75
BIRD, Leo (HB)
Shreveport, La., 1939-40-41
BISHOP, Clyde E. (SE)
Houston, Tex., 1981
BISHOP, Harold (TE)
Tuscaloosa, Ala., 1990-92
BLACKETTER, Gary (S)
Lake Charles, La., 1975-76-77
BLAKE, Jerry R. (OT)
Gretna, La., 1982
BLAKEWOOD, Eldred (Blake) (G)
Kleinwood, La., 1922-23
BLANCHARD, Mike (C)
Baton Rouge, La., 1991-92
BLASS, John P. (Jay) (DE)
Metairie, La., 1977-78-79
BOFINGER, Bill (G)
Baton Rouge, La., 1966-67
BOND, C. P. (HB)
1910
BOND, Jimmy (E)
Bogalusa, La., 1959
BOOTH, Barrett (QB)
New Orleans, La., 1936-37-38
BOOTH, Billy Joe (T)
Minden, La., 1959-60-61
BORDELON, Kenny (DE)
New Orleans, La., 1972-73-74-75
BOUDREAUX, Thomas J. (FS)
Montegut, La., 1980-81-82
BOUDREAUX, Wilfred (G-T)
Sunset, La., 1893
BOURGEOIS, Andy (E)
New Orleans, La., 1958-59-60
BOURGEOIS, Louis C., Jr. (C)
Franklin, La., 1921-22-23-24
BOURGEOIS, Rene (P)
Baton Rouge, La., 1988-89
BOURQUE, Hart (HB)
Gonzales, La., 1958-59-60
BOUTTE, Doug (OT)
Sulphur, La., 1973-74-75
BOUTTE, Marc (NG-DT)
Lake Charles, La., 1988-89-90-91
BOWMAN, Drew (ILB)
Greenville, Tenn., 1988-89
BOWMAN, George, Jr. (QB-HB)
Hammond, La., 1932-35
BOWMAN, Jimmy (FL)
Lake Charles, La., 1984
BOWMAN, Sidney S. (HB)
Hammond, La., 1929-30-31
BOWSER, Gregory M. (Greg) (NG)
Franklin, La., 1979-80-81-82
BOYD, Brad (TE)
Jennings, La., 1972-73-74
BOZEMAN, Donnie (DT-DE)
Baton Rouge, La., 1967-68-69
BRADLEY, John Edmund, Jr. (C)
Opelousas, La., 1976-77-78-79
BRADLEY, Richard (Dick) (RG)
Norristown, Pa., 1948-49
BRAINARD, Pete (G)
Artesia, N.M., 1931
BRANCATO, George (LHB)
New York, N.Y., 1952-53
BRANCH, Mel (LT)
DeRidder, La., 1958-59
BRANNON, S. W. (Red) (QB)
Pollock, La., 1905-06-07-09
BREAUX, Michael W. (ILB)
Lafayette, La., 1982
BRIAN, Alexis (Alex) (LT)
Montgomery, La., 1983-84
BRITT, James E. (CB)
Minden, La., 1978-79-80-82
BROADDUS, Bryan (C)
Dallas, Tex., 1986
BROCK, Ray (C)
Beaverton, Ore., 1984-85-86
BRODNAX, J. W. (Red) (FB-HB)
Bastrop, La., 1956-57-58
BROGAN, John E. (C)
New Orleans, La., 1901
BROGAN, Lawrence E. (G)
New Orleans, La., 1904
BROHA, Max Kent (DE)
New Orleans, La., 1976-78-79
BROMLEY, Scott (LB)
Pensacola, Fla., 1983-84-85-86
BROOKS, Kimoja (OLB)
DeRidder, La., 1992
BROOKS, Michael (OLB)
Ruston, La., 1983-84-85-86

BROOKS, Richard (Bear) (OG-OT)
Crowley, La., 1972-73-74
BROUSSARD, Billy (QB)
Jennings, La., 1973-74
BROUSSARD, Ralph A. (HB)
Abbeville, La., 1893-94
BROWN, A. D. (Andra) (G)
Laurel, Miss., 1933-34-35
BROWN, Caswell (FB)
New Orleans, La., 1951
BROWN, E. A. (Fuzzy) (C)
Minden, La., 1929
BROWN, Gerald (Buster) (FB-P)
Richlands, N.C., 1964-65
BROWN, Harry C.
Alexandria, La., 1931-32
BROWN, Lobdell P. (Bronco) (HB)
Baker, La., 1927-28-29-30
BROWN, R. Tommy (RE)
Baker, La., 1949-51
BROWN, Roland (HB)
Monroe, La., 1932-34
BROWN, Russell Louis (Rusty) (S)
Houston, Tex., 1977-78-79
BROWN, Samuel P. (G-T)
Carencro, La., 1893
BROWNDYKE, David (K)
Dallas, Tex., 1986-87-88-89
BRUE, Darryl (DT)
New Orleans, La., 1975
BRUHL, S. Kyle (NG)
Covington, La., 1979
BRUNO, Phil (QB)
New Orleans, La., 1940
BRYAN, Jack (HB)
Starkville, Miss., 1943-44
BRYANT, Willie (DB)
Ft. Walton, Fla., 1984-85-86-87
BUCK, Gordon (Charlie) (HB)
Marksville, La., 1906-07
BUCKELS, Carlton (CB)
Amite, La., 1990-91-92
BUCKLES, William (C)
Memphis, Tenn., 1944
BULLIARD, Ed (LE)
St. Martinville, La., 1950-51
BULLOCK, Farris (C)
El Dorado, Ark., 1944
BULLOCK, Ray (E)
El Dorado, Ark., 1946-47-48-49
BUNDY, Charles (SE)
Gulfport, Miss., 1965-66
BURAS, Leon (Buddy) (OG-OT)
Covington, La., 1973-74
BURGE, Pete (E)
Poplarville, Miss., 1933
BURKETT, Jeff (FB)
Laurel, Miss., 1941-42-46
BURKS, Michael P. (Mike) (OG)
Baton Rouge, La., 1979-80-81-82
BURKS, Shawn S. (ILB)
Baton Rouge, La., 1982-83-84-85
BURKS, Todd (WR)
Denham Springs, La., 1992
BURNS, Craig (S)
Baton Rouge, La., 1968-69-70
BURNS, Matthew (QB)
Lake City, Fla., 1954-55-56
BURRELL, Cinton Blane (S)
Franklin, La., 1974-75-76-78
BUSSE, Bert M. (T-G)
Alton, Ill., 1919-20-21
BUSSEY, Young (HB)
Houston, Tex., 1937-38-39
BUTAUD, Tommy (DT)
Crowley, La., 1971-72
BUTLER, David (TB)
Houma, La., 1992
BUTLER, W. E. (Bill) (HB)
Ponchatoula, La., 1929-30-31
BYRAM, James E. (C)
Bossier City, La., 1900-01
BYRD, Timothy G. (QB)

LaPlace, La., 1981-82

C

CAGER, Waldon (FS)
New Orleans, La., 1981-84-85
CAIN, Clay (OG)
Sulphur, La., 1973-74
CAJOLEAS, Jimmy (QB)
New Orleans, La., 1937-38-39
CALHOUN, Shelby (T)
Bastrop, La., 1934
CAMBON, F. Joseph (G-T)
Dulac, La., 1893
CAMP, Ivan (C)
Haynesville, La., 1951-52-53-54
CAMPBELL, Cliff C. (Shorty) (T)
Liberty, Miss., 1921-22-23-24
CAMPBELL, Edward (Bo) (LHB)
Shreveport, La., 1960-61-62
CAMPBELL, Eugene P., (E)
Vidalia, La., 1893
CAMPBELL, Irving (T)
Fayette, Ala., 1937-38-39
CAMPBELL, Raymond T. (Tommy) (C)
Winnfield, La., 1981-82-83-84
CANCIENNE, Jeff (OT)
Luling, La., 1991
CANGELOSI, Dale (CB)
Baton Rouge, La., 1971-72-73
CANNON, Billy (HB)
Baton Rouge, La., 1957-58-59
CANTRELLE, Arthur (TB)
Biloxi, Miss., 1969-70-71
CAPONE, Warren (LB)
Baton Rouge, La., 1971-72-73
CARLIN, Kent (C)
Sulphur, La., 1967
CARRIER, Chris (DB)
Eunice, La., 1984-85-86-87
CARRIERE, Oliver P. (Ike) (QB)
New Orleans, La., 1923-24-25-26
CARROLL, Paul (T)
Lake Charles, La., 1935-36-37
CARSON, Carlos (SE)
West Palm Beach, Fla., 1977-78-79
CARTER, Marcus (FL)
Mansfield, La., 1990-91
CASANOVA, Jackie (S)
Crowley, La., 1975-76-77
CASANOVA, Tommy (CB)
Crowley, La., 1969-70-71
CASCIO, Louis (LB)
Bossier City, La., 1969-70-71
CASON, Jim (HB)
Victoria, Tex., 1944-45-46-47
CASSIDY, Ed (G)
Bogalusa, La., 1955-56-57
CASSIDY, Francis (C)
Bogalusa, La. 1940-41
CASSIDY, Steve (DT)
Baton Rouge, La., 1972-73-74-75
CASTON, Toby (ILB)
Monroe, La., 1983-84-85-86
CAVIGGA, Al (G)
Jeannette, Pa., 1940-41-44
CENDOYA, Juan (ILB-OLB)
Miami, Fla., 1989-90-91-92
CHADWICK, Gene (QB)
Homer, La., 1941
CHAMBERLIN, W. Benjamin (Ben) (QB)
DeVall, La., 1897-98-99
CHAMPAGNE, Ed (T)
New Orleans, La., 1946
CHAMPAGNE, Gary (LB)
Nederland, Tex., 1971-72-73
CHAMPAGNE, Todd (OLB)
Hammond, La., 1991
CHAMPION, Joe (OT)
Ferriday, La., 1986-87
CHANDLER, Walter B. (Teeter)
Shreveport, La., 1925-26
CHATMAN, Ricky L. (LB)
Winnfield, La., 1980-81-83-84
CHAVANNE, Edmund A. M. (C)
Lake Charles, La., 1896-97-98-99
CHILDERS, John (CB)
Orlando, Fla., 1985-86-87-88
CHRISTIAN, Mickey (DE)
Magnolia, Ark., 1967-68
CLAITOR, Otto (C)
Rayne, La., 1915
CLAPP, Tommy (DL)
Gretna, La., 1984-85-86-87
CLARK, Blythe (G)
Frenchman Bayou, Ark., 1937-38
CLARK, N. Jackson (TB)
Baton Rouge, La., 1976
CLARK, Samuel M. D. (LE)
DeVall, La., 1893-94
CLAUNCH, Ed (C)
Haynesville, La., 1943-46-47-48
CLAY, Jack T. (FB)
White Castle, La., 1924-25-29
CLEGG, Robert T. (Bobby) (LHB)
Baton Rouge, La., 1947-48

COATES, Ray (HB)
New Orleans, La., 1944-45-46-47
COBB, Michael (T)
New Orleans, La., 1985
COCO, Walter A. (G)
Marksville, La., 1898
COFFEE, Al (SB)
Baton Rouge, La., 1970-72-73
COFFEE, Pat (HB)
Minden, La., 1935-36
COLE, F. E. (Estes) (C-G)
Franklin, Tex., 1929-30
COLE, John R. (Jack) (QB)
Bastrop, La., 1948-49-50
COLEMAN, John J. (HB)
New Orleans, La., 1899-1900-01-02-03
COLLE, Beau (LHB)
Pascagoula, Miss., 1963-64-65
COLLINS, Albin Harrell (Rip) (FB)
Baton Rouge, La., 1945-46-47-48
COLLINS, D. W. (Dan) (FB)
Shreveport, La., 1917
COLLINS, Ray (G)
Paradis, La., 1947-48-49
CONN, Bobby (CB)
Lake Charles, La., 1975-76-77
CONNELL, Allen P. (T)
White Creek, Tenn., 1924-25-26
CONNELL, George M. (C-T)
White Creek, Tenn., 1922-25
CONNELLY, Edwin M. (HB)
Houma, La., 1904
CONNER, John C.
Monroe, La., 1894
CONWAY, Mike (KS)
Texarkana, Ark., 1975-76-77-78
COOK, Dave (CB)
Rayne, La., 1973-74-75
COOK, Frederick W. (Freddie) (E)
Houma, La., 1901
COOLEY, Mike (DL)
Satsuma, Ala., 1984-85
COOPER, Phillip (Chief) (G)
Amite, La., 1913-14-15-16
COPES, Charles (FB)
Tylertown, Miss., 1950
CORE, Harvey (E)
Covington, La., 1944-45-46-47
CORGAN, Bill (B)
Sapulpa, Okla., 1943
CORMIER, Ken (LHB)
Jennings, La. 1963-64-65
CORMIER, Thomas (Skip) (DE)
Opelousas, La., 1971-72
COUTEE, Todd (C)
Eunice, La., 1985-86-87-88
COX, Mickey (RT)
Monroe, La., 1962-64
COYNE, Edward (Ed) (LT)
Bemis, Tenn., 1949-50-51
CRANFORD, Charles (FB)
Minden, La., 1960-61-62
CRASS, Bill (HB)
Electra, Tex., 1935-36
CRAWFORD, John Egan (G)
Liberty Hill, La., 1911-12-13
CROWELL, William (NG)
Meridian, Miss., 1991-92
CRUZ, Chris (DB)
Pensacola, Fla., 1983-84-85-86
CRYLER, Charles E. (OT)
Shreveport, La., 1981-82
CUNNINGHAM, Ed (T)
Wilmington, N.C. 1937
CUPID, George D. (LB)
Vidalia, La., 1976-77-78
CURTIS, Arthur M. (Jeff) (E)
New Orleans, La., 1921
CURTIS, Earl L. (TE)
Lafayette, La., 1982-83-84
CUSIMANO, Charles (G)
New Orleans, La. 1945-48-49
CUTBIRTH, Rob (DB)
Metairie, La., 1984-85

D

DAIGLE, Jesse (QB-WR)
Baton Rouge, La., 1990-91-92
DAILY, Ron (DE)
Houston, Tex., 1972-73-74
DALE, Jeffery D. (SS)
Winnfield, La., 1981-82-83-84
DAMPIER, Al (FB)
Sicily Island, La., 1958
DANIEL, Eugene Jr. (DB)
Baton Rouge, La., 1981-82-83
DANIEL, Loyd (OG)
Franklinton, La., 1970-71-72
DANIEL, Steve (G)
North Little Rock, Ark., 1966-67
DANTIN, Chris (TB)
Baton Rouge, La., 1970-71-72
DARK, Alvin (HB)
Lake Charles, La., 1942
DARDAR, J. Ramsey (DT)
Cecilia, La., 1980-81-82

DASPIT, Armand P. (HB)
Houma, La., 1895-96-97-98
DASPIT, Justin C. (HB)
Houma, La., 1895-96-97-98
DAVIDSON, Kenny (OT/TE/DT)
Shreveport, La., 1987-88-89
DAVIS, Arthur (T)
Pine Bluff, Ark., 1944
DAVIS, Arthur (DE-MG)
Sulphur, La., 1968-69-70
DAVIS, Brad, (TB-RB)
Hammond, La., 1972-73-74
DAVIS, Grady (LHB)
Haynesville, La., 1951-52
DAVIS, James "Bo" (NG)
Mendenhall, Miss., 1990-92
DAVIS, R. L. (Bebee) (E-T)
Monroe, La., 1920-21
DAVIS, Robert (TB)
Birmingham, Ala., 1992
DAVIS, Tommy (FB-K)
Shreveport, La., 1953-58
DAVIS, Wendell (WR)
Shreveport, La., 1984-85-86-87
DAYE, Daryl (G)
Ferriday, La., 1985
DAYE, Donnie (HB)
Ferriday, La., 1958-59-60
DeCROSTA, Bob (FB)
Hudson, N.Y., 1956-57
DeFRANK, Matt (P/K)
Ft. Walton, Fla., 1984-85-86-87
deLAUNAY, Louis F. (Lou) (OG)
Neosho, Mo., 1976-77-78
DeLEE, Robert E., Jr. (TE-OT)
Clinton, La., 1977-78-79-80
DELMORE, Jason (NG)
Gonzales, La., 1987
DELVESCOVO, Anthony (S)
Essex Fells, N.J. 1968
DEMARIE, John (OT)
Lake Charles, La., 1964-65-66
DEMARIE, Mike (OG)
Lake Charles, La., 1969-70-71
DENNIS, Gordon A.)
Shreveport, La., 1893
DENNIS, Rand (A)
Natchitoches, La., 1972-73-74
DeRUTTE, Robert (S)
Port Neches, Tex., 1978-79
DESHOTEL, Robert (ILB)
Lake Charles, La., 1991-92
DeSONIER, Richard (RE)
Morgan City, La., 1953
DESORMEAUX, Ronald Bill, Jr. (TE)
New Iberia, La. 1976
DESSELLES, Brian (P)
White Castle, La., 1992
DEUTSCHMANN, Lou (RHB)
New Orleans, La., 1953-54
DeWITT, Michael E. (WS)
Laurel, Miss., 1983-84-85-86
DIBETTA, Gawain (FB)
New Orleans, La., 1964-65-66
DICKINSON, Wayne (SB-P)
Hattiesburg, Miss., 1970
DIDIER, Melvin (C)
Baton Rouge, La., 1944-45
DILDY, Gary (C)
Bogalusa, La., 1951-52-53-54
DIMMICK, Opie, (QB-FB)
Shuteson, La., 1924-25-26
DINKLE, Gary Mitchell (Mitch) (TE)
Silsbee, Tex., 1974-75-76
DODSON, Adrian (HB)
Columbus, Miss., 1940-41
DOGGETT, Al (HB-QB)
Homer, La., 1951-52-53-54
DOLL, Shane (TE)
Kenner, La., 1988
DOMINGUE, Rusty (LB)
Port Arthur, Tex., 1975-76
DONAHUE, Patrick Michael (Pat) (OG)
Baton Rouge, La., 1974
DOUSAY, Jim (TB)
Baton Rouge, La., 1965-66-67
DOW, Robert (SE)
Jackson, Miss., 1973-74-75-76
DOYLE, Mike (DE)
Houston, Tex., 1970
DREW, Harmon C. (G)
Minden, La., 1907-09
DRY, Ronald (RT)
Fairland, Okla., 1950
DUBROC, Gregg M. (LB)
New Orleans, La., 1981-82-83-84
DUFRENE, Marty J. (C)
Larose, La., 1979-80
DUGAS, Robert W. (OT)
Luling, La., 1976-77-78
DUHE, A. J. Adam (DT)
Reserve, La., 1973-74-75-76
DUHE, Butch (QB)
New Orleans, La., 1969
DUHE, Craig (OT)
Lutcher, La., 1975-76-77

DUHON, Mike (MG)
Sulphur, La., 1964-65-66
DUHON, Steven J. (LB)
Opelousas, La., 1981
DUMAS, Bernie (E)
El Dorado, Ark., 1935-36-37
DUNBAR, Karl (DE)
Opelousas, La., 1986-87-88-89
DUNN, Lester, Jr. (FB)
Covington, La., 1979-81
DUNPHY, Robert Francis (Bo) (TE)
Houston, Tex., 1973-74-75
DUPLANTIS, Mike (OT/OG)
Mathews, La., 1990-91-92
DUPONT, John M. (E)
Houma, La., 1911-12-13-14
DUPONT, Lawrence H. (Dutch) (QB-HB)
Houma, La., 1910-11-12-13
DUPREE, Sam (G)
Baton Rouge, La., 1893-94
DURAL, Junius E. (FL)
Duson, La., 1982-83
DURKEE, Todd G. (LB)
Lafayette, La., 1981-82-84
DURRETT, Bert E.
Arcadia, La., 1925-26-27
DUTTON, John G. (Pete) (E)
Minden, La., 1917-19-21
DUTTON, Thomas W. (T)
Minden, La., 1912-13-19
DYER, Jack (T)
Baton Rouge, La., 1965-66-67

E

EARLEY, Jim (DB)
Jonesboro, La., 1968-69-70
EASTMAN, Dan (T)
New Orleans, La., 1939-40-41
EDICK, Tommy (DB)
Houston, Tex., 1987
EDMONDS, Walter R. (Ray) (E)
Lyon, N.Y., 1915-19
EDMONSON, Arthur T. (Shorty) (HB)
Marshall, Tex., 1921-22-23
EDWARDS, Bill (G)
Little Rock, Ark., 1940-41-42
EDWARDS, Frank M. (Snake) (G)
Amite, La., 1903-04-05
EDWARDS, David R. (Randy) (TE)
Lake Charles, La., 1981
EDWARDS, William E., Jr. (LB)
Metairie, La., 1976
EGAN, Raymond (G)
New Orleans, La., 1934
EGLOFF, Jay (RB)
Hanover, Pa., 1986-87-88-89
ELKINS, Brent Louis (CB)
Dallas, Tex., 1976-77-78
ELKINS, Jimmy (OG)
Crowley, La., 1970-71-72
ELKO, William (DT)
Winder, Pa., 1981-82
ELLEN, Don (LG)
Monroe, La., 1963-64-65
ELLINGTON, Eric L. (RB)
Cincinnati, Ohio, 1980
ELLIS, Frank (T-G)
Covington, La., 1927-28-29
ENSMINGER, Steven Craig (QB)
Baton Rouge, La., 1976-77-78-79
ERDMANN, Charles (HB)
New Orleans, La., 1938
ERNST, Paul (TE)
Slidell, La., 1989-90
ESTAY, Ronnie (DT)
Larose, La., 1969-70-71
ESTES, Don (LT)
Brookhaven, Miss., 1960-61-62
ESTES, Stephen Clayton (Steve) (C)
Port Arthur, Tex., 1974-75-76
ESTHAY, Terry (LT)
Lake Charles, La., 1965-66-67
EVANS, Miller (G)
Vicksburg, Miss., 1941
EVANS, W. Morton (HB-E)
Baton Rouge, La., 1910-11-12-13
EWEN, Earl L. (Tubby) (FB)
Bertrand, Neb., 1920-21-22-23
EZELL, Billy (QB)
Greenville, Miss., 1963-64-65

F

FABACHER, Tom (DB)
River Ridge, La., 1988-89
FAHEY, John K. (G)
Opelousas, La., 1903
FAKIER, Joe (SE)
Thibodaux, La., 1971-72-73
FAMBROUGH, Larry (FB)
Springhill, La., 1964-65
FARMER, Hermann (Red) (T)
Shreveport, La., 1936-37-38
FARRELL, William Y. (DE)
Pompano Beach, Fla., 1978-79

213

FATHERREE, Jesse L. (HB)
Jackson, Miss., 1933-34-35
FAY, Theodore D. (Red) (FB)
Jeanerette, La., 1923-24-25
FENTON, G. E. (Doc) (QB)
Scranton, Pa., 1907-08-09
FERGUSON, Commodore (T)
Memphis, Tenn., 1937
FERGUSON, O. K. (FB)
Woodville, Miss., 1955
FERGUSON, Pleasant L. (G)
Leesville, La., 1907
FERRER, Steve (DT-OG)
Metairie, La., 1973-74-75
FIELD, Elmer (Bubba) (HB)
Marshall, Tex., 1949
FIELD, Jimmy (QB)
Baton Rouge, La., 1960-61-62
FIFE, Robert (HB)
Waterproof, La., 1938
FLANAGAN, H. F. (Mike) (HB)
New Britain, Conn., 1916
FLEMING, Walter (Goat) (E)
Lake Charles, La., 1929-31-32
FLOOD, Martin T (G)
Shreveport, La., 1925
FLOYD, J. C. (Red) (T-G)
Jena, La., 1915-16-19
FLUKER, H. V. (E)
Monroe, La., 1913
FLURRY, Bob (LE)
Homer, La., 1960-61-62
FOGG, Ed (LT)
Slidell, La., 1953-55
FOLEY, Art (HB)
Eufala, Okla., 1931
FONTENOT, Ferdinand M. (FB)
Crowley, La., 1903
FONTENOT, Herman J. (FL)
Beaumont, Tex., 1981-82-83-84
FORDHAM, Jeff (OG)
Radnor, Pa. 1983
FORET, John (OT)
Lake Charles, La., 1971-72
FORET, Lynn (C)
Lake Charles, La., 1970
FORGEY, Charles W. M. (FB)
Berwick, La., 1923
FORTIER, Bill (T)
Jackson, Miss., 1966-67-68
FOTI, Russ (LG)
Ravenna, Ohio, 1946-47
FOURMY, James M. (QB)
Franklin, La., 1903-04
FOURNET, Emile (G)
Bogalusa, La., 1958-59
FOURNET, John B (G)
St. Martinville, La., 1917-19
FOURNET, Sidney (LG)
Bogalusa, La., 1951-52-53-54
FRANCIS, Harrison (FB)
Franklin, La., 1975-76
FRANCIS, Jerome N. (DE)
Sulphur, La., 1979
FRAYER, Jack (T)
Toledo, Ohio, 1958-59
FREEMAN, G. A. (Nubs) (G-E)
Natchitoches, La., 1927
FREEMAN, G. Chester (RHB)
Baton Rouge, La., 1949-50-51
FREY, Ignatius (FB)
New Orleans, La., 1941
FRIEND, Ben (T)
Gulfport, Miss., 1936-37-38
FRIGO, Christopher P. (L)
New Orleans, La., 1985-86
FRITCHIE, John A. (LB)
Baton Rouge, La., 1980-81-82-83
FRIZZELL, Tommy N. (LB)
Athens, Tex., 1978-79
FROECHTENICHT, W. H. (E)
Blue Point, N.Y., 1939
FRYE, Barton (CB)
Baton Rouge, La., 1966-67-68
FRYE, Lloyd (LB)
Baton Rouge, La., 1969-70-71
FUCHS, George (G)
New Orleans, La., 1899-1900-01
FUGLER, Max (C)
Ferriday, La., 1957-58-59
FULKERSON, Jack (E)
Hope, Ark., 1940-41-42
FULLER, Eddie (TB)
Leesville, La., 1986-87-88-89
FULLER, Vincent (DB/TB)
Leesville, La., 1988-90-91-92
FUSSELL, Tommy (RT)
Baton Rouge, La., 1964-65-66

G

GAINEY, Jim (DE)
Hammond, La., 1971-72
GAJAN, Howard L. (Hokie) (TB)
Baton Rouge, La., 1977-78-79-80

GAMBLE, Harry P. (E)
Natchitoches, La., 1894-95
GAMBRELL, Michael J. (C)
Slidell, La., 1980-81-82-83
GANDY, Marshall H. (Cap) (T)
Negreet, La., 1906-07-08
GARDNER, Dennis (OG)
Crowley, La., 1975-76
GARDNER, Jim W. (E)
Minden, La., 1956-57
GARLAND, Joseph M. (G-T)
Opelousas, La., 1900
GARLINGTON, John (DE)
Jonesboro, La., 1965-66-67
GARRETT, Mike (TB-WR)
The Woodlands, Tex., 1989-90-91-92
GARY, Dexter (LG)
Kaplan, La., 1960-61
GATES, Jack (RE)
Lake Charles, La., 1960-61-62
GATTO, Eddie (T)
New Orleans, La., 1936-37-38
GAUBATZ, Dennis (LB)
West Columbia, Tex., 1960-61-62
GAUTREAUX, Russell (FB)
Baton Rouge, La., 1952-53
GAYDEN, George L. (Hack) (E)
Gurley, La., 1926
GAYLE, Edwin F. (HB)
Legonier, La., 1893
GIACONE, Joe (HB)
Bogalusa, La., 1941-42
GIANELLONI, Vivian J. (G)
Baton Rouge, La., 1939-40
GILBERT, Jimmy (QB-DB-TB)
Bastrop, La., 1967-68-69
GILL, Audis (HB)
New Orleans, La., 1945
GILL, Reuben O. (Rube) (HB-E)
Ruston, La., 1907-08-09
GILLYARD, James (OLB)
Shreveport, La., 1992
GIOVANNI, Charles (Tony) (G)
Lake Charles, La., 1930-31
GIRON, Derrick (S)
Port Arthur, Tex., 1988
GLADDEN, Sterling W. (Buck) (HB)
Alexandria, La., 1919
GLAMP, Joe (HB)
Mt. Pleasant, Pa., 1942
GODCHAUX, Frank A. (QB)
Baton Rouge, La., 1897
GODFREY, Frank (C)
Pascagoula, Miss., 1989-90-91-92
GODFREY, Lola T. (Babe) (QB)
Willington, Tex., 1925-26-27
GONZALES, Vincent (Vince) (LHB)
New Orleans, La., 1952-53-54-55
GOODE, Burton (E)
DeQuincy, La., 1943
GOODRUM, James F. (G)
Mathews, La., 1985
GORE, Gary C. (Curt) (OG)
Fairhope, Ala., 1982-83-84-85
GOREE, J. W. (G)
Haynesville, La., 1938-39-40
GORHAM, Edwin S. (E)
Lake Charles, La., 1899-1900-1901
GORINSKI, Walter (FB)
Mutual, Pa., 1940-41-42
GORMLEY, Jack (E)
Tyler, Tex., 1936-37-38
GORMLEY, Richard (C)
Tyler, Tex., 1936-37-38
GOSSERAND, M. L. (Goose) (FB)
New Roads, La., 1910-11-12
GOURRIER, Samuel A. (QB-HB)
Baton Rouge, La., 1896
GRAHAM, Durwood (FB)
Vicksburg, Miss., 1955-56
GRANIER, Richard (C)
St. James, La., 1963-64
GRAVES, Soloman "Sol" (QB)
Monroe, La., 1990
GRAVES, White (LHB)
Crystal Springs, Miss., 1962-63-64
GRAY, Dale (LHB)
El Dorado, Ark., 1946-47-48
GREEN, Robby (S)
Gretna, La., 1989-90-91
GREEN, V. E. (Chick) (FB)
DeRidder, La., 1914
GREEN, Winfred C. (Poss) (HB)
DeRidder, La., 1913-14-15-16
GREENWOOD, Bobby (C)
Lake Charles, La., 1958-59
GREER, Ed (QB)
Minden, La., 1964
GREMILLION, F. V. (T)
1899-1900
GREVEMBERG, Albert (T)
Savannah, Ga., 1927
GREVEMBERG, Joseph H. (E)
Savannah, Ga., 1926-27
GREZAFFI, Sammy (S)
New Roads, La., 1965-66-67

GRIFFIN, Benny (LB)
Baton Rouge, La., 1965-66-67
GRIFFIN, John (K)
Gloster, Miss., 1987
GRIFFITH, Brian (P)
Memphis, Tenn., 1988-89-90-91
GRIFFITH, Carroll (HB-QB)
N. Little Rock, Ark., 1943-47-48-49
GRIFFITH, J. H. (John) (E)
Jackson, Mich., 1905
GRIVOT, Maurice
New Orleans, La., 1894
GROS, Earl (FB)
Houma, La., 1959-60-61
GUENO, Albert J. (E)
Crowley, La., 1901-02-03
GUGLIELMO, Al (RE)
Lutcher, La., 1951-52-53
GUIDRY, J. W. (T)
Opelousas, La., 1901-02-03
GUIDRY, Kevin (DB)
Lake Charles, La., 1984-85-86-87
GUIDRY, Mickey J. (QB)
Gretna, La., 1985-86-87-88
GUILLOT, Jerry (RG)
Thibodaux, La., 1966-67-68
GUILLOT, Rodney (T)
Baton Rouge, La., 1960-62
GUILLOT, Rodney (Monk) (RG)
New Orleans, La., 1959-60-61
GUILLOT, Stephen Roch (Rocky) (C)
Shreveport, La., 1976-77-78
GUNNELS, William D., Jr. (DE)
Hahnville, La., 1977

H

HABERT, Ed (G)
Vicksburg, Miss. 1960-61-62
HAGUE, Perry G. (QB-HB)
Baton Rouge, La., 1919-20
HALEY, Otis (B)
Tyler, Tex., 1943
HALIBURTON, Ronnie (TE)
Port Arthur, Tex., 1986-87-88-89
HALL, Fred (Skinny) (E-T-G)
Haynesville, La., 1941-42-46
HALL, J. O. (Doc) (E)
Lake Charles, La., 1909-10-11-12
HALL, Marc (DL)
Patterson, La., 1984
HAMIC, Garland (Buddy) (FB)
Crowley, La., 1961-62-63
HAMIC, Jimmy (RG)
Crowley, La., 1965-66
HAMILTON, Andy (SB)
Ruston, La., 1969-70-71
HAMILTON, W. J. (QB)
Winnfield, La., 1907
HAMLETT, Bob (TE)
Bossier City, La., 1966-67-68
HAMMOND, M. R. (Bull) (HB-FB)
Jennings, La., 1910-11
HANDY, Beverly B. (Spaghetti) (QB)
Monroe, La., 1907
HANLEY, William B. (Red) (G-T)
Crowville, La., 1919
HARE, Derik K. (WR)
Milton, Fla. 1985
HARGETT, Dan (C)
Lafayette, La., 1960-61
HARMON, Rudy (LB)
Beaumont, Tex., 1987-88
HARP, James F.
Bonita, La., 1896
HARRELL, John F., Jr. (OT)
Alexandria, La., 1982-83-84
HARRELL, Louis (Tee-Tee) (QB)
Baton Rouge, La., 1929
HARRIS, Bill (LT)
Bossier City, La., 1953
HARRIS, Clinton (Bo) (LB)
Shreveport, La., 1972-73-74
HARRIS, L. B. (T)
Denham Springs, La., 1904
HARRIS, Leonard (DT)
Baton Rouge, La., 1989-90
HARRIS, Mickey (RB)
Mandeville, La., 1984-85-86-87
HARRIS, Sulcer (HB)
Baton Rouge, La., 1941-42
HARRIS, Wendell (HB)
Baton Rouge, La., 1959-60-61
HARRISON, Pollard E. (E)
Colfax, La., 1913
HARTLEY, Hugh (T-HB)
Marksville, La., 1906
HARTLEY, Joe (T)
St. Petersburg, Fla., 1943
HATCHER, George R. (E)
Clinton, La., 1927
HAYES, George (LHB)
Clinton, La., 1963-64-65
HAYNES, Everette H. (Hinkey) (HB)
Lineville, Ala., 1925-26-27

HAYNES, Fred (QB)
Minden, La., 1966-67-68
HAYES, George (LHB)
Clinton, La., 1963-64-66
HAZARD, John (DT)
Metairie, La., 1983-84-85-86
HAZARD, Nicky (LB)
Metairie, La., 1984-85-86-87
HEALD, Russell (OT)
Texas City, Tex., 1971-72-73
HEARD, Holley (RT)
Haynesville, La., 1942-47
HEARD, T. J. (Fatty) (G)
Marksville, La., 1904-05
HEBERT, Mike (OLB)
New Orleans, La., 1986-87-88
HEDGES, Lee (QB)
Shreveport, La., 1949-50-51
HELM, Newton C. (Dirty) (E)
Bunkie, La., 1919-20-21-22
HELMS, Lee (E)
Homewood, La. 1926
HELSCHER, Harold (HB)
New Orleans, La., 1941
HELVESTON, Osborn (Butch) (G)
Biloxi, Miss., 1933-34-35
HEMPHILL, Don (E)
Bogalusa, La., 1945-46-47
HEMPHILL, Fred Bruce (SE)
Sulphur, La., 1974-75-76
HENDRICK, Bruce (QB)
Birmingham, Ala., 1938
HENDRIX, Billy R. (E)
Rayville, La., 1966-67-68
HENDRIX, Billy R., Jr. (NG)
Bunkie, La., 1981-83-84
HENDRIX, John A. (Johnnie) (HB)
Olla, La., 1928-29-30
HENDRIX, Sid W. (QB)
Baton Rouge, La., 1922
HENRIQUEZ, George (DE-NG)
New Orleans, La., 1984-86-87
HENRY, Thomas J. (HB-FB)
Alton, Ill., 1916
HENSLEY, James Craig (LB)
Lake Charles, La., 1976-77-78
HEBERT, Arthur W. (Doc) (G)
Alexandria, La., 1916-17
HEREFORD, Robert M. (T)
Lake Charles, La., 1920-21
HERGET, George Caldwell (Warm-Up) (E)
Baton Rouge, La., 1925-26
HERNANDEZ, Jude B. (FB)
Baton Rouge, La., 1978-79-80-81
HEROMAN, Alfred (LHB)
Baton Rouge, La., 1946-47-48
HERPIN, Joseph O. (E)
Lafayette, La., 1899-1901
HERRINGTON, James (G)
Lake Providence, La., 1944
HEWETT, Lem F. (E)
Lexington, Neb., 1920
HEWITT, Mike (OLB)
Slidell, La., 1990-91-92
HIGHTOWER, Gerald (HB)
Arcadia, La., 1939-40-41
HILL, Chris (TE)
Mansfield, La., 1992
HILL, Eric D. (OLB)
Galveston, Tex., 1985-86-87-88
HILL, Jerry D. (LB)
Midwest City, Okla., 1978-79
HILL, Terry (LB)
Baton Rouge, La., 1973-74-75
HILLIARD, Dalton (TB)
Patterson, La., 1982-83-84-85
HILLIARD, Ivory (S)
Patterson, La., 1991-92
HILLMAN, Mike (QB)
Lockport, La., 1967-68-69
HILLMAN, William A. (G)
Minden, La., 1906-07-08-09
HIMES, Levi A. (Lee) (QB)
Baton Rouge, La., 1906-07-08-09
HINTON, Lora (TB-RB)
Chesapeake, Va., 1973-74-75
HOBLEY, Liffort W. (FS)
Shreveport, La., 1980-82-83-84
HODGE, Abner A.
Natchez, Miss., 1894
HODGES, Harry (C)
Baton Rouge, La., 1954-55

HODGINS, Leo M. (TE)
Metairie, La., 1976
HODGINS, Norman (DB-SB)
Metairie, La., 1971-72-73
HODSON, Tommy (QB)
Mathews, La., 1986-87-88-89
HOGAN, BILL (QB-C)
Laurel, Miss., 1939-40-41
HOLDEN, T. D. (E)
Picayune, Miss., 1929-30
HOLLAND, Pershing (G-E)
Plain Dealing, La., 1941-42
HOLLAND, Woodrow (E)
Plain Dealing, La., 1942
HOLT, Glenn (WR)
Miami, Fla., 1984-85
HORNE, Frank (RT)
Fayette, Ala., 1952
HOUSTON, Tony (DB)
Ruston, La., 1987-88-89
HOVER, Allen (T)
Memphis, Tenn., 1948-49-50
HOWARD, Jamie (QB)
Lafayette, La., 1992
HOWARD, Tommy (OLB)
Columbus, Mo., 1983-85-86
HOWELL, Robert C. (E)
Wilcox, La., 1903
HOWELL, Roland B. (Billiken) (QB)
Thibodaux, La., 1909-11
HOWELL, William C. (E)
St. Francisville, La., 1897
HUBBELL, Michael R. (Mickey) (SB)
Metairie, La., 1978
HUBICZ, Jim (OT/OG)
Sharon, Pa., 1986-87-88-89
HUCKLEBRIDGE, Robbie (LG)
Bossier City, La., 1961-62-63
HUERKAMP, Matt (PK)
Shalimar, Fla., 1992
HUEY, James M.
Ruston, La., 1893
HUFFMAN, Alva S. (Brute) (T)
DeRidder, La., 1926-27-28
HUFFMAN, Ryan (QB)
Houston, Texas, 1992
HUGHES, Clyde B. (Red) (T)
Baton Rouge, La., 1921-23
HUMBLE, John (C)
Monroe, La., 1944
HUNSICKER, George R. (E)
Shreveport, La., 1905
HUNT, Ralph (T)
Shreveport, La., 1943
HUNTER, Guy N.
Waterproof, La., 1894
HUNTER, Louis T.
Waterproof, La., 1894
HUNTER, Robert (LE)
Los Angeles, Cal., 1950
HURD, Roy (K)
Covington, La., 1967
HUTCHINSON, Roger (OT)
Gonzales, La., 1988-89
HUTCHINSON, Thos. C. (Chris) (CB)
Monroe, La., 1981
HUYCK, Phillip P. (G)
Baton Rouge, La., 1895-96-97-99

I

INDEST, Adalphe (G)
New Orleans, La., 1944
IPPOLITO, Mark A. (LB)
New Orleans, La., 1978-79
IVES, Clarence A. (Fatty) (HB)
Baton Rouge, La., 1917-19-20-21

J

JACKSON, Augustus W. (Gus) (FB)
Lecompte, La., 1922-23-24
JACKSON, Dalton (Rusty) (KS)
Chatom, Ala., 1972-73-74
JACKSON, Gregory A. (S)
Miami, Fla., 1985-86-87-88
JACKSON, Steve Loran (S)
Chatom, Ala., 1974-75-76
JACOB, Wesley (FL)
Crowley, La., 1989-90-91-92
JACQUET, James (TB)
St. Martinville, La., 1991
JAMES, Albert (S)
Covington, La., 1940-41
JAMES, Clint (DE)
New Orleans, La., 1986-87-88-89
JAMES, Garry M. (TB)
Gretna, La., 1982-83-84-85
JAMES, Tory (WR)
Marrero, La., 1992
JANNECK, Carl (G)
New Orleans, La., 1943-44
JAUBERT, Jack (C)
Lafayette, La., 1969-70-71
JEAN-BATISTE, Garland (FB)
St. Martinville, La., 1983-84-85-86

JEFFERSON, Norman
Marrero, La., 1983-84-85-86
JENKINS, Brian (TE)
Palestine, Texas, 1990
JENKINS, Darryl (QB)
Franklinton, La., 1958-59-60
JENKINS, Harry (E)
Crowley, La., 1904
JENKINS, Marvin (QB)
Tupelo, Miss., 1939-40
JENNINGS, Joe Patrick (DE)
Baker, La., 1974-75-76
JETER, Ronald (G)
Ferriday, La., 1965-66-67
JOFFRION, A. Bush (HB)
Lecompte, La., 1904-05
JOHNS, Levi (Chuck) (LHB)
Rayville, La., 1953-54-55
JOHNSON, Charles (E)
Conroe, Tex., 1938-39-40
JOHNSON, David R. (KS)
Tempe, Ariz., 1980-81
JOHNSON, Jay (TB)
Waco, Texas, 1992
JOHNSON, Melvin F. (HB)
Lake Charles, La., 1912
JOHNSON, Michael K. (LB)
Franklin, La., 1970
JOHNSON, Mike (LB)
Baton Rouge, La., 1984-85
JOHNSON, Phil (C)
Shreveport, La., 1965-66
JOHNSON, Ray L. (C)
Electra, Tex., 1932
JOHNSON, William C. (OT)
Athens, Tex., 1976-77-78
JOHNSTON, Craig (OT)
Crosby, Texas, 1990
JOHNSTON, Jerry (HB)
Waynesboro, Miss., 1956
JOHNSTON, Mark A. (FL)
Rayville, La., 1981-82
JOHNSTON, Ronnie (HB)
Bastrop, La., 1956
JOINER, Timothy L. (LB)
Baton Rouge, La., 1980-81-82
JONES, Benjamin M. (Ben) (SE)
Ruston, La., 1972-73-74
JONES, Bertram H. (Bert) (QB)
Ruston, La., 1970-71-72
JONES, Carroll (HB)
Ruston, La., 1941
JONES, David (DB)
West Monroe, La., 1966-67
JONES, Keith E. (G)
Winnfield, La., 1915-16-17
JONES, Larry (C)
Little Rock, Ark., 1953-54
JONES, LeRoid E. (FB)
Baton Rouge, La., 1977-80
JONES, LeRoyal A. (CB)
Baton Rouge, La., 1977-80
JONES, Mike (OG)
Shreveport, La., 1975
JONES, Norwood (Chubby) (C)
Lake Providence, La., 1927-28-29
JONES, Richard (SE)
West Monroe, La., 1965-66
JONES, Victor T. (RB)
Zachary, La., 1985-87-88-89
JONES, William A. "Dub" (HB)
Ruston, La., 1942
JORDAN, Jeff (G)
Baton Rouge, La., 1985
JOSEPH, Jerry (DB)
Baton Rouge, La., 1964-65-66

K

KAFFIE, Leopold (C)
Natchitoches, La., 1897-98
KAHLDEN, Larry (G)
Weimar, Tex., 1956-57-58
KAISER, Bradley (OT)
New Orleans, La., 1975
KALIL, Emile (LT)
McComb, Miss., 1952
KARAPHILLIS, John M. (S)
Tarpon Springs, Fla., 1976
KAVANAUGH, Ken, Sr. (E)
Little Rock, Ark., 1937-38-39
KAVANAUGH, Ken, Jr. (SE)
Ft. Washington, Pa., 1969-70-71
KEIGLEY, Gerald (SB-SE)
Greenville, Miss., 1970-71-72
KELLER, Joe L. (HB)
Reserve, La., 1930-31-32
KELLUM, Bill (E)
Haynesville, La., 1945
KELLY, Angus H. (E)
Colfax, La., 1906
KELLY, Charlie (RT)
Natchez, Miss., 1951
KENDRICK, Herbert (T)
Homer, La., 1939-40-41

KENDRICK, Robert (Bob) (FB)
Homer, La., 1939
KENNEDY, Ralph M. (HB)
Los Angeles, Calif., 1901-02-03
KENT, Gerry (CB)
Jackson, Miss., 1966-67-68
KENT, John (C)
Amite, La., 1931-32-33
KENNON, Robert F. (C)
Minden, La., 1924
KHOURY, Ed (Big Ed) (T)
Lake Charles, La., 1929-30-31
KILLEEN, Frank H. (CB)
New Orleans, La., 1982
KILLEEN, Logan (C)
McDade, La. 1971-72-73
KIMBLE, Dennis J. (S)
Baton Rouge, La., 1977-78-79
KINCHEN, Brian (TE)
Baton Rouge, La., 1984-85-86-87
KINCHEN, Gary (C)
Baton Rouge, La., 1960-61-62
KINCHEN, Gaynell (Gus) (E)
Baton Rouge, La., 1958-59-60
KINCHEN, Todd (WR)
Baton Rouge, La., 1989-90-91
KING, Bobby Joe (DT)
Shreveport, La., 1968-69-70
KING, Larry (E)
New Orleans, La., 1937
KING, Larry (FB)
Lake Charles, La., 1955
KING, Mark (OG)
Houma, La., 1992
KING, Shawn (OLB)
Monroe, La., 1990-91
KINGERY, Don (TB)
Lake Charles, La., 1943
KINGERY, Wayne (HB)
Lake Charles, La., 1945
KITTO, Armand (RE)
New Orleans, La., 1948-49-50
KITTOK, Eric D. (DT)
New Orleans, La., 1982-86
KIZER, Roland C. (Chesty) (QB)
Monticello, Ark., 1922
KNECHT, Jas. Doyle (CB)
Natchitoches, La., 1972-73-74
KNIGHT, Alex A. (Butch) (DE)
Baton Rouge, La., 1974-75-76
KNIGHT, Gene (Red) (FB)
Bossier City, La., 1943-44-45-46
KNIGHT, ROY (C)
EL Dorado, Ark., 1935
KLOCK, Arthur E. (G)
Cheneyville, La., 1912-13-14-16
KLOCK, E. L. (G)
Cheneyville, La., 1902-03-04-05
KOBER, Jerry (E)
Souderton, Pa., 1967-69
KOCK, David T. (OT)
Houston, Tex., 1979-80-81
KONZ, Kenneth (LHB)
Weimar, Tex., 1948-49-50
KOSMAC, Andrew (C)
Plains, Pa., 1942-45
KREMENTZ, F. B. (Freddy) (E)
Baton Rouge, La., 1915-16

L

LABAT, Leroy (HB)
LaPlace, La., 1951-52
LABRUZZO, Joe (LHB)
Lockport, La., 1963-64-65
LAFAUCI, Tyler (OG-DT)
New Orleans, La., 1971-72-73
LaFLEUR, Gregory L. (SE)
Ville Platte, La., 1977-79-80
LALLY, Michael F. (HB)
Jessup, Pa., 1908-10
LAMBERT, James (Coot) (S)
Canton, Miss., 1967-68
LAMBERT, Sam (FB)
Baton Rouge, La., 1895-96
LAND, Fred N. (T)
N. Little Rock, Ark., 1944-45-46-47
LANDRY, Ben H. (T)
Lake Charles, La., 1929
LANDRY, Darron (OG)
Ponchatoula, La., 1989-90-91-92
LANDRY, Henry E. (FB)
Garyville, La., 1899-1900-02
LANDRY, M. J. (HB)
Baton Rouge, La., 1945
LANDRY, Walter M. (Bud) (G)
Westwego, La., 1921-22
LANDRY, Willard (LHB)
Baton Rouge, La., 1945-46
LANE, Clifton R. (Cliff) (TE)
Monroe, La., 1976-77-78
LANE, Robert H. (QB-S)
Monroe, La., 1979
LANG, Gene E. (RB)
Pass Christian, Miss., 1980-81-82-83

LANGAN, John (C)
Carbondale, Ill., 1957-58-59
LANGFORD, Kevin R. (OG)
Florence, Miss., 1982-83-84
LANGLEY, Leroy (HB)
Jennings, La., 1932-33
LANGLEY, Willis (RT)
Basile (Oberlin), La., 1962-63
LANOUX, Paul R., III (OT)
New Orleans, La., 1974-75-56
LANSING, Bill (RG)
Magnolia, Miss., 1950-51-52
LaSUEUR, Leon J. (G)
Baton Rouge, La., 1902
LATOUR, Brandon (LB)
Baton Rouge, La., 1990
LAVIN, Jim (T)
New Orleans, La., 1956-57
LAWRASON, Charles M. (E)
St. Francisville, La., 1899
LAWRENCE, Bob (LT)
Brilliant, Ala., 1962-63
LAWRENCE, Oliver C. (LB)
Monroe, La., 1985-86-87-89
LAWRIE, Joe (QB)
St. Petersburg, Fla., 1933-34-35
LAWSON, Jamie (RB)
Raceland, La., 1984-85
LAWTON, Jack E. Jr. (Jackie) (CB)
Sulphur, La., 1976-77
LAY, Andrew (HB)
Homer, La., 1944
LEACH, Joe (E)
Shreveport, La., 1946-47
LEAKE, Sam (RT)
Woodville, Miss., 1953
LeBLANC, Allen (T)
New Iberia, La., 1965-66-67
LeBLANC, Lynn (T)
Crowley, La., 1957-58-59
LeBLANC, Maurice (SB)
Lafayette, La., 1966-67-68
LeBLANC, Troy (RB)
Lafayette, La., 1989
LEBLEU, Claude A. (E)
Lake Charles, La., 1929
LEDBETTER, Wiltz M. (G)
Summerfield, La., 1895-96
LeDOUX, Jimmy (SE)
Sulphur, La., 1970-71-72
LEE, Alvin (WR)
Beaumont, Tex., 1986-87-88-89
LEE, David (DE)
Bastrop, La., 1973
LEE, Felix (Buddy) (QB)
Zachary, La., 1969-70
LEGGETT, Earl (T)
Jacksonville, Fla., 1955-56
LEISK, Wardell (G)
Shreveport, La., 1935-36
LELEKACS, Steve (LB)
Angleton, Tex., 1972-73-74
LEMAK, Charles W. (TB)
Duquesne, Pa., 1937
LEMOINE, Hampton T. (Tick) (G)
Marksville, La., 1899
LEONARD, Michael B. (Mike) (S)
Shreveport, La., 1974-75-76
LEOPARD, Duane (C)
Baton Rouge, La., 1957-58-59
LeSAGE, Joe (QB)
Homer, La., 1948
LESTER, Gordon (T)
Lockhart, Tex., 1935-37
LeSUEUR, George B. (Heck) (FB)
Baton Rouge, La., 1897-98-99
LEVY, Julius M.
Evergreen, La., 1897
LEWIS, Freddie L. (LB)
Lake Charles, La., 1981-83-84
LEWIS, James (LG)
Tyler, Tex., 1943-47-48
LEWIS, John W. (Johnnie) (E)
Opelousas, La., 1920-21
LEWIS, Ron (K)
New Orleans, La., 1984-85-86-87
LEWIS, William J. (QB-HB)
Ruston, La., 1894
LEWIS, William S. (Bill) (HB)
DeRidder, La., 1915-16
LINDSEY, Clyde (T)
Kilgore, Tex., 1944-45-46
LIPKIS, Bernie (C-E)
New Orleans, La., 1939-40
LOBDELL, W. Y. (Bill) (QB)
Baton Rouge, La., 1932-33
LOFLIN, Jim (E)
New Orleans, La., 1946-47
LOFTIN, Billy (E)
DeRidder, La., 1967-68
LOFTON, Andy (WR)
Hammond, La., 1988-89
LONERGAN, Patrick M. (Pat) (OG)
New Orleans, La., 1978
LOTT, Bobby (E)
Texarkana, Ark., 1956

LOTT, Tommy (G)
  Texarkana, Ark., 1957-58-59
LOUP, Chad (QB)
  Baton Rouge, La., 1990-91-92
LOUSTALOT, Albert L. (HB)
  Franklin, La., 1903
LOUSTALOT, Matthew L. (Matt) (C)
  Franklin, La., 1923
LOUVIERE, William H. (Chick) (C)
  Houma, La., 1914
LUKER, J. B. (E)
  Alexandria, La., 1928-29-30
LUMPKIN, Mark (KS)
  Lake Charles, La., 1967-68-69
LYLE, Jim (Egg) (LE)
  El Dorado, Ark., 1948-49-50
LYLE, Mel (LE)
  El Dorado, Ark., 1946-47-48-49
LYLES, William M. (Buffalo) (T)
  Leesville, La., 1904-07
LYONS, Frederick G. (QB)
  New Orleans, La., 1893
LYONS, Pat (QB)
  Midland, Tex., 1975-76-77
LYONS, Paul (QB)
  Midland, Tex., 1970-71-72

M

MACKEY, Guy (SE)
  Lake Charles, La., 1983
MADDEN, Bryan (OT)
  Indianapolis, Ind., 1991-92
MAGEE, Rogee (WR)
  Bogalusa, La., 1984-85-86-87
MAGGIORE, Ernest (LT)
  Norco, La., 1963-64-65
MAHFOUZ, Robert P. (QB)
  Lafayette, La., 1979-80
MAHTOOK, Michael A. (ILB)
  Lafayette, La., 1982
MAHTOOK, Robert A., Jr. (LB)
  Lafayette, La., 1978-79
MALANCON, Rydell J. (LB)
  Vacherie, La., 1980-81-82-83
MALBROUGH, Darren (LB)
  Metairie, La., 1984-86-87
MALONE, Jim (G-T)
  Reform, Ala., 1930-31-32
MAMOUDIS, Charles G. (Chuck) (FL)
  Chesapeake, Va., 1974-75
MANGHAM, Mickey (E)
  Kensington, Md., 1958-59-60
MANTON, Ronnie (G)
  Brookhaven, Miss., 1965-66-67
MARCHAND, Jerry (LHB)
  Baton Rouge, La., 1952-53
MARIX, Michael (OL)
  Plaquemine, La., 1990-91
MARSHALL, Anthony (S)
  Mobile, Ala., 1990-91
MARSHALL, Leonard A. (DT)
  Franklin, La., 1979-80-81-82
MARTIN, Andy (OT)
  DeRidder, La., 1988-89-90-91
MARTIN, C. Y. (G)
  Bowie, La., 1910
MARTIN, Curtis (SE)
  Golden Meadow, La., 1969
MARTIN, Eric W. (SE)
  Van Vleck, Tex., 1981-82-83-84
MARTIN, G. H. (G)
  Crowley, La., 1914
MARTIN, Jackie (FB)
  Haynesville, La., 1950
MARTIN, Sammy (TB)
  New Orleans, La., 1984-85-86-87
MARTIN, Steve (DT-OG)
  Houston, Tex., 1968-70
MARTIN, Wade O. (Skinny) (E)
  Arnaudville, La., 1902-03-04
MASON, C. C. (Charlie) (QB)
  Shreveport, La., 1926-27-28
MASTERS, Billy (E-SB)
  Olla, La., 1964-65-66
MATHERNE, Durel (QB)
  Lutcher, La., 1958-59
MATLOCK, Oscar (RG)
  Shreveport, La., 1936
MATTE, Frank (SB)
  Jennings, La., 1966-67-68
MATTHEWS, Lawrence R. (Tubbo) (FB)
  St. Francisville, La., 1922-23
MAWAE, John (NG)
  Leesville, La., 1992
MAWAE, Kevin (OT/OG/C)
  Leesville, La., 1990-91-92
MAY, Bill (QB-FB)
  El Dorado, Ark., 1934-35-36
MAY, Joe (HB)
  Shreveport, La., 1954-55-56
MAY, William J. (Jon) (DT)
  Homer, La., 1977
MAY, Joe (HB)
  Shreveport, La., 1954-55-56

MAYES, Michael O. (CB)
  DeRidder, La., 1985-87-88
MAYET, Jay (LB)
  Galliano, La., 1986
McCABE, Raymond J., III (DT)
  Metairie, La., 1981
McCAGE, Samuel V. (TE)
  Baytown, Tex., 1977-78-79
McCALL, Henry L. (Mac) (E)
  Lake Charles, La., 1923-26
McCANN, John (RG)
  Baton Rouge, La., 1968-69-70
McCANN, M. G. (Mickey) (HB)
  New Orleans, La., 1927
McCARSON, Paul (HB)
  Batesville, Ark., 1944
McCARTY, Dave (T-E)
  Rayville, La., 1958-59
McCASKILL, Larry (C)
  Baton Rouge, La., 1967-68
McCLAIN, Jess (C)
  Covington, La., 1930-31
McCLAIN, Scotty (E)
  Smackover, Ark., 1957-58-59
McCLELLAND, William (RG)
  Crowley, La., 1943-44-47-48
McCOLLAM, Andrew M. (HB)
  Houma, La., 1909
McCORMICK, Dave (LT)
  Rayville, La., 1963-64-65
McCORVEY, Derriel (S)
  Pensacola, Fla., 1989-90-91-92
McCREADY, James M. (QB)
  Metairie, La., 1982
McCREEDY, Ed (G)
  Biloxi, Miss., 1958-59-60
McDANIEL, Orlando K. (SE)
  Lake Charles, La., 1978-79-80-81
McDONALD, Robert (LE)
  Franklin, La., 1960
McDUFF, Chas. H. (OT)
  Baton Rouge, La., 1978-79
McFARLAND, Reggie A. (HB)
  Baton Rouge, La., 1919-20-21-22
McFERIN, Sherman S. (Mack) (G)
  Pleasant Hill, La., 1929
McHENRY, Barney G. (Mac) (T)
  Monroe, La., 1910-11
McINGVALE, Ralph C. (OT)
  Dallas, Tex., 1977
McKINNEY, Billy (HB)
  Jackson, Tenn., 1939-41
McKINNEY, Jim (HB)
  Bogalusa, La., 1939
McLEOD, James (E)
  Laurel, Miss., 1941-42-47
McLEOD, Ralph (LE)
  Beaumont, Tex., 1950-51-52
McNAIR, Dan (OG)
  Monroe, La., 1973
McNEESE, Oswald W. (E)
  Lake Charles, La., 1900-01
McSHERRY, Robert (LB)
  Monroe, La., 1967-68
MELANCON, Keith (OL)
  Hahnville, La., 1984-85-86
MENETRE, Ralph (LHB)
  Covington, La., 1945
MERCER, John (RHB)
  Bossier City, La., 1961-62
MERO, Pershing (Joe) (CB)
  New Orleans, La., 1990-91
MESSA, Rene A. (FB)
  Santiago, Cuba, 1904-05
MESSINA, Jake (G)
  Port Arthur, Tex., 1937-38-39
MESTAYER, Otto (E)
  New Iberia, La., 1914
MICHAELSON, Fred (MG-T)
  Foley, Ala., 1967-68-69
MICHAELSON, Julius (Jay) (TE)
  Foley, Ala., 1969-70-71
MICIOTTO, Charles (Binks) (DE)
  Lafayette, La., 1971-72-73
MICKAL, Abe (HB)
  McComb, Miss., 1933-34-35
MIDDLETON, Eric (ILB)
  Corsicana, Tex., 1988
MIHALICH, John (Mickey) (E)
  Lorain, Ohio, 1934-35-36
MILEY, Mike (QB)
  Metairie, La., 1972-73
MILLER, Ben R. (E)
  Shreveport, La., 1923-24-25
MILLER, Blake (OG/C)
  Alexandria, La., 1987-88-89-90
MILLER, Charles (Chip) (DT)
  New Orleans, La., 1972-73
MILLER, Dale (FB)
  Franklinton, La., 1971
MILLER, Fred (RT)
  Homer, La., 1960-61-62
MILLER, Herd (T-G)
  Springfield, La., 1943-44-45-46
MILLER, Nate (DT)
  Tuscaloosa, Ala., 1991-92

MILLER, Paul (LT)
  Baton Rouge, La., 1950-52-53
MILLER, Willie (G)
  Minden, La., 1940-41-42
MILLET, Walter (CB)
  Pasadena, Tex., 1973
MILLICAN, Samuel (Buddy) (DE)
  Baton Rouge, La., 1968-69-70
MILNER, Guy (Cotton) (HB)
  Alexandria, La., 1936-37-38
MINALDI, Thad (FB)
  Lake Charles, La., 1975-76-77-78
MISTRETTA, Albert (T)
  Covington, La., 1943
MITCHELL, George (Gee) (G)
  Rayville, La., 1932-33
MITCHELL, Jim (E)
  Baton Rouge, La., 1952-53-56
MIXON, Neil (HB)
  Amite, La., 1931-32-33
MOBLEY, Larry (RE)
  Baton Rouge, La., 1952-54
MOBLEY, T. R. (Ray) (G-C)
  Coushatta, La., 1913-14
MODICUT, Joseph (LG)
  Baton Rouge, La., 1951-52
MONGET, Gayle (C)
  Baton Rouge, La., 1937-38-39
MONSOUR, Eli (Mike) (E)
  Shreveport, La., 1927
MONTZ, Michael C. (RB)
  Lutcher, La., 1980-81-82
MONTGOMERY, William (FB)
  Murphysboro, Ill., 1942-43-45
MOOCK, Chris (QB)
  Greenwell Springs, La., 1988-89-90
MOORE, Charles (E)
  Chattanooga, Tenn., 1964-65
MOORE, Charles F. (SB)
  Plaquemine, La., 1964-65
MOORE, D. Haywood (G-T)
  Jonesboro, La., 1928-29-31
MOORE, Frank E. (Specks) (E)
  Douglas, Ariz., 1932-33-34
MOORE, Sean B. (LB)
  Poplar Bluff, Mo., 1981-82
MOREAU, Doug (LE)
  Baton Rouge, La., 1963-64-65
MOREAU, Kenneth R. (Bobby) (QB-LB)
  Alexandria, La., 1975-76-77
MOREL, Tommy (SE)
  New Orleans, La., 1966-67-68
MORGAN, John (DT-NG)
  Rayne, La., 1989-90-91-92
MORGAN, Mike (RE)
  Natchez, Miss., 1961-62-63
MORGAN, Paul C. (FB-HB)
  Elba, Ala., 1927
MORGAN, Sam R. (T)
  Elba, Ala., 1924-25-26
MORRIS, John E. (T)
  West Monroe, La., 1895
MORTIMER, Eugene H. (HB)
  Laurel, Miss., 1900
MORTON, Arthur (Slick) (HB-TB)
  Tallulah, La., 1935-36-37
MOSES, Phil (C)
  Sulphur, La., 1972-73-74
MOSS, Tony (WR)
  Shreveport, La., 1986-87-88-89
MOUTON, Clayton (DT)
  Beaumont, Tex., 1989-90-91-92
MULLER, J. C. (E)
  Washington, La., 1904-05
MULLINS, William B. (E)
  Simsboro, La., 1894
MUNDINGER, Adam G. (Addie) (T)
  Baton Rouge, La., 1900-01-02
MURLA, Mike (LB)
  New Orleans, La., 1986-87-88-89
MURPHREE, Jerry D. (TB)
  Birmingham, Ala., 1977-78-79
MURPHY, Sammy (RE)
  Baker, La., 1952-53-54
MURRAY, Keith E. (P)
  Theodore, Ala., 1985
MURRAY, Phil (OT)
  Franklinton, La., 1970-71-72
MYLES, Jesse J. (TB)
  Gray, La., 1979-80-81-82
MYLES, Lonny (SE)
  Franklinton, La., 1967-68
MYRICK, Basil (LE)
  El Dorado, Ark., 1936

N

NAGATA, Joe (HB)
  Eunice, La., 1942-43
NAGLE, John (CB)
  Gloster, Miss., 1969-70-71
NEALY, Wrendall (RE)
  Homer, La., 1951-52
NECK, Tommy (HB)
  Marksville, La., 1959-60-61

NELKEN, William
  Natchitoches, La., 1894
NELSON, Manson (G)
  Ferriday, La., 1958-59
NELSON, Robert J.
  Monroe, La., 1894
NEPHEW, Tony (ILB)
  Willis, Tex., 1983
NESOM, Guy W. (T)
  Tickfaw, La., 1926-27-28
NEUMANN, Danny (E)
  Tallulah, La., 1961-62-63
NEUMANN, Leonard (TB)
  Tallulah, La., 1964-65-66
NEVILS, Ab (T)
  Lake Charles, La., 1931-32-33
NEWFIELD, Kenny (FB)
  New Orleans, La., 1966-67-68
NEWELL, Edward T. J.
  St. Joseph, La., 1894
NICAR, Randy (DT)
  Morgan City, La., 1971
NICHOLSON, Gordon B. (HB)
  Baton Rouge, La., 1894-95-96-97
NICOLO, Sal (HB)
  Saugus, Mass., 1952-54
NOBLET, Oren H. (Babe) (G)
  Denham Springs, La., 1904-05-07-08
NOONAN, James (DT)
  New Orleans, La., 1976
NORFLEET, Fred (FB)
  Memphis, Tenn., 1989
NORRIS, Craig (DE)
  Cicero, N.Y., 1988
NORSWORTHY, Bill (DT)
  New Orleans, La., 1968-69-70
NORTHERN, Gabe (OLB)
  Baton Rouge, La., 1992
NORWOOD, Don (E)
  Baton Rouge, La., 1957-58-59
NORWOOD, Ralph E. (OT)
  New Orleans, La., 1985-86-87-88
NUNNERY, R. B. (RT)
  Summit, Miss., 1954-55

O

OAKLEY, Charles (FB)
  Lake Charles, La., 1951-52-53
O'BRIEN, Robert (Bob) (E)
  New Orleans, La., 1964-65-66
O'CALLAGHAN, Joe (HB)
  Summerville, Mass., 1952
ODOM, Sammy Joe (LB)
  Minden, La., 1961
O'DONNELL, Joe (HB)
  Ovett, Miss., 1940
OGDEN, Don G. (QB)
  Baton Rouge, La., 1929-30
OLIVER, George (RT)
  Little Rock, Ark., 1952
OLIVER, L. A. (E)
  Lafayette, La., 1901
O'QUIN, Arthur (Mickey) (E)
  Shreveport, La., 1914-15-16-17
O'QUIN, Leon (QB)
  Natchitoches, La., 1914
OSBORNE, Clarence (DT)
  Baton Rouge, La., 1983-84
OUSTALET, Jimmy (C)
  Lake Arthur, La., 1972-73-75
OWENS, Daryl W. (WR)
  Beaumont, Tex., 1985
OWENS, Richard (Ricki) (LB)
  Homer, La., 1967-68-69

P

PACKNETT, Robert (OT)
  New Orleans, La., 1987-88-89
PARDO, Diego (QB)
  Panama, 1944
PARIS, Ted (C)
  Leesville, La., 1954-55-56
PARKER, Enos (T)
  Mobile, Ala., 1953-54-55-56
PARKER, James C. (Clay) (KS)
  Grayson, La., 1982-83-84
PARNHAM, Spencer (T)
  Hawthorne, N.J. 1945
PEEBLES, Leo (Les) (HB)
  Shreveport, La., 1928-29

PEGUES, Gary (SE-CB)
Fort Walton, Fla., 1991-92
PEGUES, William T. (T)
Mansfield, La., 1900
PERE, Ralph (LT)
Larose, La., 1961-62-63
PERCY, Chaille (FB)
Baton Rouge, La., 1968-69
PERRY, Boyd (LB)
Orange, Tex., 1970-71
PETTAWAY, Chris (OG-OT)
Miami, Fla., 1989
PEVEY, Charles (QB)
Jackson, Miss., 1946-47-48-49
PHARIS, Mike (C)
Shreveport, La., 1965-66
PHELPS, Joe R. (Polly) (QB)
Shreveport, La., 1927
PHILLIPS, Darrell P. (NG)
Franklin, La., 1983-86-87-88
PHILLIPS, Ivan J. (DT)
New Orleans, La., 1977-78-79
PHILLIPS, Marty (DT)
Baton Rouge, La., 1973-74
PICKETT, Garland (E)
Temple, Tex., 1933
PICOU, Richard (LB)
Gonzales, La., 1969-70-71
PIERCE, Spike (DB)
Baton Rouge, La., 1965
PIERSON, James (DB)
New Orleans, La., 1984-85-86-87
PIKE, Mike (S)
Metairie, La., 1973-74-75
PILLOW, Dudley (E)
Greenwood, Miss., 1939-40
PILLOW, Walter (TE)
Greenwood, Miss., 1963-64-65
PITALO, Alex M. (C)
Biloxi, Miss., 1950
PITCHER, James E. (Jim) (HB)
Hammond, La., 1917
PITCHER, William (HB)
Hammond, La., 1922-23-24
PITTMAN, Albert (G)
New Orleans, La., 1944
PITTMAN, J. S. (Big Pitt) (G)
Lake Providence, La., 1914-15
PITTMAN, Paul (T)
Hot Springs, Ark., 1937
PLATOU, R. (HB)
Brooklyn, N.Y., 1915
PLEASANT, Ruffin G. (QB)
Farmerville, La., 1893
POLLOCK, William M. (Judge) (T)
Bernice, La., 1908-09-10
POLOZOLA, Steve (CB)
Baton Rouge, La., 1967-68-69
POPE, Derek (FB)
New Orleans, La., 1990-91
PORTA, Ray (Coon) (QB)
Baton Rouge, La., 1948
PORTER, Tracy R. (SB)
Baton Rouge, La., 1979-80
POTTER, Ray (T)
Peabody, Mass., 1949-50-51
POTTS, John H. (E)
Baton Rouge, La., 1910
POWELL, R. H. (Bob) (T)
Quitman, La., 1929-30-31
POWELL, Doug (QB)
Houston, Tex., 1984-85-86
POWELL, Tommy (RT)
Bogalusa, La., 1963-64-65
PRATHER, Trey (QB)
Shreveport, La., 1966
PRATT, George K. (T)
New Orleans, La., 1899
PRATT, Joel M. (E)
Baton Rouge, La., 1893
PRESCOTT, Aaron (RT)
Washington, La., 1893
PRESCOTT, Dickie (HB)
St. Francisville, La., 1951-52-54
PRESCOTT, Willis B. (FB)
Washington, La., 1893-94
PRESSBURG, Joel W. (G)
Baton Rouge, La., 1929-30
PRICE, Marcus (OT)
Port Arthur, Texas, 1991-92
PRICE, T. J. (HB)
Alexandria, La., 1939
PRICKETT, Greg (DE)
Houston, Tex., 1975-76
PRUDHOMME, Remi (LG)
Opelousas, La., 1962-63-64
PULLETT, Ike (DT)
Baton Rouge, La., 1992
PURVIS, Don (Scooter) (HB)
Crystal Springs, Miss., 1957-58-59

Q

QUINN, Marcus (SB-SS)
New Orleans, La., 1977-78-79-80
QUINTELLA, Mike (SE)
Port Arthur, Tex., 1975-76-77-78
QUIRK, Lewis A. W. (T)
Washington, La., 1894-95

R

RABB, Carlos C. (DT)
Ferriday, La., 1966-67-68
RABB, Warren (QB)
Baton Rouge, La., 1957-58-59
RABENHORST, Oscar D. (Dudley) (QB)
Baton Rouge, La., 1921-22
RACINE, Frank (S)
Shreveport, La., 1971-72-73
RADECKER, Gary (OG)
New Orleans, La., 1975-77-78
RAIFORD, Albert (Rock) (DT-OG)
Destrehan, La., 1972-73-74-75
RATHJEN, Craig (FB)
Houston, Tex., 1983-84-85-86
RAY, Eddie (FB)
Vicksburg, Miss., 1967-68-69
RAY, Scott (WR)
Baton Rouge, La., 1990-91-92
RAYMOND, Corey (CB/S)
New Iberia, La., 1988-89-90-91
RAYMOND, Gregory P. (OT)
Metairie, La., 1979-80
READING, Steve (OL)
Belle Chase, La., 1990
REAGAN, C. R. (Jerry) (HB)
Jackson, La., 1915
REBSAMEN, Paul (QB)
Eudora, Ark., 1955
REDHEAD, J. A. (T)
Vicksburg, Miss., 1901
REDING, Joe (LT-G)
Bossier City, La., 1966-67-68
REED, J. T. (Rock) (HB)
Haynesville, La., 1934-35-36
REEDY, Frank (T)
Baton Rouge, La., 1929
REEVES, W. A. (Dobie) (HB)
Lake Charles, La., 1928-29-30
REHAGE, Steve (CB)
Metairie, La., 1983-84-85-86
REID, Alfred J. (Alf) (FB)
Lake Charles, La., 1912-13-14-15
REID, Joseph (Joe) (G)
Meridian, Miss., 1948-49-50
REILY, Charles S. (T)
Clinton, La., 1910-11-12
RENFROE, John C. (Cherry) (HB-QB)
San Antonio, Tex., 1927, 1929-30
RENFROE, Olin (HB)
Ft. Myers, Fla., 1956
REYNOLDS, Gerald (Jerry) (G)
Baton Rouge, La., 1947-48
REYNOLDS, M. C. (QB)
Mansfield, La., 1955-56
RHODES, H. J. (G)
Vicksburg, Miss., 1900-01-02
RICE, George (T)
Baton Rouge, La., 1963-64-65
RICE, R. E. (Red) (C)
West Plains, Mo., 1915-16
RICE, Robert (T)
Lake Charles, La., 1962
RICH, Christopher J. (Chris) (OT)
San Antonio, Tex., 1976-77-78
RICHARDS, Bobby (T)
Oak Ridge, Tenn., 1960-61
RICHARDSON, Albert J., III (LB)
Baton Rouge, La., 1979-80-82
RICHARDSON, Lyman (QB)
Shreveport, La., 1940-41-42
RICHMOND, Dilton (E)
Nacogdoches, Tex. 1941-42-46
RICHTER, David (OG)
Opelousas, La., 1987
RINAUDO, Martin (B)
New Roads, La., 1943
RIPPLE, Steve (LB)
Metairie, La., 1975-76-77
RISHER, Alan D. (QB)
Slidell, La., 1980-81-82
RITTINER, Chris M. (SB)
New Orleans, La., 1976
RIVERO, V. Victor (HB-E)
Monterrey, Mex., 1904
ROANE, James A. (RG)
Vienna, La., 1893
ROBERTS, Henry Lee (HB)
North Little Rock, Ark., 1958
ROBERTSON, Archie Ed (FB)
Plaquemine, La., 1896
ROBICHAUX, Al (T)
Taft, La., 1951-52-53
ROBICHAUX, Mike (E)
Raceland, La., 1965-66
ROBINSON, Dwight (DB)
Ponchatoula, La., 1961-62-63
ROBINSON, Johnny (HB)
Baton Rouge, La., 1957-58-59
ROBISKIE, Terry (RB-TB)
Lucy, La., 1973-74-75-76
ROCA, Juan (KS)
Metairie, La., 1972-73-74
RODRIGUE, J. C. (Friday) (HB-FB)
Duboin, La., 1915-16
RODRIGUE, Ruffin, Sr. (C)
Thibodaux, La., 1962-63-64
RODRIGUE, Ruffin, Jr. (OG)
Thibodaux, La., 1986-87-88-89

ROGER, Don (LB)
Garland, Tex., 1972-73-74
ROGERS, Steve (TB-RB)
Ruston, La., 1972-73-74
ROHM, Charles (Pinky) (HB)
New Orleans, La., 1935-36-37
ROMAIN, Richard (FL)
Gretna, La., 1973-74
ROSHTO, James (Jimmy) (HB)
Baton Rouge, La., 1949-50-51
ROSS, George (LB)
Lake Charles, La., 1975
ROUSSELL, Terry (NG)
Lutcher, La., 1983
ROUSSOS, George (G)
Santa Ana, Cal., 1949-50
ROWAN, Elwyn (FB)
Memphis, Tenn., 1944
RUKAS, Justin (Ruke) (T)
Gary, Ind., 1933-34-35
RUSH, Gordy (WR)
Gretna, La., 1988-89-90
RUSSELL, Randy (OT)
West Monroe, La., 1971-72
RUSSELL, Tony (G)
Tallulah, La., 1967-68-69
RUTLAND, James (Pepper) (LB)
Baton Rouge, La., 1970-71-72
RUTLEDGE, D. H. (Don) (E)
Robeline, La., 1917
RYAN, Mike (DB)
Mooringsport, La., 1967
RYAN, Warren (Pat) (G-T)
New Orleans, La., 1908-09
RYDER, Robert (Red) (OT)
Alexandria, La., 1968-69

S

SAGE, John (T)
Houston, Tex., 1968-69-70
SAIA, S. J. (LB)
Baton Rouge, La., 1975-76
ST. DIZIER, Roger V. (Blue) (E-G)
New Roads, La., 1916-17
SALASSI, John R. (G)
French Settlement, La., 1894-95-96
SANCHEZ, A. C. (G)
Santa Lucia, Cuba, 1914
SANCHO, Ron (OLB)
Avondale, La., 1985-86-87-88
SANDERS, Al (Apple) (C)
Baton Rouge, La., 1945-56
SANDERS, James W. (C)
Franklin, La., 1895
SANDIFER, Dan (HB)
Shreveport, La., 1944-45-46-47
SANDRAS, Jules (T)
Westwego, La., 1956
SANFORD, James (Jim) (T)
Covington, La., 1951-52
SANFORD, Joseph H. (QB)
Baton Rouge, La., 1901
SAUCIER, Jeff (PK)
New Orleans, La., 1991
SAULSBERRY, Derrick (WR)
Thibodaux, La., 1986
SCAVO, Charles (LB)
Carbondale, Pa., 1988
SCHEXNAILDRE, Merle (FB)
Houma, La., 1958-59
SCHNEIDER, Edward D. (Pete) (LG)
Lake Providence, La., 1920
SCHNEIDER, F.H. (Teddy) (G)
Lake Providence, La., 1929-30
SCHNEIDER, Frederick H. (G)
Lake Providence, La., 1894-95-96
SCHOENBERGER, George C. (E)
Buras, La., 1893-96
SCHROLL, Charles (C)
Alexandria, La., 1946
SCHROLL, William (FB)
Alexandria, La., 1943, 1946-47-48
SCHWAB, Don (FB)
Thibodaux, La., 1963-64-65
SCHWALB, Gerald (Jerry) (G)
Baton Rouge, La., 1954-57
SCHWING, Ivan H. (QB)
Lake Charles, La., 1899-1900
SCOFIELD, Dale (QB)
River Ridge, La., 1992
SCOTT, E.E. (C)
Kingston, La., 1893-94
SCOTT, Edwin A. (Ned) (T-L)
Wilson, La., 1893-94-95-96-97
SCOTT, Malcolm M. (TE)
New Orleans, La., 1979-80-81-82
SCREEN, Pat (QB)
New Orleans, La., 1963-64-65
SCULLY, Don (G)
St. Petersburg, Fla., 1955-56
SEAGO, Ernest (Son) (FB)
Temple, Tex., 1933-34-35
SEAMSTER, Sammy (FB)
Minden, La., 1990-91-92
SEBSTIAN, James A. (HB-E)
Spring Ridge, La., 1901
SESSIONS, Wayne (SE)
Springhill, La., 1965-66
SEIP, John J. (E)
Allentown, Pa., 1907-08-09-10

SETTERS, Ross (OT)
Memphis, Mo., 1990-91-92
SHARP, Linden E. (C)
Baton Rouge, La., 1902
SHAW, Elton (E)
Kentwood, La., 1952
SHEEHY, Billy (E)
Mobile, Ala., 1956
SHERBURNE, Thomas L. (G)
Baton Rouge, La., 1897-98
SHIRER, Joe (HB)
New Orleans, La., 1950-51
SHOAF, James (Jim) (T)
Greensburg, Pa., 1948-49-50
SHOREY, Allen (TB)
Ruston, La., 1969-70-71
SHURTZ, Hubert (T)
Pinckneyville, Ill., 1946-47
SIBLEY, Llewellyn R. (Lew) (DE)
Longview, Tex., 1974-75-76-77
SIGREST, Ed (E)
Bogalusa, La., 1944-45
SIMES, Ashford (HB)
Houston, Tex., 1938-39
SIMMONS, Charles (T)
Moss Point, Miss., 1962-64
SIMMONS, Kelly (FB)
Houston, Tex., 1975-76-77
SIMMONS, Ray (HB)
El Dorado, Ark., 1952
SIMNICHT, Ronnie (DT/OT)
Ocean Springs, Miss., 1990-91-92
SIMON, Phillip (OT)
St. Martinville, La., 1991-92
SKIDMORE, Claude (Skid) (QB)
Winchester, Tenn., 1931-32
SKIDMORE, Jim (Big Skid) (T)
Winchester, Tenn., 1930-31-32
SLAUGHTER, William S. (E)
Port Hudson, La., 1894-95-96-97-98
SMEDES, William C (C)
Vicksburg, Miss., 1893-94
SMITH, Benny (Gunboat) (E)
Bossier City, La., 1919
SMITH, Billy (E)
Ruston, La., 1955-56-57
SMITH, Charlie (T)
El Dorado, Ark., 1950-51
SMITH, Clarence I. (HB)
Albion, Mich., 1905-06-08
SMITH, David C. (SB)
Natchez, Miss., 1976
SMITH, Glenn (TB)
New Orleans, La., 1967-68
SMITH, Guy (LE)
Marshall, Tex., 1952
SMITH, John Hugh (HB)
Shreveport, La., 1936-37-38
SMITH, Lance (OT)
Kannapolis, N.C., 1981-82-83-84
SMITH, Robert C. (OT)
Cleveland, Ohio, 1981
SMITH, Rollis (E)
Dubach, La., 1944
SMITH, Spencer L. (OG)
Baton Rouge, La., 1976-77-78
SMITH, Thielen (LB)
Metairie, La., 1973-74-75
SMITH, Tom (FB)
Alexandria, La., 1929-30-31
SMITH, Tommy (LB)
Brookhaven, Miss., 1970
SMITH, V. E. (Bob) (HB)
Albion, Mich., 1905-08
SMOOT, Raymond (OT)
Leesville, La., 1990-92
SMOTHERS, Jason (TE)
Destrehan, La., 1991
SNYDER, John E. (Texas) (QB)
Georgetown, Tex., 1894-95
SOARES, Fred (ILB)
Santa Ana, Cal., 1990
SOEFKER, Buddy (HB)
Memphis, Tenn., 1961-62-63
SOILEAU, Danny L. (FB)
Elton, La., 1977-78-79
SOWELL, Claude (HB)
Crowville, La., 1926
SPENCE, Ray (T)
Shreveport, La., 1956-57
SPENCER, Curtis (HB)
Grove, La., 1925
SPENCER, Floyd W. (E)
Grove, La., 1912-13
SPENCER, Fritz L. (C)
Grove, La., 1919-20-21
SPENCER, George B. (G)
Grove, La., 1911-13-14
SPENCER, Hugh Frank (T-G-C)
Grove, La., 1916-17
SPERIER, Joseph (RB)
Covington, La., 1988
STAFFORD, David Grove (HB-FB)
Alexandria, La., 1919
STAGG, Jack (B)
Eunice, La., 1943-44
STAGGS, John (S)
Texas City, Tex., 1970-71-72
STANFORD, John T.
Baton Rouge, La., 1898-99
STANTON, Edward J. (OT)
Friendswood, Tex., 1977-78

217

STAPLES, Duncan P.
Alexandria, La., 1894-97
STAPLES, Jake (FB)
Calhoun, La., 1937-38-39
STAUDINGER, Louis P. (QB)
New Orleans, La., 1904
STAYTON, William D. (Judge) (C)
Keatchie, La., 1903-04
STEELE, John E. (Pug) (T)
Yadkin Valley, N.C., 1921-23-24-25
STELL, J. H. (Jabbo) (HB)
Shreveport, La., 1937-38
STELLY, Brandon (TE)
Opelousas, La., 1992
STEPHENS, Harold (LB)
Baton Rouge, La., 1966-67-68
STEPTEAU, Mike (CB)
San Antonio, Texas, 1992
STEVENS, Ed (HB-QB)
Picayune, Miss., 1930-31
STEVENS, Norman (QB)
Picayune, Miss. 1950-51-52
STEVENS, Norman G. (Steve) (HB)
Picayune, Miss., 1922-23-24-25
STEWART, Marvin (Moose) (C)
Picayune, Miss., 1934-35-36
STINSON, Don (HB)
Shreveport, La., 1954-55
STOBER, Bill (E)
Rockford, Ohio, 1967-68-69
STOKLEY, Nelson (QB)
Crowley, La., 1965-66-67
STONECIPHER, Wade (E)
Haynesville, La., 1939
STOVALL, Hefley H. (Hank) (QB)
Dodson, La., 1927-28
STOVALL, Jerry (HB)
West Monroe, La., 1960-61-62
STOVALL, Lloyd J. (C)
Dodson, La., 1932-33-34
STOVALL, Robert L. (Strauss) (C)
Dodson, La., 1906-07-08-09
STOVALL, Rowson R. (HB)
Dodson, La., 1907-08-09
STRANGE, Charles (Bo) (T)
Baton Rouge, La., 1958-59-60
STRANGE, Clarence (Pop) (T)
El Dorado, Ark., 1935-36
STRANGE, David (G)
Baton Rouge, La., 1963-64-65
STREETE, Jon G. (LB)
Lake Charles, La., 1974-75-76
STREETE, Steve (OG-OT)
Lake Charles, La., 1971-72
STRICKLAND, Tom (OT)
Houston, Tex., 1972-73
STRINGFIELD, Cliff (QB)
Bogalusa, La., 1951-52-53
STROTHER, Howard (T)
Baton Rouge, La., 1945-48
STUART, Charles (OT)
Sterlington, La., 1969-70-71
STUART, Roy J. (OG)
Jackson, Miss., 1974-75-76
STUMPH, John C. (Shorty) (G)
New Orleans, La., 1926
STUPKA, Frank (T)
Bogalusa, La., 1934-35
STUPKA, Mike (G)
Bogalusa, La., 1958-59
SUAREZ, Pedro (PK)
Hialeah, Fla., 1989-90-91-92
SULLIVAN, Walter (Sully) (HB)
Hazelhurst, Miss., 1932-33-34
SWAN, Roovelroe (OLB)
Shreveport, La., 1990-91-92
SWANSON, A. E. (Nip) (E-T)
Quitman, La., 1926-27-28
SWANSON, Arthur L. (Red) (G-FB-T)
Quitman, La., 1923-24-25
SYKES, Gene (E)
Covington, La., 1960-61-62

T

TALBOT, Edward L. (HB)
Napoleonville, La., 1912
TALLEY, Jim (C)
Houston, Tex., 1941-42
TARASOVIC, George (C)
Bridgeport, Conn., 1951
TAYLOR, Jimmy (FB)
Baton Rouge, La., 1956-57
TEAL, Willie, Jr. (CB)
Texarkana, Tex., 1976-77-78-79
TEXADA, James C. (G-T)
Alexandria, La., 1906
THIBODEAUX, Chester B. (Benjy) (DT)
Rayne, La., 1977-78-79-80
THIBODEAUX, Robert (DT)
River Ridge, La., 1992
THOMAS, Alvin J. (CB)
Donaldsonville, La., 1979-80-81-82
THOMAS, Arthur J. (Tommy) (G)
Baton Rouge, La., 1908-09-10-11
THOMAS, Henry
Houston, Tex., 1983-84-85-86
THOMAS, Stanley (DT)
Marshall, Texas,1990-91
THOMASON, Bill (LB)
Sulphur, La., 1967-68-69

THOMPSON, Leon (TE)
Shreveport, La., 1973
THOMPSON, Steve (FB)
Winnsboro, La., 1956
THORNALL, Bill (C)
Metuchen, N.J. 1942
THORNTON, Sam B. (T-G)
Pitkin, La., 1922-23
TILLY, L. R. (E)
St. Martinville, La., 1909
TINSLEY, Gaynell (Gus) (E)
Homer, La., 1934-35-36
TINSLEY, Jess D. (T)
Haynesville, La., 1926-27-28
TISDALE, Charles H. (HB)
New Orleans, La., 1983
TITTLE, Billy (Mgr.)
New Orleans, La., 1976
TITTLE, Y. A. (QB-HB)
Marshall, Tex., 1944-45-46-47
TOCZYLOSKI, Edward (QB)
1940
TOLBERT, Tyke (WR)
Conroe, Tex., 1988-90
TOLER, Jack
Baker, La., 1943-44
TOMLINSON, Todd (P)
Miami, Fla., 1986
TOMS, Randy (TE)
Hodge, La., 1969-70
TOOMER, Robert (FB)
Sylvester, Ga., 1992
TORRANCE, Jack (Baby Jack) (G-T-C)
Oak Grove, La., 1931-32-33
TOTH, Zollie (FB)
Pocahontas, Va., 1945-47-48-49
TRAPANI, Felix (G)
Donaldsonville, La., 1943-45
TRICHE, Phillip J. (LB)
Metairie, La., 1975-76-77
TRICHEL, Walter S. (FB)
Natchitoches, La., 1893
TRIMBLE, Carl Otis (QB-SB)
Tallulah, La., 1974-75-76
TROSCLAIR, Milton (T)
Thibodaux, La., 1962-63-64
TRUAX, Bill (E)
New Orleans, La., 1961-62-63
TRUAX, Chris (OG)
Richardson, Tex., 1988-89-90-91
TUCKER, Tim (NG)
Meraux, La., 1987
TULLOS, Earl R. (T)
Bogalusa, La., 1943-44-45-46
TULLY, Thomas N. (OG)
Baton Rouge, La., 1979-80-81
TUMINELLO, Joe (E)
Brookhaven, Miss., 1952-53-54-55
TURNER, J. Michael (Mike) (LB-OG)
Shreveport, La., 1978-79-80-82
TURNER, Jim (G)
Baton Rouge, La., 1962-63
TURNER, Tom (DT)
Bastrop, La., 1992
TURNER, Win (QB)
Baton Rouge, La., 1953-54-56-57

V

VAIRIN, Kenny (E)
New Orleans, La., 1963-64
VALENTINE, Leonard (QB)
Marrero, La., 1987
VALENTINE, Miles S. (OG)
Ft. Walton Beach, Fla., 1979
VALENTINO, Eric (OLB)
Houston, Texas, 1992
VAN BUREN, Ebert (HB)
Metairie, La., 1948-49-50
VAN BUREN, Steve (HB)
New Orleans, La., 1941-42-43
VENABLE, Jack
Covington, La., 1943
VENABLE, John
Camden, Ark., 1951
VENTRESS, Nigel (OLB)
Port Arthur, Tex., 1989
VERNON, Benton R. (C)
Ruston, La., 1923-24-25
VICKERS, Donald G. (C)
Greenwell Springs, La., 1979
VINCENT, Mike (LB)
Sulphur, La., 1963-64-65
VINEYARD, Hershal (Sleepy) (G)
Albertville, Ala., 1926-27
VIRGETS, Warren (E)
Baton Rouge, La., 1950-51
VOSS, Harold (T)
Baton Rouge, La., 1948-49-50

W

WADDILL, George D.
Baton Rouge, La., 1894
WAGNER, James, Jr., (KS)
New Orleans, La., 1981
WALDEN, Henry E. (E)
Marksville, La., 1913-14
WALET, P. H. (HB)
New Iberia, La., 1911

WALKER, Delmar (Del) (TB)
Baton Rouge, La., 1969-70-71
WALKER, Jack (HB)
Houma, La., 1936
WALKER, R. F. (Foots) (G-T)
Dodson, La., 1913-16
WALKER, Reggie (ILB)
New Orleans, La., 1989-90-91
WALKUP, David (ILB)
The Woodlands, Tex., 1989-90-91-92
WALL, Benjamin B. (HB)
Alexandria, La., 1898-99
WALLIS, Lionel J. (SE)
Houma, La., 1977-78-79-80
WALSH, Ewell (G)
Tempe, Ariz., 1949-50
WALTON, R. H. (Tough) (T-G)
Albermarie, La., 1914-15
WARD, Steve (FB)
Baton Rouge, La., 1960-61-62
WARMBROD, James (C)
Belvidere, Tenn., 1936-37
WARNER, Ambrose D. (HB)
Robert, La., 1922-23-25
WASHINGTON, Ricardo (TE-ILB)
Bogalusa, La., 1990-91-92
WATERMEIER, Chris (DS)
Metairie, La., 1992
WATKINS, Slip (TB-FL)
Ft. Lauderdale, Fla., 1988-89
WATSON, A. Scott (S)
Pensacola, Fla., 1979-82
WATSON, John D. (S)
Bossier City, La., 1977-78-79-80
WEATHERSBY, Robert B. (Bob) (OT)
Athens, Ga., 1980-82
WEAVER, A. V. (Tubbo) (T)
Natchitoches, La., 1924
WEAVER, Odell (HB)
Homer, La., 1940-41
WEAVER, Otto L. (T)
Natchitoches, La., 1924-25
WEBB, Charles (E)
McComb, Miss., 1943-44
WEBB, Kendall (DT)
Metairie, La., 1992
WEBER, S. R. (Chink) (E)
Baton Rouge, La., 1924
WEBSTER, Rene J.
Jeanerette, La., 1894
WEIL, Edgar E. (FB)
Alexandria, La., 1905-06
WEIMAR, John
Baton Rouge, La., 1943
WEINSTEIN, John (DT)
Opelousas, La., 1970
WEST, Billy (FB)
Natchitoches, La., 1949-50-51
WEST, Jim (SB)
Bossier City, La., 1967-68-69
WEST, Kerry L. (OT)
Pineville, La., 1978-79-80
WESTBROOK, John T. (E)
Baton Rouge, La., 1894-95-96-97
WHARTON, Scott (NG)
Baton Rouge, La., 1988-89-90-91
WHITE, Corey (OLB)
Shreveport, La., 1990-91-92
WHITE, James R. (TE)
Rayville, La., 1981-84
WHITE, Lyman D., Jr. (DE)
Franklin, La., 1977-78-79-80
WHITFILL, Steve (DE-LB)
Dallas, Tex., 1973-74
WHITLATCH, Blake (LB)
Baton Rouge, La., 1975-76-77
WHITLEY, John (Jay) (C)
Baton Rouge, La., 1976-77-78
WHITMAN, Ralph (T)
Jennings, La., 1938-39
WHYTE, Vernon
Tyler, Tex., 1943
WICKERSHAM, Jeff (QB)
Merritt Island, Fla., 1983-84-85
WILBANKS, T. E. (HB)
Shreveport, La., 1917
WILKINS, Ray (HB)
Homer, La., 1960-61-62
WILLIAMS, Anthony (ILB-TE)
Monroe, La., 1989-90-91-92
WILLIAMS, Bobby (ILB-OLB)
Ruston, La., 1991-92
WILLIAMS, Chris A. (CB)
Tioga, La., 1977-78-79-80
WILLIAMS, Darrell (FB-TE)
Hempstead, Tex., 1988-90-91
WILLIAMS, Germaine (FB)
Donaldsonville, La., 1990-91-92
WILLIAMS, Harvey (FB)
Hempstead, Tex., 1986-87-89-90
WILLIAMS, Henry L. (E)
Baton Rouge, La., 1906
WILLIAMS, Lawrence (LB)
Lake Charles, La., 1980-81-82
WILLIAMS, Lee (ILB)
Monroe, La., 1992
WILLIAMS, Mike (CB)
Covington, La., 1972-73-74
WILLIAMS, T. Demetri (DT)
Plaquemine, La., 1978-79-80

WILLIAMS, Wayne (WR-CB)
Brazoria, Tex., 1988-89-90-91
WILLIAMS, Willie (TE)
Houston, Tex., 1987-88-89
WILLIAMSON, Charles (Chuck) (TE)
Baton Rouge, La., 1971-72
WINDOM, Calvin (TB)
Orlando, Fla., 1988-89-90
WILSON, Barry (C)
New Orleans, La., 1965-66-67
WILSON, Karl (DT)
Baton Rouge, La., 1983-84-85-86
WILSON, N. A. (Fats) (G)
Shreveport, La., 1926-27-28
WILSON, Roy (E-G)
Bossier City, La., 1930-31-32
WILSON, Sheddrick (WR)
Thomasville, Ga., 1992
WIMBERLY, Abner (E)
Oak Ridge, La., 1943-46-47-48
WINKLER, Joe (S)
New Orleans, La., 1971-72-73
WINSTON, Roy (Moonie) (G)
Baton Rouge, La., 1959-60-61
WINTLE, James V. (Wee Willie) (QB-HB)
Leesville, La., 1921-22
WOLF, Sidney K. (Izzy) (HB)
Baton Rouge, La., 1920
WOOD, John (DE)
Lake Charles, La., 1970-71-72
WOOD, John (E)
Lake City, Fla., 1954-55-56
WOODARD, Risdon E. (Red) (T)
Dubberly, La., 1919-20-22
WOODLEY, David E. (QB)
Shreveport, La., 1977-78-79
WORKMAN, Tori (DT)
Winston-Salem, N.C., 1992
WORLEY, Mitch (LB-P)
Dallas, Tex., 1966
WORLEY, Wren (G)
El Dorado, Ark., 1946-47-48
WRIGHT, Mike (RT)
Sulphur, La., 1968-69-70

Y

YATES, Bertis (Bert) (FB)
Haynesville, La., 1932-33-34
YATES, Jesse (E)
N. Little Rock, Ark., 1949-50-51
YEAGER, Rudy (T)
Philadelphia, Pa., 1951
YEARBY, Ronnie (OL)
Columbia, La., 1984
YOKUBAITIS, Mark (LB)
Houston, Tex., 1972
YOUNG, Charles G. (T-G)
Homer, La., 1893-94
YOUNG, Jerry (G)
Lafayette, La., 1962-63
YOUNG, Jimmy (CB)
San Antonio, Tex., 1987-88-89
YOUNG, Rodney (S)
Grambling, La., 1991-92
YOUNGBLOOD, Tommy (DE)
Shreveport, La., 1967-68

Z

ZAUNBRECHER, Godfrey (C)
Crowley, La., 1967-68-69
ZERINGUE, Brian (FB)
Raceland, La., 1973
ZICK, Francis (T)
Phillipsburg, N.J., 1941-42
ZIEGLER, Paul (G)
Crowley, La., 1954-55-56

218

1893 Record: 0-1-0 SIAA: 0-1-0
Coach Dr. Charles E. Coates
Captain: Ruffin G. Pleasant (QB)

Nov. 25	Tulane	L	0-34	New Orleans

1894 Record: 2-1-0 SIAA: 0-1-0
Coach Albert P. Simmons
Captain: Samuel Marmaduke Dinwidie Clark (FB)

Nov. 30	Natchez AC	W	26-0	Natchez, Miss.
Dec. 3	Mississippi	L	6-26	Baton Rouge
Dec. 21	Centenary	W	30-0	Baton Rouge

1895 Record: 3-0-0 SIAA: 2-0-0
Coach Albert P. Simmons
Captain: J.E. Snyder (QB)

Oct. 26	Tulane	W	8-4	Baton Rouge
Nov. 2	Centenary	W	16-6	Jackson, La.
Nov. 18	Alabama	W	12-6	Baton Rouge

1896 Record: 6-0-0 SIAA: 3-0-0
Coach Allen W. Jeardeau
Captain: Edwin Allen (Ned) Scott (T)

Oct. 10	Centenary	W	46-0	Baton Rouge
Oct. 24	Tulane	W	6-0	New Orleans
Nov. 13	Mississippi	W	12-4	Vicksburg, Miss.
Nov. 16	Texas	W	14-0	Baton Rouge
Nov. 20	Miss. State	W	52-0	Baton Rouge
Nov. 28	Southern AC	W	6-0	New Orleans

1897 Record: 1-1-0 SIAA: 0-0-0
Coach Allen W. Jeardeau
Captain: Edwin Allen (Ned) Scott (T)

Dec. 20	Montgomery AC	W	28-6	Baton Rouge
Jan. 8	Cincinnati	L	0-26	Baton Rouge

1898 Record: 1-0-0 SIAA: 1-0-0
Coach Edmond A. Chavanne
Captain: Edmond A. Chavanne (T)

Dec. 14	Tulane	W	37-0	Baton Rouge

1899 Record: 1-4-0 SIAA: 1-2-0
Coach John P. Gregg
Captain: Hulette F. Aby (T)

Nov. 3	Mississippi	L	0-11	Meridian, Miss.
Nov. 10	*Lake Charles HS	W	48-0	Lake Charles, La.
Nov. 12	Sewanee	L	0-34	Baton Rouge
Nov. 30	Texas	L	0-29	Austin
Dec. 2	Texas A&M	L	0-52	College Station
Dec. 8	Tulane	W	38-0	Baton Rouge

*-exhibition game

1900 Record: 2-2-0 SIAA: 0-1-0
Coach Edmond A. Chavanne
Captain: I.H. Schwing (QB)

Nov. 11	Millsaps	W	70-0	Baton Rouge
Nov. 17	Tulane	L	0-29	New Orleans
Nov. 30	Millsaps	L	5-6	Jackson, Miss.
Dec. 5	LSU Alumni	W	10-0	Baton Rouge

1901 Record: 5-1-0 SIAA: 2-1-0
Coach W. S. Borland
Captain: E.L. Gorham (HB)

Oct. 28	Louisiana Tech	W	57-0	Ruston, La.
Nov. 7	Mississippi	W	46-0	Baton Rouge
Nov. 16	Tulane	W	11-0	New Orleans
Nov. 20	Auburn	L	0-28	Baton Rouge
Nov. 28	YMCA-N.O.	W	38-0	Baton Rouge
Dec. 5	Arkansas	W	15-0	Baton Rouge

1902 Record: 6-1-0 SIAA: 4-1-0
Coach W.S. Borland
Captain: Henry E. Landry (FB)

Oct. 16	Southwestern La.	W	42-0	Lafayette, La.
Oct. 18	Texas-S.A.	W	5-0	San Antonio, Texas
Oct. 27	Auburn	W	5-0	Baton Rouge
Nov. 8	Mississippi	W	6-0	New Orleans
Nov. 17	Vanderbilt	L	5-27	Baton Rouge
Nov. 27	Miss. State	W	6-0	Starkville
Nov. 29	Alabama	W	11-0	Tuscaloosa

1903 Record: 4-5-0 SIAA: 0-4-0
Coach W. S. Borland
Captain: J.J. Coleman (HB)

Oct. 14	LSU Alumni	W	16-0	Baton Rouge
Oct. 24	Eagles-N.O.	W	33-0	Baton Rouge
Oct. 30	Louisiana Tech	W	16-0	Ruston, La.
Oct. 31	Shreveport AC	W	5-0	Shreveport, La.
Nov. 7	Miss. State	L	0-11	Starkville
Nov. 9	Alabama	L	0-18	Tuscaloosa
Nov. 11	Auburn	L	0-12	Auburn, Ala.
Nov. 16	Cumberland	L	0-41	Baton Rouge
Nov. 21	Mississippi	L	0-11	New Orleans

1904 Record: 3-4-0 SIAA: 1-2-0
Coach Dan A. Killian
Captain: E.L. Klock (T)

Oct. 16	Louisiana Tech	W	17-0	Baton Rouge
Oct. 22	Shreveport AC	L	0-16	Shreveport, La.
Oct. 23	Louisiana Tech	L	0-6	Ruston, La.
Nov. 5	Mississippi	W	5-0	Baton Rouge
Nov. 10	Nashville Med	W	16-0	Baton Rouge
Nov. 19	Tulane	L	0-5	New Orleans
Dec. 1	Alabama	L	0-11	Baton Rouge

1905   Record: 3-0-0   SIAA: 2-0-0
Coach Dan A. Killian
Captain: Frank M. Edwards (G)

Nov. 18	Louisiana Tech	W	16-0	Baton Rouge
Nov. 25	Tulane	W	5-0	New Orleans
Dec. 1	Miss. State	W	15-0	Baton Rouge

1906   Record: 2-2-2   SIAA: 0-1-1
Coach Dan A. Killian
Captain: E.E. Weil (FB)

Oct. 10	Monroe AC	W	5-0	Baton Rouge
Oct. 20	Mississippi	L	0-9	Baton Rouge
Oct. 27	Miss. State	T	0-0	Starkville
Nov. 9	Louisiana Tech	W	17-0	Baton Rouge
Nov. 19	Texas A&M	L	12-21	Baton Rouge
Nov. 29	Arkansas	T	6-6	Baton Rouge

1907   Record: 7-3-0   SIAA: 2-1-0
Coach Edgar R. Wingard
Captain: Solle W. Brannon (QB)

Oct. 11	Louisiana Tech	W	28-0	Baton Rouge
Oct. 19	Texas	L	5-12	Austin
Oct. 21	Texas A&M	L	5-11	College Station
Oct. 28	Howard	W	57-0	Baton Rouge
Nov. 6	Arkansas	W	17-12	Baton Rouge
Nov. 9	Miss. State	W	23-11	Baton Rouge
Nov. 16	Mississippi	W	23-0	Jackson
Nov. 23	Alabama	L	4-6	Mobile
Nov. 30	Baylor	W	48-0	Baton Rouge
Dec. 25	Havana U	W	56-0	Havana, Cuba

1908   Record: 10-0-0   SIAA: 2-0-0
Coach Edgar R. Wingard
Captain: Marshall H. (Cap) Gandy (T)

Oct. 3	YMGC-N.O.	W	41-0	Baton Rouge
Oct. 11	Jackson Br.-N.O.	W	81-5	Baton Rouge
Oct. 17	Texas A&M	W	26-0	New Orleans
Oct. 26	Southwestern, Tenn.	W	55-0	Baton Rouge
Oct. 31	Auburn	W	10-2	Auburn, Ala.
Nov. 7	Miss. State	W	50-0	Baton Rouge
Nov. 10	Baylor	W	89-0	Baton Rouge
Nov. 16	Haskell	W	32-0	New Orleans
Nov. 23	Louisiana Tech	W	22-0	Ruston, La.
Nov. 26	Arkansas	W	36-4	Little Rock

1909   Record: 6-2-0   SIAA: 3-1-0
Coaches Joe G. Pritchard/John W. Mayhew
Captain: R.L. (Big) Stovall (C)

Oct. 2	Jackson Br.-N.O.	W	70-0	Baton Rouge
Oct. 9	Mississippi	W	10-0	Baton Rouge
Oct. 16	Miss. State	W	15-0	Baton Rouge
Oct. 30	Sewanee	L	6-15	New Orleans
Nov. 4	Louisiana Tech	W	23-0	Alexandria, La.
Nov. 13	Arkansas	L	0-16	Memphis, Tenn.
Nov. 18	Transylvania	W	52-0	Baton Rouge
Nov. 25	Alabama	W	12-6	Birmingham

1910   Record: 1-5-0   SIAA: 0-3-0
Coach John W. Mayhew
Captain: Bill Seip (E)

Oct. 15	Miss. College	W	40-0	Baton Rouge
Oct. 21	Miss. State	L	0-3	Columbus, Miss.
Oct. 29	Sewanee	L	5-31	New Orleans
Nov. 5	Vanderbilt	L	0-22	Nashville, Tenn.
Nov. 19	Texas	L	0-12	Austin
Nov. 24	Arkansas	L	0-51	Little Rock

1911   Record: 6-3-0   SIAA: 1-1-0
Coach James K. (Pat) Dwyer
Captain: Arthur J. (Tommy) Thomas (G)

Oct. 7	Southwestern La.	W	42-0	Baton Rouge
Oct. 14	Louisiana Normal	W	46-0	Baton Rouge
Oct. 20	Miss. College	W	40-0	Baton Rouge
Oct. 28	Meteor AC	W	40-0	Baton Rouge
Nov. 4	Baylor	W	6-0	Waco, Texas
Nov. 12	Miss. State	L	0-6	Gulfport, Miss.
Nov. 18	SW Texas	L	6-17	Houston
Nov. 30	Arkansas	L	0-11	Little Rock
Dec. 9	Tulane	W	6-0	Baton Rouge

1912   Record: 4-3-0   SIAA: 1-3-0
Coach James K. (Pat) Dwyer
Captain: Charles S. Reiley (T)

Oct. 5	Southwestern La.	W	85-3	Baton Rouge
Oct. 11	Miss. College	W	45-0	Baton Rouge
Oct. 19	Mississippi	L	7-10	Baton Rouge
Nov. 2	Miss. State	L	0-7	Baton Rouge
Nov. 9	Auburn	L	0-7	Mobile, Ala.
Nov. 16	Arkansas	W	7-6	Little Rock
Nov. 28	Tulane	W	21-3	New Orleans

1913   Record: 6-1-2   SIAA: 1-1-1
Coach James K. (Pat) Dwyer
Captain: T.W. (Tom) Dutton (C)

Oct. 4	Louisiana Tech	W	20-2	Ruston, La.
Oct. 11	Southwestern La.	W	26-0	Lafayette, La.
Oct. 18	Jefferson College	W	45-6	Baton Rouge
Oct. 23	Baylor	W	50-0	Baton Rouge
Nov. 1	Auburn	L	0-7	Mobile, Ala.
Nov. 8	Arkansas	W	12-7	Shreveport, La.
Nov. 15	Miss. State	T	0-0	Starkville, Miss.
Nov. 22	Tulane	W	40-0	Baton Rouge
Nov. 27	Texas A&M	T	7-7	Houston

1914   Record: 4-4-1   SIAA: 0-1-1
Coach E.T. McDonald
Captain: George B. Spencer (T)

Sept. 27	Southwestern La.	W	54-0	Baton Rouge
Oct. 3	Louisiana Tech	W	60-0	Baton Rouge
Oct. 10	Miss. College	W	14-0	Baton Rouge
Oct. 17	Mississippi	L	0-21	Baton Rouge
Oct. 24	Jefferson College	W	14-13	Baton Rouge
Oct. 31	Texas A&M	L	9-63	Dallas
Nov. 7	Arkansas	L	12-20	Shreveport, La.
Nov. 14	Haskell	L	0-31	New Orleans
Nov. 26	Tulane	T	0-0	New Orleans

1915 **Record: 6-2-0** **SIAA: 3-1-0**
Coach E.T. McDonald
Captain: Alfred J. Reid (FB)

Oct. 1	Jefferson College	W	42-0	Baton Rouge
Oct. 8	Miss. College	W	14-0	Baton Rouge
Oct. 15	Mississippi	W	28-0	Oxford
Oct. 22	Georgia Tech	L	7-36	New Orleans
Oct. 29	Miss. State	L	10-0	Baton Rouge
Nov. 5	Arkansas	W	13-7	Shreveport, La.
Nov. 17	Rice	L	0-6	Houston
Nov. 25	Tulane	W	12-0	Baton Rouge

1916 **Record: 7-1-2** **SIAA: 2-1-1**
Coach E.T. McDonald/I.R. Pray/D.X. Bible
Captain: Phillip Cooper (T)

Sept. 30	Southwestern	W	24-0	Lafayette, La.
Oct. 7	Jefferson College	W	59-0	Baton Rouge
Oct. 14	Texas A&M	W	13-0	Galveston, Texas
Oct. 21	Miss. College	W	50-7	Baton Rouge
Oct. 28	Sewanee	L	0-7	New Orleans
Nov. 5	Arkansas	W	17-7	Shreveport, La.
Nov. 12	Miss. State	W	13-3	Starkville
Nov. 19	Mississippi	W	41-0	Baton Rouge
Nov. 24	Rice	W	7-7	Baton Rouge
Nov. 30	Tulane	T	14-14	New Orleans

1917 **Record: 3-5-0** **SIAA: 1-3-0**
Coach Wayne Sutton
Captain: Arthur (Mickey) O'Quinn (E)

Oct. 6	Southwestern La.	W	20-6	Baton Rouge
Oct. 13	Mississippi	W	52-7	Oxford
Oct. 20	Sewanee	L	0-3	New Orleans
Oct. 27	Texas A&M	L	0-27	San Antonio
Nov. 3	Arkansas	L	0-14	Shreveport, La.
Nov. 10	Miss. College	W	34-0	Baton Rouge
Nov. 17	Miss. State	L	0-9	Baton Rouge
Nov. 29	Tulane	L	6-28	Baton Rouge

1918 **No Team (World War I)**

1919 **Record: 6-2-0** **SIAA: 2-2-0**
Coach Irving R. Pray
Captain: T.W. Dutton (C)

Oct. 4	Southwestern, La.	W	39-0	Baton Rouge
Oct. 11	Jefferson College	W	38-0	Baton Rouge
Oct. 18	Mississippi	W	13-0	Baton Rouge
Oct. 25	Arkansas	W	20-0	Shreveport, La.
Nov. 1	Miss. State	L	0-6	Starkville
Nov. 8	Miss. College	W	24-0	Baton Rouge
Nov. 15	Alabama	L	0-23	Baton Rouge
Nov. 22	Tulane	W	27-6	New Orleans

1920 **Record: 5-3-1** **SIAA: 0-3-0**
Coach Branch Bocock
Captain: Roy L. Benoit (QB)

Oct. 2	Jefferson College	W	81-0	Baton Rouge
Oct. 2	Louisiana Normal	W	34-0	Baton Rouge
Oct. 9	Spring Hill	W	40-0	Baton Rouge
Oct. 16	Texas A&M	T	0-0	College Station
Oct. 23	Miss. State	L	7-12	Baton Rouge
Oct. 30	Miss. College	W	41-9	Baton Rouge
Nov. 6	Arkansas	W	3-0	Shreveport, La.
Nov. 13	Alabama	L	0-21	Tuscaloosa
Nov. 25	Tulane	L	0-21	Baton Rouge

1921 **Record: 6-1-1** **SIAA: 2-1-1**
Coach Branch Bocock
Captain: F.L. (Fritz) Spence (E)

Oct. 8	Louisiana Normal	W	78-0	Baton Rouge
Oct. 15	Texas A&M	W	6-0	Baton Rouge
Oct. 22	Spring Hill	W	41-7	Baton Rouge
Oct. 29	Alabama	T	7-7	New Orleans
Nov. 5	Arkansas	W	10-7	Shreveport, La.
Nov. 12	Mississippi	W	21-0	Baton Rouge
Nov. 19	Tulane	L	0-21	New Orleans
Dec. 3	Miss. State	W	17-14	Starkville

1922 **Record: 3-7-0** **SIAA: 1-2-0**
Coach Irving R. Pray
Captain: E.L. (Tubby) Ewen (E)

Sept. 30	Louisiana Normal	W	13-0	Baton Rouge
Oct. 7	Loyola	L	0-7	Baton Rouge
Oct. 14	SMU	L	0-51	Dallas, Texas
Oct. 20	Texas A&M	L	0-47	College Station
Oct. 28	Arkansas	L	6-40	Shreveport, La.
Nov. 2	Spring Hill	W	25-7	Baton Rouge
Nov. 7	Rutgers	L	0-25	New York, N.Y.
Nov. 10	Alabama	L	3-47	Tuscaloosa
Nov. 18	Miss. State	L	0-7	Baton Rouge
Nov. 30	Tulane	W	25-14	Baton Rouge

1923 **Record: 3-5-1** **SIC: 0-3-0**
Coach Mike Donahue
Captain: E.L. (Tubby) Ewen (E)

Sept. 29	Louisiana Normal	W	40-0	Baton Rouge
Oct. 6	Southwestern, La.	W	7-3	Baton Rouge
Oct. 13	Spring Hill	W	33-0	Baton Rouge
Oct. 20	Texas A&M	L	0-28	Baton Rouge
Oct. 27	Arkansas	L	13-26	Shreveport, La.
Nov. 2	Miss. College	T	0-0	Vicksburg, Ms.
Nov. 16	Alabama	L	3-30	Montgomery, Ala.
Nov. 24	Tulane	L	0-20	New Orleans
Dec. 1	Miss. State	L	7-14	Starkville

1924 **Record: 5-4-0** **SIC: 0-3-0**
Coach Mike Donahue
Captain: C.C. (Cliff) Campbell (T)

Sept. 27	Spring Hill	W	7-6	Baton Rouge
Oct. 4	Southwestern La.	W	31-7	Baton Rouge
Oct. 11	Indiana	W	20-14	Indianapolis
Oct. 18	Rice	W	12-0	Houston, Texas
Oct. 25	Auburn	L	0-3	Birmingham, Ala.
Nov. 1	Arkansas	L	7-10	Shreveport, La.
Nov. 8	Georgia Tech	L	7-28	Atlanta
Nov. 15	Louisiana Normal	W	40-0	Baton Rouge
Nov. 25	*Tulane	L	0-13	Baton Rouge

*First game in Tiger Stadium

1925 **Record: 5-3-1** **SIC: 0-2-1**
Coach Mike Donahue
Captain: Jonathan Edward Steele (G)

Sept. 26	Louisiana Normal	W	27-0	Baton Rouge
Oct. 3	Southwestern La.	W	38-0	Baton Rouge
Oct. 10	Alabama	L	0-42	Baton Rouge
Oct. 17	LSU Freshman	W	6-0	Baton Rouge
Oct. 24	Tennessee	T	0-0	Knoxville, Tenn.
Oct. 31	Arkansas	L	0-12	Shreveport, La.
Nov. 7	Rice	W	6-0	Baton Rouge
Nov. 14	Loyola	W	13-0	New Orleans
Nov. 21	Tulane	L	0-16	Baton Rouge

1926   Record: 6-3-0   SIC: 3-3-0

Coach Mike Donahue
Captain: L.T. (Babe) Godfrey (HB)

Sept. 25	Louisiana Normal	W	47-0	Baton Rouge
Oct. 2	Southwestern La.	W	34-0	Baton Rouge
Oct. 9	Tennessee	L	7-14	Baton Rouge
Oct. 16	Auburn	W	10-0	Montgomery, Ala.
Oct. 23	Miss. State	L	6-7	Jackson
Oct. 30	Alabama	L	0-24	Tuscaloosa
Nov. 6	Arkansas	W	14-0	Shreveport, La.
Nov. 13	Mississippi	W	3-0	Baton Rouge
Nov. 25	Tulane	W	7-0	New Orleans

1927   Record: 4-4-1   SIC: 2-3-1

Coach Mike Donahue
Captain: L.T. (Babe) Godfrey (FB)

Sept. 24	Louisiana Tech	W	45-0	Baton Rouge
Oct. 1	Southwestern La.	W	52-0	Baton Rouge
Oct. 8	Alabama	T	0-0	Birmingham, Ala.
Oct. 15	Auburn	W	9-0	Montgomery, Ala.
Oct. 22	Miss. State	W	9-7	Jackson
Oct. 29	Arkansas	L	0-28	Shreveport, La.
Nov. 5	Mississippi	L	7-12	Oxford
Nov. 12	Georgia Tech	L	0-23	Atlanta
Nov. 24	Tulane	L	6-13	Baton Rouge

1928   Record: 6-2-1   SIC: 3-1-1

Coach Russ Cohen
Captain: Jess Tinsley (T)

Oct. 6	Southwestern La.	W	46-0	Baton Rouge
Oct. 13	Louisiana College	W	41-0	Baton Rouge
Oct. 20	Miss. State	W	31-0	Jackson
Oct. 27	Spring Hill	W	30-7	Baton Rouge
Nov. 3	Arkansas	L	0-7	Shreveport, La.
Nov. 10	Mississippi	W	19-6	Baton Rouge
Nov. 17	Georgia	W	13-12	Athens
Nov. 29	Tulane	T	0-0	New Orleans
Dec. 8	Alabama	L	0-13	Birmingham

1929   Record: 6-3-0   SIC: 3-1-0

Coach Russ Cohen
Captain: Frank Ellis (T)

Sept. 28	Louisiana College	W	58-0	Baton Rouge
Oct. 5	Southwestern La.	W	58-0	Baton Rouge
Oct. 12	Sewanee	W	27-14	Baton Rouge
Oct. 19	Miss. State	W	31-6	Jackson
Oct. 26	Louisiana Tech	W	53-7	Baton Rouge
Nov. 2	Arkansas	L	0-32	Shreveport, La.
Nov. 9	Duke	L	6-32	Durham, N.C.
Nov. 16	Mississippi	W	13-6	Baton Rouge
Nov. 28	Tulane	L	0-21	Baton Rouge

1930   Record: 6-4-0   SIC: 2-3-0

Coach Russ Cohen
Captain: Walter (Dobie) Reeves (HB)

Sept. 20	S.D. Wesleyan	W	76-0	Baton Rouge
Sept. 27	Louisiana Tech	W	71-0	Baton Rouge
Oct. 4	Southwestern La.	W	85-0	Baton Rouge
Oct. 11	South Carolina	L	6-7	Columbia
Oct. 18	Miss. State	L	6-8	Jackson
Oct. 25	Sewanee	W	12-0	Baton Rouge
Nov. 1	Arkansas	W	27-12	Shreveport, La.
Nov. 8	Mississippi	W	6-0	Baton Rouge
Nov. 15	Alabama	L	0-33	Montgomery
Nov. 27	Tulane	L	7-12	New Orleans

1931   Record: 5-4-0   SIC: 2-2-0

Coach Russ Cohen
Captain: Edward Khoury (T)

Sept. 26	TCU	L	0-3	Fort Worth, Texas
Oct. 3	*Spring Hill	W	35-0	Baton Rouge
Oct. 10	South Carolina	W	19-12	Baton Rouge
Oct. 17	Miss. State	W	31-0	Baton Rouge
Oct. 24	Arkansas	W	13-6	Shreveport, La.
Oct. 31	Sewanee	L	6-12	Baton Rouge
Nov. 7	Army	L	0-20	West Point, NY
Nov. 14	Mississippi	W	26-3	Jackson
Nov. 28	Tulane	L	7-34	New Orleans

*First night game in Tiger Stadium

1932   Record: 6-3-1   SIC: 3-0-0

Coach Lawrence M. (Biff) Jones
Captain: Walter Fleming (E)

Sept. 24	TCU	T	3-3	Baton Rouge
Oct. 1	Rice	L	8-10	Houston, Texas
Oct. 8	Spring Hill	W	80-0	Baton Rouge
Oct. 15	Miss. State	W	24-0	Monroe, La.
Oct. 22	Arkansas	W	14-0	Shreveport, La.
Oct. 29	Sewanee	W	38-0	Baton Rouge
Nov. 5	South Carolina	W	6-0	Columbia
Nov. 12	Centenary	L	0-6	Shreveport, La.
Nov. 26	Tulane	W	14-0	Baton Rouge
Dec. 17	Oregon	L	0-12	Baton Rouge

1933   Record: 7-0-3   SEC: 3-0-2

Coach Lawrence M. (Biff) Jones
Captain: Jack Torrance (T)

Sept. 30	Rice	W	13-0	Baton Rouge
Oct. 7	Millsaps	W	40-0	Baton Rouge
Oct. 14	Centenary	T	0-0	Baton Rouge
Oct. 21	Arkansas	W	20-0	Shreveport, La.
Oct. 28	Vanderbilt	T	7-7	Baton Rouge
Nov. 4	South Carolina	W	30-7	Baton Rouge
Nov. 18	Mississippi	W	31-0	Baton Rouge
Nov. 25	Miss. State	W	21-6	Monroe, La.
Dec. 2	Tulane	T	7-7	New Orleans
Dec. 9	Tennessee	W	7-0	Baton Rouge

1934   Record: 7-2-2   SEC: 4-2-0

Coach Lawrence M. (Biff) Jones
Captain: Bert Yates (HB)

Sept. 29	Rice	T	9-9	Houston, Texas
Oct. 6	SMU	T	14-14	Baton Rouge
Oct. 13	Auburn	W	20-6	Baton Rouge
Oct. 20	Arkansas	W	16-0	Shreveport, La.
Oct. 27	Vanderbilt	W	29-0	Nashville, Tenn.
Nov. 3	Miss. State	W	25-3	Baton Rouge
Nov. 10	George Washington	W	6-0	Washington, D.C.
Nov. 17	Mississippi	W	14-0	Jackson
Dec. 1	Tulane	L	12-13	Baton Rouge
Dec. 8	Tennessee	L	13-19	Knoxville
Dec. 15	Oregon	W	14-13	Baton Rouge

SEC CHAMPION

1935   Record: 9-2-0   SEC: 5-0-0

Coach Bernie H. Moore
Captain: W.J. Barrett (E)

Sept. 28	Rice	L	7-10	Baton Rouge
Oct. 5	Texas	W	18-6	Baton Rouge
Oct. 12	Manhattan	W	32-0	New York, NY
Oct. 19	Arkansas	W	13-7	Shreveport, La.
Oct. 26	Vanderbilt	W	7-2	Nashville, Tenn.
Nov. 2	Auburn	W	6-0	Baton Rouge
Nov. 9	Miss. State	W	28-13	Baton Rouge
Nov. 16	Georgia	W	13-0	Athens
Nov. 23	Southwestern La.	W	56-0	Baton Rouge
Nov. 30	Tulane	W	41-0	New Orleans
SUGAR BOWL				
Jan. 1	TCU	L	2-3	New Orleans

SEC CHAMPION

1936   Record: 9-1-1   SEC: 6-0-0

Coach Bernie H. Moore
Captain: Bill May (QB-FB)

Sept. 26	Rice	W	20-7	Baton Rouge
Oct. 3	Texas	T	6-6	Austin
Oct. 10	Georgia	W	47-7	Baton Rouge
Oct. 17	Mississippi	W	13-0	Baton Rouge
Oct. 24	Arkansas	W	19-7	Shreveport, La.
Oct. 31	Vanderbilt	W	19-0	Nashville, Tenn.
Nov. 7	Miss. State	W	12-0	Baton Rouge
Nov. 14	Auburn	W	19-6	Birmingham
Nov. 21	Southwestern La.	W	93-0	Baton Rouge
Nov. 28	Tulane	W	33-0	Baton Rouge
SUGAR BOWL				
Jan. 1	Santa Clara	L	14-21	New Orleans

1937   Record: 9-2-0   SEC: 5-1-0

Coach Bernie H. Moore
Captain: Art (Slick) Morton (HB-TB)

Sept. 25	Florida	W	19-0	Baton Rouge
Oct. 2	Texas	W	9-0	Baton Rouge
Oct. 9	Rice	W	13-0	Houston
Oct. 16	Mississippi	W	13-0	Baton Rouge
Oct. 23	Vanderbilt	L	6-7	Nashville, Tenn.
Oct. 30	Loyola	W	52-6	Baton Rouge
Nov. 6	Miss. State	W	41-0	Baton Rouge
Nov. 13	Auburn	W	9-7	Baton Rouge
Nov. 20	Louisiana Normal	W	52-0	Baton Rouge
Nov. 27	Tulane	W	20-7	New Orleans
SUGAR BOWL				
Jan. 1	Santa Clara	L	0-6	New Orleans

1938   Record: 6-4-0   SEC: 2-4-0

Coach Bernie H. Moore
Captain: Ben Friend (T)

Sept. 24	Mississippi	L	7-20	Baton Rouge
Oct. 1	Texas	W	20-0	Austin
Oct. 8	Rice	W	3-0	Baton Rouge
Oct. 15	Loyola	W	47-0	Baton Rouge
Oct. 22	Vanderbilt	W	7-0	Baton Rouge
Oct. 29	Tennessee	L	6-14	Knoxville, Tenn.
Nov. 5	Miss. State	W	32-7	Baton Rouge
Nov. 12	Auburn	L	6-28	Birmingham
Nov. 19	Southwestern La.	W	32-0	Baton Rouge
Nov. 26	Tulane	L	0-14	Baton Rouge

1939   Record: 4-5-0   SEC: 1-5-0

Coach Bernie H. Moore
Captain: Young Bussey (HB)

Sept. 30	Mississippi	L	7-14	Baton Rouge
Oct. 7	Holy Cross	W	26-7	Worcester, Mass.
Oct. 14	Rice	W	7-0	Baton Rouge
Oct. 21	Loyola	W	20-0	Baton Rouge
Oct. 28	Vanderbilt	W	12-6	Nashville, Tenn.
Nov. 4	Tennessee	L	0-20	Baton Rouge
Nov. 11	Miss. State	L	12-15	Baton Rouge
Nov. 18	Auburn	L	7-21	Baton Rouge
Dec. 2	Tulane	L	20-33	New Orleans

1940   Record: 6-4-0   SEC: 3-3-0

Coach Bernie H. Moore
Captain: Charles Anastasio (HB)

Sept. 21	Louisiana Tech	W	39-7	Baton Rouge
Sept. 28	Mississippi	L	6-19	Baton Rouge
Oct. 5	Holy Cross	W	25-0	Baton Rouge
Oct. 12	Rice	L	0-23	Houston
Oct. 19	Mercer	W	20-0	Baton Rouge
Oct. 26	Vanderbilt	W	7-0	Baton Rouge
Nov. 2	Tennessee	L	0-28	Knoxville, Tenn.
Nov. 9	Miss. State	L	7-22	Baton Rouge
Nov. 16	Auburn	W	21-13	Birmingham
Nov. 30	Tulane	W	14-0	Baton Rouge

1941   Record: 4-4-2   SEC: 2-2-2

Coach Bernie H. Moore
Captain: Leo Bird (HB)

Sept. 20	Louisiana Tech	W	25-0	Baton Rouge
Sept. 27	Holy Cross	L	13-19	Baton Rouge
Oct. 4	Texas	L	0-34	Austin
Oct. 11	Miss. State	T	0-0	Baton Rouge
Oct. 18	Rice	W	27-0	Baton Rouge
Oct. 25	Florida	W	10-7	Baton Rouge
Nov. 1	Tennessee	L	6-13	Baton Rouge
Nov. 8	Mississippi	L	12-13	Baton Rouge
Nov. 15	Auburn	T	7-7	Baton Rouge
Nov. 29	Tulane	W	19-0	New Orleans

1942   Record: 7-3-0   SEC: 3-2-0

Coach Bernie H. Moore
Captain: Willie Miller (G)

Sept. 19	Louisiana Normal	W	40-0	Baton Rouge
Sept. 26	Texas A&M	W	16-7	Baton Rouge
Oct. 3	Rice	L	14-27	Houston
Oct. 10	Miss. State	W	16-6	Baton Rouge
Oct. 17	Mississippi	W	21-7	Baton Rouge
Oct. 24	Georgia Navy	W	34-0	Baton Rouge
Oct. 31	Tennessee	L	0-26	Knoxville, Tenn.
Nov. 7	Fordham	W	26-13	New York, N.Y.
Nov. 14	Auburn	L	7-25	Birmingham
Nov. 26	Tulane	W	18-6	Baton Rouge

1943   Record: 6-3-0   SEC: 2-2-0

Coach Bernie H. Moore
Captain: Steve Van Buren (HB)

Sept. 25	Georgia	W	34-27	Baton Rouge
Oct. 2	Rice	W	20-7	Baton Rouge
Oct. 9	Texas A&M	L	13-28	Baton Rouge
Oct. 16	La. Army (STU)	W	28-7	Baton Rouge
Oct. 23	Georgia	W	27-6	Columbus, Ga.
Oct. 30	TCU	W	14-0	Baton Rouge
Nov. 6	Georgia Tech	L	7-42	Atlanta, Ga.
Nov. 20	Tulane	L	0-27	New Orleans
ORANGE BOWL				
Jan. 1	Texas A&M	W	19-14	Miami, Fla.

1944 **Record: 2-5-1** **SEC: 2-3-1**
Coach Bernie H. Moore
Captain: Al Cavigga (G)

Sept. 30	Alabama	T	27-27	Baton Rouge
Oct. 7	Rice	L	13-14	Houston
Oct. 14	Texas A&M	L	0-7	Baton Rouge
Oct. 21	Miss. State	L	6-13	Baton Rouge
Oct. 28	Georgia	W	15-7	Atlanta
Nov. 4	Tennessee	L	0-13	Baton Rouge
Nov. 18	Georgia Tech	L	6-14	Baton Rouge
Nov. 30	Tulane	W	25-6	Baton Rouge

1945 **Record: 7-2-0** **SEC: 5-2-0**
Coach Bernie H. Moore
Captain: Andy Kosmac (QB)

Sept. 29	Rice	W	42-0	Baton Rouge
Oct. 6	Alabama	L	7-26	Baton Rouge
Oct. 13	Texas A&M	W	31-12	Baton Rouge
Oct. 20	Georgia	W	32-0	Athens
Oct. 27	Vanderbilt	W	39-7	Baton Rouge
Nov. 3	Mississippi	W	32-13	Baton Rouge
Nov. 10	Miss. State	L	20-27	Baton Rouge
Nov. 17	Georgia Tech	W	9-7	Atlanta
Dec. 1	Tulane	W	33-0	New Orleans

1946 **Record: 9-1-1** **SEC: 5-1-0**
Coach Bernie H. Moore
Captain: Dilton Richmond (E)

Sept. 28	Rice	W	7-6	Houston
Oct. 5	Miss. State	W	13-6	Baton Rouge
Oct. 12	Texas A&M	W	33-9	Baton Rouge
Oct. 19	Georgia Tech	L	7-26	Baton Rouge
Oct. 26	Vanderbilt	W	14-0	Nashville, Tenn.
Nov. 2	Mississippi	W	34-21	Baton Rouge
Nov. 9	Alabama	W	31-21	Baton Rouge
Nov. 15	Miami (Fla.)	W	20-7	Miami, Fl.
Nov. 22	Fordham	W	40-0	Baton Rouge
Nov. 29	Tulane	W	41-27	Baton Rouge
COTTON BOWL				
Jan. 1	Arkansas	T	0-0	Dallas, Texas

1947 **Record: 5-3-1** **SEC: 2-3-1**
Coach Bernie H. Moore
Captain: Jim Cason (HB)

Sept. 27	Rice	W	21-14	Baton Rouge
Oct. 4	Georgia	L	19-35	Athens
Oct. 11	Texas A&M	W	19-13	Baton Rouge
Oct. 17	Boston College	W	14-13	Boston, Mass.
Oct. 25	Vanderbilt	W	19-13	Baton Rouge
Nov. 1	Mississippi	L	18-20	Baton Rouge
Nov. 15	Miss. State	W	21-6	Baton Rouge
Nov. 22	Alabama	L	12-41	Tuscaloosa
Dec. 6	Tulane	T	6-6	New Orleans

1948 **Record: 3-7-0** **SEC: 1-5-0**
Coach Gaynell (Gus) Tinsley
Captain: Ed Claunch (C)

Sept. 18	Texas	L	0-33	Austin
Oct. 2	Rice	W	26-13	Baton Rouge
Oct. 9	Texas A&M	W	14-13	Baton Rouge
Oct. 16	Georgia	L	0-22	Baton Rouge
Oct. 23	North Carolina	L	7-34	Chapel Hill
Oct. 30	Mississippi	L	19-49	Baton Rouge
Nov. 6	Vanderbilt	L	7-48	Nashville, Tenn.
Nov. 13	Miss. State	L	0-7	Baton Rouge
Nov. 20	Alabama	W	26-6	Baton Rouge
Nov. 27	Tulane	L	0-46	Baton Rouge

1949 **Record: 8-3-0** **SEC: 4-2-0**
Coach Gaynell (Gus) Tinsley
Captain: Mel Lyle (E)

Sept. 24	Kentucky	L	0-19	Baton Rouge
Oct. 1	Rice	W	14-7	Baton Rouge
Oct. 8	Texas A&M	W	34-0	Baton Rouge
Oct. 14	Georgia	L	0-7	Athens
Oct. 22	North Carolina	W	13-7	Baton Rouge
Oct. 29	Mississippi	W	34-7	Baton Rouge
Nov. 5	Vanderbilt	W	33-13	Baton Rouge
Nov. 12	Miss. State	W	34-7	Baton Rouge
Nov. 19	SE Louisiana	W	48-7	Baton Rouge
Nov. 26	Tulane	W	21-0	New Orleans
Sugar Bowl				
Jan. 1	Oklahoma	L	0-35	New Orleans

1950 **Record: 4-5-2** **SEC: 2-3-2**
Coach Gaynell (Gus) Tinsley
Captain: Ebert Van Buren (HB)

Sept. 23	Kentucky	L	0-14	Lexington
Sept. 30	Pacific	W	19-0	Baton Rouge
Oct. 7	Rice	L	20-35	Houston, Texas
Oct. 14	Georgia Tech	L	0-13	Baton Rouge
Oct. 21	Georgia	T	13-13	Baton Rouge
Nov. 4	Mississippi	W	40-14	Baton Rouge
Nov. 11	Vanderbilt	W	33-7	Nashville, Tenn.
Nov. 18	Miss. State	L	7-13	Baton Rouge
Nov. 24	Villanova	W	13-7	Baton Rouge
Dec. 2	Tulane	T	14-14	New Orleans
Dec. 9	Texas	L	6-21	Austin

1951 **Record: 7-3-1** **SEC: 4-2-1**
Coach Gaynell (Gus) Tinsley
Captains: Ray Potter (T), Chester Freeman (RHB)

Sept. 22	Southern Miss.	W	13-0	Baton Rouge
Sept. 29	Alabama	W	13-7	Mobile
Oct. 6	Rice	W	7-6	Baton Rouge
Oct. 13	Georgia Tech	L	7-25	Atlanta
Oct. 20	Georgia	W	7-0	Athens
Oct. 27	Maryland	L	0-27	Baton Rouge
Nov. 3	Mississippi	T	6-6	Baton Rouge
Nov. 10	Vanderbilt	L	13-20	Baton Rouge
Nov. 17	Miss. State	W	3-0	Baton Rouge
Nov. 24	Villanova	W	45-7	Shreveport, La.
Dec. 1	Tulane	W	14-13	Baton Rouge

1952 **Record: 3-7-0** **SEC: 2-5-0**
Coach Gaynell (Gus) Tinsley
Captains: Norm Stevens (QB), Joe Modicut (LG), Bill Lansing (RG), Leroy Labat (HB), Jim Sanford (T), Ralph McLeod (LE)

Sept. 20	Texas	L	14-35	Baton Rouge
Sept. 27	Alabama	L	20-21	Baton Rouge
Oct. 4	Rice	W	27-7	Houston, Texas
Oct. 11	Kentucky	W	34-7	Lexington
Oct. 18	Georgia	L	14-27	Baton Rouge
Oct. 25	Maryland	L	6-34	College Park
Nov. 1	Mississippi	L	0-28	Oxford
Nov. 8	Tennessee	L	3-22	Baton Rouge
Nov. 15	Miss. State	L	14-33	Baton Rouge
Nov. 29	Tulane	W	16-0	New Orleans

1953   **Record: 5-3-3**   **SEC: 2-3-3**

Coach Gaynell Tinsley
Captains: Jerry Marchand (LHB), Charley Oakley (FB)

Sept. 19	Texas	W	20-7	Baton Rouge
Sept. 26	Alabama	T	7-7	Mobile
Oct. 3	Boston College	W	42-6	Baton Rouge
Oct. 10	Kentucky	T	6-6	Baton Rouge
Oct. 17	Georgia	W	14-6	Athens
Oct. 24	Florida	T	21-21	Gainesville
Oct. 31	Mississippi	L	16-27	Baton Rouge
Nov. 7	Tennessee	L	14-32	Knoxville
Nov. 14	Miss. State	L	13-26	Baton Rouge
Nov. 21	Arkansas	W	9-8	Little Rock
Nov. 28	Tulane	W	32-13	Baton Rouge

1954   **Record: 5-6-0**   **SEC: 2-5-0**

Coach Gaynell (Gus) Tinsley
Captain: Sid Fournet (LG)

Sept. 18	Texas	L	6-20	Austin
Sept. 25	Alabama	L	0-12	Baton Rouge
Oct. 2	Kentucky	L	6-7	Lexington
Oct. 9	Georgia Tech	L	20-30	Atlanta
Oct. 16	Texas Tech	W	20-13	Baton Rouge
Oct. 23	Florida	W	20-7	Baton Rouge
Oct. 30	Mississippi	L	6-21	Baton Rouge
Nov. 6	Chattanooga	W	26-19	Baton Rouge
Nov. 13	Miss. State	L	0-25	Baton Rouge
Nov. 20	Arkansas	W	7-6	Shreveport, La.
Nov. 27	Tulane	W	14-13	New Orleans

1955   **Record: 3-5-2**   **SEC: 2-3-1**

Coach Paul Dietzel
Captains: Joe Tuminello (E), O.K. Ferguson (FB)

Sept. 17	Kentucky	W	19-7	Baton Rouge
Sept. 24	Texas A&M	L	0-28	Dallas
Oct. 1	Rice	T	20-20	Houston
Oct. 8	Georgia Tech	L	0-7	Baton Rouge
Oct. 15	Florida	L	14-18	Gainesville
Oct. 29	Mississippi	L	26-29	Baton Rouge
Nov. 5	Maryland	L	0-13	College Park
Nov. 12	Miss. State	W	34-7	Baton Rouge
Nov. 19	Arkansas	W	13-7	Little Rock
Nov. 26	Tulane	T	13-13	Baton Rouge

1956   **Record: 3-7-0**   **SEC: 1-5-0**

Coach Paul Dietzel
Captain: Don Scully (G)

Sept. 29	Texas A&M	L	6-9	Baton Rouge
Oct. 6	Rice	L	14-23	Houston
Oct. 13	Georgia Tech	L	7-39	Atlanta
Oct. 20	Kentucky	L	0-14	Lexington
Oct. 27	Florida	L	6-21	Baton Rouge
Nov. 3	Mississippi	L	17-46	Baton Rouge
Nov. 10	Oklahoma A&M	W	13-0	Baton Rouge
Nov. 17	Miss. State	L	13-32	Baton Rouge
Nov. 24	Arkansas	W	21-7	Shreveport
Dec. 1	Tulane	W	7-6	New Orleans

1957   **Record: 5-5-0**   **SEC: 4-4-0**

Coach Paul Dietzel
Captain: Alvin Aucoin (LT)

Sept. 21	Rice	L	14-20	Baton Rouge
Sept. 28	Alabama	W	28-0	Baton Rouge
Oct. 5	Texas Tech	W	19-14	Lubbock
Oct. 12	Georgia Tech	W	20-13	Baton Rouge
Oct. 19	Kentucky	W	21-0	Baton Rouge
Oct. 26	Florida	L	14-22	Gainesville
Nov. 2	Vanderbilt	L	0-7	Nashville, Tenn.
Nov. 9	Mississippi	L	12-14	Oxford
Nov. 16	Miss. State	L	6-14	Baton Rouge
Nov. 30	Tulane	W	25-6	Baton Rouge

NATIONAL CHAMPION
SEC CHAMPION

1958   **Record: 11-0-0**   **SEC: 6-0-0**

Coach Paul Dietzel
Captain: Billy Hendrix (E)

Sept. 20	Rice	W	26-6	Houston
Sept. 27	Alabama	W	13-3	Mobile
Oct. 4	Hardin-Simmons	W	20-6	Baton Rouge
Oct. 10	Miami (Fla.)	W	41-0	Miami, Fla.
Oct. 18	Kentucky	W	32-7	Baton Rouge
Oct. 25	Florida	W	10-7	Baton Rouge
Nov. 1	Mississippi	W	14-0	Baton Rouge
Nov. 8	Duke	W	50-18	Baton Rouge
Nov. 15	Miss. State	W	7-6	Jackson
Nov. 22	Tulane	W	62-0	New Orleans
SUGAR BOWL				
Jan. 1	Clemson	W	7-0	New Orleans TV

1959   **Record: 9-2-0**   **SEC: 5-1-0**

Coach Paul Dietzel
Captain: Lynn LeBlanc (T)

Sept. 19	Rice	W	26-3	Baton Rouge	TV
Sept. 26	TCU	W	10-0	Baton Rouge	
Oct. 3	Baylor	W	22-0	Shreveport, La.	
Oct. 10	Miami (Fla.)	W	27-3	Baton Rouge	
Oct. 17	Kentucky	W	9-0	Lexington	
Oct. 24	Florida	W	9-0	Gainesville	
Oct. 31	Mississippi	W	7-3	Baton Rouge	
Nov. 7	Tennessee	L	13-14	Knoxville	
Nov. 14	Miss. State	W	27-0	Baton Rouge	
Nov. 21	Tulane	W	14-6	Baton Rouge	
SUGAR BOWL					
Jan. 1	Mississippi	L	0-21	New Orleans	TV

1960   **Record: 5-4-1**   **SEC: 2-3-1**

Coach Paul Dietzel
Captain: Charles (Bo) Strange (C)

Sept. 17	Texas A&M	W	9-0	Baton Rouge	
Oct. 1	Baylor	L	3-7	Baton Rouge	
Oct. 8	Georgia Tech	L	2-6	Atlanta	
Oct. 15	Kentucky	L	0-3	Lexington	
Oct. 22	Florida	L	10-13	Baton Rouge	
Oct. 29	Mississippi	T	6-6	Oxford	TV
Nov. 5	South Carolina	W	35-6	Baton Rouge	
Nov. 12	Miss. State	W	7-3	Baton Rouge	
Nov. 19	Wake Forest	W	16-0	Baton Rouge	
Nov. 26	Tulane	W	17-6	New Orleans	

SEC CHAMPION

1961   Record: 10-1-0   SEC: 6-0-0

Coach Paul Dietzel
Captain: Roy (Moonie) Winston (G)

Sept. 23	Rice	L	3-16	Houston	
Sept. 30	Texas A&M	W	16-7	Baton Rouge	
Oct. 7	Georgia Tech	W	10-0	Baton Rouge	
Oct. 14	South Carolina	W	42-0	Columbia	
Oct. 21	Kentucky	W	24-14	Baton Rouge	
Oct. 28	Florida	W	23-0	Gainesville	
Nov. 4	Mississippi	W	10-7	Baton Rouge	
Nov. 11	North Carolina	W	30-0	Chapel Hill	TV
Nov. 18	Miss. State	W	14-6	Baton Rouge	
Nov. 25	Tulane	W	62-0	Baton Rouge	
ORANGE BOWL					
Jan. 1	Colorado	W	25-7	Miami, Fla.	TV

1962   Record: 9-1-1   SEC: 5-1-0

Coach Charles McClendon
Captain: Fred Miller (RT)

Sept. 22	Texas A&M	W	21-0	Baton Rouge	
Sept. 29	Rice	T	6-6	Baton Rouge	
Oct. 6	Georgia Tech	W	10-7	Atlanta	TV
Oct. 13	Miami (Fla.)	W	17-3	Baton Rouge	
Oct. 20	Kentucky	W	7-0	Lexington	
Oct. 27	Florida	W	23-0	Baton Rouge	
Nov. 3	Mississippi	L	7-15	Baton Rouge	
Nov. 10	TCU	W	5-0	Baton Rouge	
Nov. 17	Miss. State	W	28-0	Jackson	
Nov. 24	Tulane	W	38-3	New Orleans	
COTTON BOWL					
Jan. 1	Texas	W	13-0	Dallas, Texas	TV

1963   Record: 7-4-0   SEC: 4-2-0

Coach Charles McClendon
Captain: Bill Truax (E)

Sept. 21	Texas A&M	W	14-6	Baton Rouge	
Sept. 28	Rice	L	12-21	Houston	
Oct. 5	Georgia Tech	W	7-6	Baton Rouge	
Oct. 11	Miami (Fla.)	W	3-0	Miami, Fla.	
Oct. 19	Kentucky	W	28-7	Baton Rouge	
Oct. 26	Florida	W	14-0	Gainesville	
Nov. 2	Mississippi	L	3-37	Baton Rouge	TV
Nov. 9	TCU	W	28-14	Baton Rouge	
Nov. 16	Miss. State	L	6-7	Jackson	
Nov. 23	Tulane	W	20-0	Baton Rouge	
BLUEBONNET BOWL					
Dec. 21	Baylor	L	7-14	Houston, Texas	TV

1964   Record: 8-2-1   SEC: 4-2-1

Coach Charles McClendon
Captain: Richard Granier (C)

Sept. 19	Texas A&M	W	9-6	Baton Rouge	
Sept. 26	Rice	W	3-0	Houston	
Oct. 10	North Carolina	W	20-3	Baton Rouge	
Oct. 17	Kentucky	W	27-7	Lexington	
Oct. 24	Tennessee	T	3-3	Baton Rouge	TV
Oct. 31	Mississippi	W	11-10	Baton Rouge	
Nov. 7	Alabama	L	9-17	Birmingham	
Nov. 14	Miss. State	W	14-10	Baton Rouge	
Nov. 21	Tulane	W	13-3	New Orleans	
Nov. 28	Florida	L	6-20	Baton Rouge	
SUGAR BOWL					
Jan. 1	Syracuse	W	13-10	New Orleans	TV

1965   Record: 8-3-0   SEC: 3-3-0

Coach Charles McClendon
Captains: Billy Ezell (QB), John Aaron (RG)

Sept. 18	Texas A&M	W	10-0	Baton Rouge	
Sept. 25	Rice	W	42-14	Baton Rouge	
Oct. 2	Florida	L	7-14	Gainesville	
Oct. 9	Miami (Fla.)	W	34-27	Miami, Fla.	
Oct. 16	Kentucky	W	31-21	Baton Rouge	
Oct. 23	South Carolina	W	21-7	Baton Rouge	
Oct. 30	Mississippi	L	0-23	Jackson	
Nov. 6	Alabama	L	7-31	Baton Rouge	TV
Nov. 13	Miss. State	W	37-20	Baton Rouge	
Nov. 20	Tulane	W	62-0	Baton Rouge	
COTTON BOWL					
Jan. 1	Arkansas	W	14-7	Dallas, Texas	TV

1966   Record: 5-4-1   SEC: 3-3-0

Coach Charles McClendon
Captains: Leonard Neumann (TB), Gawain DiBetta (FB)

Sept. 17	South Carolina	W	28-12	Baton Rouge	
Sept. 24	Rice	L	15-17	Houston	
Oct. 1	Miami (Fla.)	W	10-8	Baton Rouge	
Oct. 8	Texas A&M	T	7-7	Baton Rouge	
Oct. 15	Kentucky	W	30-0	Lexington	
Oct. 22	Florida	L	7-28	Baton Rouge	
Oct. 29	Mississippi	L	7-17	Baton Rouge	
Nov. 5	Alabama	L	0-21	Birmingham	TV
Nov. 12	Miss. State	W	17-7	Baton Rouge	TV
Nov. 19	Tulane*	W	21-7	New Orleans	

* Designated as conference game by the SEC

1967   Record: 7-3-1   SEC: 3-2-1

Coach Charles McClendon
Captains: Barry Wilson (C), Benny Griffin (LB)

Sept. 23	Rice	W	20-14	Baton Rouge	
Sept. 30	Texas A&M	W	17-6	Baton Rouge	
Oct. 7	Florida	W	37-6	Gainesville	
Oct. 14	Miami (Fla.)	L	15-17	Baton Rouge	
Oct. 21	Kentucky	W	30-7	Baton Rouge	
Oct. 28	Tennessee	L	14-17	Knoxville	
Nov. 4	Mississippi	T	13-13	Jackson	TV
Nov. 11	Alabama	L	6-7	Baton Rouge	
Nov. 18	Miss. State	W	55-0	Baton Rouge	
Nov. 25	Tulane	W	41-27	Baton Rouge	
SUGAR BOWL					
Jan. 1	Wyoming	W	20-13	New Orleans	TV

1968   Record: 8-3-0   SEC: 4-2-0

Coach Charles McClendon
Captains: Barton Frye (CB), Jerry Guillot (RG)

Sept. 21	Texas A&M	W	13-12	Baton Rouge	
Sept. 28	Rice	W	21-7	Houston	
Oct. 5	Baylor	W	48-16	Baton Rouge	
Oct. 12	Miami (Fla.)	L	0-30	Miami, Fla.	
Oct. 19	Kentucky	W	13-3	Baton Rouge	
Oct. 26	TCU*	W	10-7	Baton Rouge	
Nov. 2	Mississippi	L	24-27	Baton Rouge	
Nov. 9	Alabama	L	7-16	Birmingham	
Nov. 16	Miss. State	W	20-16	Baton Rouge	
Nov. 23	Tulane*	W	34-10	Baton Rouge	
PEACH BOWL					
Dec. 30	Florida State	W	31-27	Atlanta, Ga.	TV

* Designated as conference game by the SEC

1969 Record: 9-1-0 SEC: 4-1-0
Coach Charles McClendon
Captains: George Bevan (LB), Robert (Red) Ryder (OT)

Sept. 20	Texas A&M	W	35-6	Baton Rouge	
Sept. 27	Rice	W	42-0	Houston	
Oct. 4	Baylor	W	63-8	Baton Rouge	
Oct. 10	Miami (Fla.)	W	20-0	Miami, Fla.	
Oct. 18	Kentucky	W	37-10	Lexington	
Oct. 25	Auburn	W	21-20	Baton Rouge	TV
Nov. 1	Mississippi	L	23-26	Jackson	TV
Nov. 8	Alabama	W	20-15	Baton Rouge	
Nov. 15	Miss. State	W	61-6	Baton Rouge	
Nov. 22	Tulane	W	27-0	Baton Rouge	

SEC CHAMPION
1970 Record: 9-3-0 SEC: 5-0-0
Coach Charles McClendon
Captains: Buddy Lee (QB), John Sage (T)

Sept. 19	Texas A&M	L	18-20	Baton Rouge	
Sept. 26	Rice	W	24-0	Baton Rouge	
Oct. 3	Baylor	W	31-10	Baton Rouge	
Oct. 10	Pacific	W	34-0	Baton Rouge	
Oct. 17	Kentucky	W	14-7	Baton Rouge	
Oct. 24	Auburn	W	17-9	Auburn, Ala.	
Nov. 7	Alabama	W	14-9	Birmingham	TV
Nov. 14	Miss. State	W	38-7	Baton Rouge	
Nov. 21	Notre Dame	L	0-3	South Bend, Ind.	
Nov. 28	Tulane	W	26-14	New Orleans	
Dec. 5	Mississippi	W	61-17	Baton Rouge	TV
Orange Bowl					
Jan. 1	Nebraska	L	12-17	Miami, Fla.	TV

1971 Record: 9-3 SEC: 3-2-0
Coach Charles McClendon
Captains: Louis Cascio (LB), Mike Demarie (OG)

Sept. 11	Colorado	L	21-31	Baton Rouge	
Sept. 18	Texas A&M	W	37-0	Baton Rouge	
Sept. 25	Wisconsin	W	38-28	Madison, Wis.	
Oct. 2	Rice	W	38-3	Baton Rouge	
Oct. 9	Florida	W	48-7	Baton Rouge	
Oct. 16	Kentucky	W	17-13	Lexington	
Oct. 30	Mississippi	L	22-24	Jackson	
Nov. 6	Alabama	L	7-14	Baton Rouge	TV
Nov. 13	Miss. State	W	28-3	Jackson	
Nov. 20	Notre Dame	W	28-8	Baton Rouge	TV
Nov. 27	Tulane	W	36-7	Baton Rouge	
SUN BOWL					
Dec. 18	Iowa State	W	33-15	El Paso, Texas	TV

1972 Record: 9-2-1 SEC: 4-1-1
Coach Charles McClendon
Captains: Paul Lyons (QB), Pepper Rutland (LB)

Sept. 16	Pacific	W	31-13	Baton Rouge	
Sept. 23	Texas A&M	W	42-17	Baton Rouge	
Sept. 30	Wisconsin	W	27-7	Baton Rouge	
Oct. 7	Rice	W	12-6	Houston	
Oct. 14	Auburn	W	35-7	Baton Rouge	
Oct. 21	Kentucky	W	10-0	Baton Rouge	
Nov. 4	Mississippi	W	17-16	Baton Rouge	
Nov. 11	Alabama	L	21-35	Birmingham	TV
Nov. 18	Miss. State	W	28-14	Baton Rouge	
Nov. 25	Florida	T	3-3	Gainesville	
Dec. 2	Tulane	W	9-3	New Orleans	
ASTRO-BLUEBONNET BOWL					
Dec. 30	Tennessee	L	17-24	Houston, Texas	TV

1973 Record: 9-3-0 SEC: 5-1-0
Coach Charles McClendon
Captains: Tyler Lafauci (OG-DT), Binks Miciotto (DE)

Sept. 15	Colorado	W	17-6	Baton Rouge	
Sept. 22	Texas A&M	W	28-23	Baton Rouge	
Sept. 29	Rice	W	24-9	Baton Rouge	
Oct. 6	Florida	W	24-3	Baton Rouge	
Oct. 13	Auburn	W	20-6	Auburn, Ala.	
Oct. 20	Kentucky	W	28-21	Baton Rouge	
Oct. 27	South Carolina	W	33-29	Columbia	
Nov. 3	Mississippi	W	51-14	Jackson	TV
Nov. 17	Miss. State	W	26-7	Baton Rouge	
Nov. 22	Alabama	L	7-21	Baton Rouge	TV
Dec. 1	Tulane	L	0-14	New Orleans	
ORANGE BOWL					
Jan. 1	Penn State	L	9-16	Miami, Fla.	TV

1974 Record: 5-5-1 SEC: 2-4-0
Coach Charles McClendon
Captains: Brad Boyd (TE), Steve Lelekacs (LB)

Sept. 14	Colorado	W	42-14	Baton Rouge	
Sept. 21	Texas A&M	L	14-21	Baton Rouge	
Sept. 28	Rice	T	10-10	Houston	
Oct. 5	Florida	L	14-24	Gainesville	
Oct. 12	Tennessee	W	20-10	Baton Rouge	
Oct. 19	Kentucky	L	13-20	Lexington	
Nov. 2	Mississippi	W	24-0	Baton Rouge	
Nov. 9	Alabama	L	0-30	Birmingham	TV
Nov. 16	Miss. State	L	6-7	Jackson	
Nov. 23	Tulane	W	24-22	Baton Rouge	
Nov. 30	Utah	W	35-10	Baton Rouge	

1975 Record: 5-6-0 SEC: 2-4-0
Coach Charles McClendon
Captains: Greg Bienvenu (C), Steve Cassidy (G)

Sept. 13	Nebraska	L	7-10	Lincoln	
Sept. 20	Texas A&M	L	8-39	Baton Rouge	
Sept. 27	Rice	W	16-13	Shreveport, La.	
Oct. 4	Florida	L	6-34	Baton Rouge	
Oct. 11	Tennessee	L	10-24	Knoxville	
Oct. 18	Kentucky	W	17-14	Baton Rouge	
Oct. 25	South Carolina	W	24-6	Baton Rouge	
Nov. 1	Mississippi	L	13-17	Jackson	TV
Nov. 8	Alabama	L	10-23	Baton Rouge	
Nov. 15	*Miss. State	W	6-16	Baton Rouge	
Nov. 22	Tulane	W	42-6	New Orleans	
*-forfeited to LSU by NCAA

1976 Record: 7-3-1 SEC: 3-3-0
Coach Charles McClendon
Captains: Roy Stuart (OG), Butch Knight (DE)

Sept. 11	Nebraska	T	6-6	Baton Rouge	
Sept. 18	Oregon State	W	28-11	Baton Rouge	
Sept. 25	Rice	W	31-0	Baton Rouge	
Oct. 2	Florida	L	23-28	Gainesville	
Oct. 9	Vanderbilt	W	33-20	Baton Rouge	
Oct. 16	Kentucky	L	7-21	Lexington	
Oct. 30	Mississippi	W	45-0	Baton Rouge	
Nov. 6	Alabama	L	17-28	Birmingham	
Nov. 13	*Miss. State	W	13-21	Jackson	
Nov. 20	Tulane	W	17-7	Baton Rouge	
Nov. 27	Utah	W	35-7	Baton Rouge	
*-forfeited to LSU by NCAA

1977   Record: 8-4-0   SEC: 4-2-0

Coach Charles McClendon
Captains: Kelly Simmons (FB), Steve Ripple (LB)

Sept. 17	Indiana	L	21-24	Bloomington	
Sept. 24	Rice	W	77-0	Baton Rouge	
Oct. 1	Florida	W	36-14	Baton Rouge	
Oct. 8	Vanderbilt	W	28-15	Nashville, Tenn.	
Oct. 15	Kentucky	L	13-33	Baton Rouge	
Oct. 22	Oregon	W	56-17	Baton Rouge	
Oct. 29	Mississippi	W	28-21	Jackson	TV
Nov. 5	Alabama	L	3-24	Baton Rouge	TV
Nov. 12	Miss. State	W	27-24	Baton Rouge	
Nov. 19	Tulane	W	20-17	New Orleans	
Nov. 26	Wyoming	W	66-7	Baton Rouge	
		SUN BOWL			
Dec. 31	Stanford	L	14-24	El Paso, Texas	TV

1978   Record: 8-4-0   SEC: 3-3-0

Coach Charles McClendon
Captains: Charles Alexander (TB), Thad Minaldi (FB)

Sept. 16	Indiana	W	24-17	Baton Rouge	
Sept. 23	Wake Forest	W	13-11	Baton Rouge	
Sept. 30	Rice	W	37-7	Houston	
Oct. 7	Florida	W	34-21	Gainesville	
Oct. 14	Georgia	L	17-24	Baton Rouge	
Oct. 21	Kentucky	W	21-0	Lexington	
Nov. 4	Mississippi	W	30-8	Baton Rouge	TV
Nov. 11	Alabama	L	10-31	Birmingham	TV
Nov. 18	Miss. State	L	14-16	Jackson	
Nov. 25	Tulane	W	40-21	Baton Rouge	
Dec. 2	Wyoming	W	24-17	Baton Rouge	
		LIBERTY BOWL			
Dec. 23	Missouri	L	15-20	Memphis, Tenn.	TV

1979   Record: 7-5-0   SEC: 4-2-0

Coach Charles McClendon
Captains: John Ed Bradley (C), Willie Teal (CB), Rusty Brown (S)

Sept. 15	Colorado	W	44-0	Boulder	
Sept. 22	Rice	W	47-3	Baton Rouge	
Sept. 29	Southern Cal	L	12-17	Baton Rouge	
Oct. 6	Florida	W	20-3	Baton Rouge	
Oct. 13	Georgia	L	14-21	Athens	
Oct. 20	Kentucky	W	23-19	Baton Rouge	
Oct. 27	Florida State	L	19-24	Baton Rouge	TV
Nov. 3	Mississippi	W	28-24	Jackson	
Nov. 10	Alabama	L	0-3	Baton Rouge	
Nov. 17	Miss. State	W	21-3	Baton Rouge	
Nov. 24	Tulane	L	13-24	New Orleans	TV
		TANGERINE BOWL			
Dec. 22	Wake Forest	W	34-10	Orlando, Fla.	TV

1980   Record: 7-4-0   SEC: 4-2-0

Coach Jerry Stovall
Captains: Hokie Gajan (FB), Lyman White (OLB)

Sept. 6	Florida State	L	0-16	Baton Rouge	
Sept. 13	Kansas State	W	21-0	Baton Rouge	
Sept. 20	Colorado	W	23-20	Baton Rouge	
Sept. 27	Rice	L	7-17	Houston	
Oct. 4	Florida	W	24-7	Gainesville	
Oct. 11	Auburn	W	21-17	Baton Rouge	
Oct. 18	Kentucky	W	17-10	Lexington	
Nov. 1	Mississippi	W	38-16	Baton Rouge	TV
Nov. 8	Alabama	L	7-28	Tuscaloosa	
Nov. 15	Miss. State	L	31-55	Jackson	
Nov. 22	Tulane	W	24-7	Baton Rouge	

1981   Record: 3-7-1   SEC: 1-4-1

Coach Jerry Stovall
Captains: James Britt (CB), Tom Tully (OG)

Sept. 5	Alabama	L	7-24	Baton Rouge	TV
Sept. 12	Notre Dame	L	9-27	South Bend, Ind.	TV
Sept. 19	Oregon State	W	27-24	Baton Rouge	
Sept. 26	Rice	W	28-14	Baton Rouge	
Oct. 3	Florida	L	10-24	Baton Rouge	
Oct. 10	Auburn	L	7-19	Auburn, Ala.	
Oct. 17	Kentucky	W	24-10	Baton Rouge	
Oct. 24	Florida State	L	14-38	Baton Rouge	
Oct. 31	Mississippi	T	27-27	Jackson	
Nov. 14	Miss. State	L	9-17	Baton Rouge	
Nov. 28	Tulane	L	7-48	New Orleans	

1982   Record: 8-3-1   SEC: 4-1-1

Coach Jerry Stovall
Captains: Alan Risher (QB), James Britt (CB)

Sept. 18	Oregon State	W	45-7	Baton Rouge	
Sept. 25	Rice	W	52-13	Baton Rouge	
Oct. 2	Florida	W	24-13	Gainesville	
Oct. 9	Tennessee	T	24-24	Baton Rouge	
Oct. 16	Kentucky	W	34-10	Lexington	
Oct. 23	South Carolina	W	14-6	Baton Rouge	
Oct. 30	Mississippi	W	45-8	Baton Rouge	
Nov. 6	Alabama	W	20-10	Birmingham	
Nov. 13	Miss. State	L	24-27	Starkville	TV
Nov. 20	Florida State	W	55-21	Baton Rouge	
Nov. 27	Tulane	L	28-31	Baton Rouge	
		ORANGE BOWL			
Dec. 1	Nebraska	L	20-21	Miami, Fla.	TV

1983   Record: 4-7-0   SEC: 0-6-0

Coach Jerry Stovall
Captains: John Fritchie (ILB), Mike Gambrell (C)

Sept. 10	Florida State	L	35-40	Baton Rouge	TV
Sept. 17	Rice	W	24-10	Houston	
Sept. 24	Washington	W	40-14	Baton Rouge	
Oct. 1	Florida	L	17-31	Baton Rouge	
Oct. 8	Tennessee	L	6-20	Knoxville	TV
Oct. 15	Kentucky	L	13-21	Baton Rouge	
Oct. 22	South Carolina	W	20-6	Baton Rouge	
Oct. 29	Mississippi	L	24-27	Jackson	
Nov. 5	Alabama	L	26-32	Baton Rouge	TV
Nov. 12	Miss. State	L	26-45	Baton Rouge	
Nov. 19	Tulane	W	20-7	New Orleans	TV

1984   Record: 8-3-1   SEC: 4-1-1

Coach Bill Arnsparger
Captains: Gregg Dubroc (OLB), Liffort Hobley (FS), Kevin Langford (OG), Jeff Wickersham (QB)

Sept. 8	Florida	T	21-21	Gainesville	TV
Sept. 15	Wichita State	W	47-7	Baton Rouge	
Sept. 22	Arizona	W	27-26	Baton Rouge	
Sept. 29	Southern Cal	W	23-3	Los Angeles, Calif.	
Oct. 13	Vanderbilt	W	34-27	Baton Rouge	TV
Oct. 20	Kentucky	W	36-10	Lexington	TV
Oct. 27	Notre Dame	L	22-30	Baton Rouge	TV
Nov. 3	Mississippi	W	32-29	Baton Rouge	
Nov. 10	Alabama	W	16-14	Birmingham	
Nov. 17	Miss. State	L	14-16	Starkville	
Nov. 24	Tulane	W	33-15	Baton Rouge	
		SUGAR BOWL			
Jan. 1	Nebraska	L	10-28	New Orleans	TV

1985 Record: 9-2-1 SEC: 4-1-1

Coach Bill Arnsparger
Captains: Shawn Burks (ILB), Dalton Hilliard (RB), Jeff Wickersham (QB), Karl Wilson (DE)

Sept. 14	North Carolina	W	23-13	Chapel Hill	
Sept. 21	Colorado State	W	17-3	Baton Rouge	
Oct. 5	Florida	L	0-20	Baton Rouge	
Oct. 12	Vanderbilt	W	49-7	Nashville, Tenn.	
Oct. 19	Kentucky	W	10-0	Baton Rouge	TV
Nov. 2	Mississippi	W	14-0	Jackson	TV
Nov. 9	Alabama	T	14-14	Baton Rouge	TV
Nov. 16	Miss. State	W	17-15	Baton Rouge	
Nov. 23	Notre Dame	W	10-7	South Bend, Ind.	TV
Nov. 30	Tulane	W	31-19	New Orleans	
Dec. 7	East Carolina	W	35-15	Baton Rouge	
			LIBERTY BOWL		
Dec. 27	Baylor	L	7-21	Memphis, Tenn.	TV

SEC CHAMPION

1986 Record: 9-3-0 SEC: 5-1-0

Coach Bill Arnsparger
Captains: Eric Andolsek (OG), Michael Brooks (OLB), John Hazard (OT), Karl Wilson (DE)

Sept. 13	Texas A&M	W	35-17	Baton Rouge	TV
Sept. 20	Miami (Ohio)	L	12-21	Baton Rouge	
Oct. 4	Florida	W	28-17	Gainesville	
Oct. 11	Georgia	W	23-14	Baton Rouge	
Oct. 18	Kentucky	W	25-16	Lexington	
Oct. 25	North Carolina	W	30-3	Baton Rouge	
Nov. 1	Mississippi	L	19-21	Baton Rouge	TV
Nov. 8	Alabama	W	14-10	Birmingham	TV
Nov. 15	Miss. State	W	47-0	Jackson	
Nov. 22	Notre Dame	W	21-19	Baton Rouge	TV
Nov. 29	Tulane	W	37-17	Baton Rouge	
			USF&G Sugar Bowl		
Jan. 1	Nebraska	L	15-30	New Orleans	TV

1987 Record: 10-1-1 SEC: 5-1-0

Coach Mike Archer
Captains: Eric Andolsek (OG), Tommy Clapp (DE), Wendell Davis (SE), Nicky Hazard (ILB)

Sept. 5	Texas A&M	W	17-3	College Station	TV
Sept. 12	Cal St. Fullerton	W	56-12	Baton Rouge	
Sept. 19	Rice	W	49-16	Baton Rouge	
Sept. 26	Ohio State	T	13-13	Baton Rouge	TV
Oct. 3	Florida	W	13-10	Baton Rouge	TV
Oct. 10	Georgia	W	26-23	Athens	TV
Oct. 17	Kentucky	W	34-9	Baton Rouge	TV
Oct. 31	Mississippi	W	42-13	Jackson	
Nov. 7	Alabama	L	10-22	Baton Rouge	TV
Nov. 14	Miss. State	W	34-14	Baton Rouge	
Nov. 21	Tulane	W	41-36	New Orleans	
			MAZDA GATOR BOWL		
Dec. 31	South Carolina	W	30-13	Jacksonville, Fla.	TV

SEC CHAMPION

1988 Record: 8-4-0 SEC: 6-1

Coach Mike Archer
Captains: Tommy Hodson (QB), Todd Coutee (C), Ralph Norwood (OT), Eric Hill (OLB), Greg Jackson (WS)

Sept. 3	Texas A&M	W	27-0	Baton Rouge	
Sept. 17	Tennessee	W	34-9	Knoxville	TV
Sept. 24	Ohio State	L	33-36	Columbus, Ohio	TV
Oct. 1	Florida	L	6-19	Gainesville	TV
Oct. 8	Auburn	W	7-6	Baton Rouge	TV
Oct. 15	Kentucky	W	15-12	Baton Rouge	
Oct. 29	Mississippi	W	31-20	Baton Rouge	TV
Nov. 5	Alabama	W	19-18	Tuscaloosa, Ala.	TV
Nov. 12	Miss. State	W	20-3	Starkville, Miss.	
Nov. 19	Miami (Fla.)	L	3-44	Baton Rouge	TV
Nov. 26	Tulane	W	44-14	Baton Rouge	
			Hall of Fame Bowl		
Jan. 2	Syracuse	L	10-23	Tampa, Fla.	TV

1989 Record: 4-7-0 SEC: 2-5

Coach Mike Archer
Captains: Tommy Hodson (QB), Karl Dunbar (DT)

Sept. 2	Texas A&M	L	16-28	College Station	TV
Sept. 16	Florida State	L	21-31	Baton Rouge	TV
Sept. 30	Ohio	W	57-6	Baton Rouge	
Oct. 7	Florida	L	13-16	Baton Rouge	
Oct. 14	Auburn	L	6-10	Auburn, Ala.	TV
Oct. 21	Kentucky	L	21-27	Lexington, Ky.	
Oct. 28	Tennessee	L	39-45	Baton Rouge	TV
Nov. 4	Ole Miss	W	35-30	Oxford, Miss.	
Nov. 11	Alabama	L	16-32	Baton Rouge	TV
Nov. 18	Miss. State	W	44-20	Baton Rouge	
Nov. 25	Tulane	W	27-7	New Orleans	

1990 Record: 5-6-0 SEC: 2-5

Coach Mike Archer
Captains: Sol Graves (QB), Marc Boutte (DT)

Sept. 8	Georgia	W	18-13	Baton Rouge	
Sept. 15	Miami (Ohio)	W	35-7	Baton Rouge	
Sept. 22	Vanderbilt	L	21-24	Nashville	TV
Sept. 29	Texas A&M	W	17-8	Baton Rouge	
Oct. 6	Florida	L	8-34	Gainesville, Fla.	TV
Oct. 20	Kentucky	W	30-20	Baton Rouge	
Oct. 27	Florida State	L	3-42	Tallahassee, Fla.	TV
Nov. 3	Ole Miss	L	10-19	Baton Rouge	
Nov. 10	Alabama	L	3-24	Tuscaloosa, Ala.	
Nov. 17	Miss. State	L	22-34	Jackson, Miss.	
Nov. 24	Tulane	W	16-13	Baton Rouge	

1991 Record: 5-6-0 SEC: 3-4

Coach Curley Hallman
Captains: Todd Kinchen (SE), Marc Boutte (DT), Darrell Williams (special teams)

Sept. 7	Georgia	L	10-31	Athens	TV
Sept. 14	Texas A&M	L	7-45	College Station	
Sept. 21	Vanderbilt	W	16-14	Baton Rouge	
Oct. 5	Florida	L	0-16	Baton Rouge	
Oct. 12	Arkansas State	W	70-14	Baton Rouge	
Oct. 19	Kentucky	W	29-26	Lexington	TV
Oct. 26	Florida State	L	16-27	Baton Rouge	TV
Nov. 2	Ole Miss	W	25-22	Jackson	
Nov. 9	Alabama	L	17-20	Baton Rouge	TV
Nov. 16	Miss. State	L	19-28	Baton Rouge	
Nov. 23	Tulane	W	39-20	New Orleans	

1992 Record: 2-9 SEC: 1-7

Coach Curley Hallman
Captains: Darron Landry (OG), Anthony Williams (ILB), Carlton Buckels (special teams)

Sept. 5	Texas A&M	L	22-31	Baton Rouge	TV
Sept. 12	Miss. State	W	24-3	Baton Rouge	
Sept. 19	Auburn	L	28-30	Auburn	TV
Sept. 26	Colorado State	L	14-17	Baton Rouge	
Oct. 3	Tennessee	L	0-20	Baton Rouge	TV
Oct. 10	Florida	L	21-28	Gainesville	
Oct. 17	Kentucky	L	25-27	Baton Rouge	
Oct. 31	Ole Miss	L	0-32	Jackson	
Nov. 7	Alabama	L	11-31	Baton Rouge	TV
Nov. 21	Tulane	W	24-12	Baton Rouge	
Nov. 27	Arkansas	L	6-30	Fayetteville	TV